BLACK'S

GUIDE TO THE COUNTY

OF SUSSEX

AND ITS WATERING-PLACES

SEVENTH EDITION

With Map, Charts, and numerous Wood Engravings

EDINBURGH

ADAM AND CHARLES BLACK

1885

CHICHESTER,

WITH VIEW OF THE CATHEDRAL AND THE DETACHED CAMPANILE OR BELFRY.

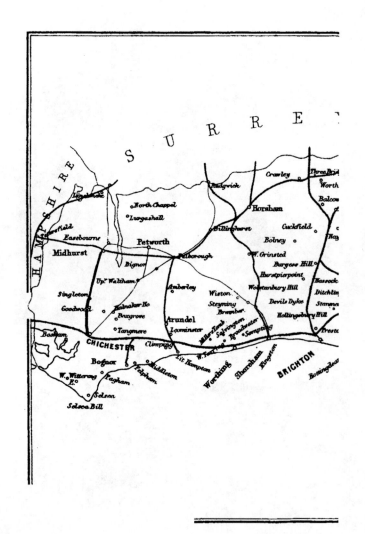

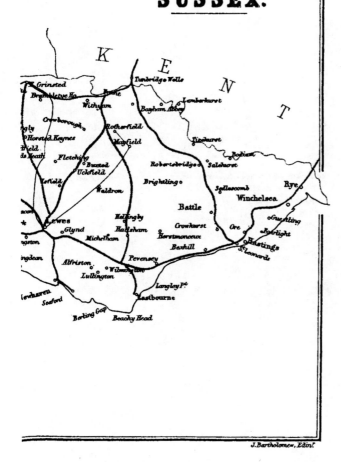

SKETCH MAP
OF
SUSSEX.

J.Bartholomew, Edin.

CONTENTS.

PREFACE.

THE county of Sussex divides itself into two distinct lines or districts of travel and research—one along the northern and middle portions, amid the woodland scenery of St. Leonard's and Tilgate forests, near Horsham, or that which abounds in Ashdown forest and the lovely country south of Tunbridge Wells and East Grinstead; —the other along the South Downs, whether below their escarpments towards the north, or along their slopes and cliffs coming down to the sea on the south. By far the best way of visiting the various scenes of interest is not to make any connected tour through the county, but— now that abundant facilities are offered by the network of railways—to fix on definite stopping-places, making them centres of operation for diverging excursions. In all the small towns of Sussex good, comfortable inns, with cleanliness, civility, and moderate charges, will be found—domestic hostelries—which are often to be preferred to the more pretentious hotels in the watering-places. The following will be found excellent central stations of this kind :—

PETWORTH, from whence can be visited the Great House with its galleries, Midhurst and Cowdray, and the lovely hill scenery from Burton to Ladyholt on the Hampshire border.

CHICHESTER, with Goodwood, Stanstead, Charlton forest, Bognor, and Boxgrove, at convenient distances.

ARUNDEL, with its castle and park, Amberley, Par ham, Storrington, and a wide tract both of down and valley.

HORSHAM, with St. Leonard's forest, exhibiting fine studies of wooded dells, rivulets, ruined towers, ancient village churches.

BALCOMBE and HAYWARD'S HEATH, two railway stations with good small inns, in the very heart of the Wealden district, where some of the most interesting manor-houses may be seen—including those near Cuckfield northward; Hurstpierpoint, Poynings, Danny, etc., towards the south.

EAST GRINSTEAD, one of the choicest spots in Sussex, giving ready access to Ashdown forest, Brambletye, Buckhurst, etc., and rich in ancient residences and churches.

LEWES, in the centre of the best Down scenery.

FRANT, for the old iron-working country, Eridge Castle, Bayham Abbey, Lamberhurst, and the forest district; Mayfield, Brightling and its Down, and the fine views near Heathfield.

BRIGHTON and WORTHING, and the adjacent sea-coast.

HASTINGS, Pevensey, and Eastbourne; Battle, with its *sanguelac, mal-fosse,* and the choir of its abbatial church—the spot of Harold's death; Bodiam Castle; Rye and Winchelsea; Camber Castle, and the scenery of the coast.

INTRODUCTION.

I.—DIMENSIONS AND DIVISIONS.

THE county of Sussex consists of an oblong territory, stretching along the southern coast of England. The line of its coast, following the indentations, is nearly ninety miles long; the extreme length of the county in a straight line, from Ladyholt Park on the west, to the end of Kent Ditch on the east, is seventy-six miles; while the extreme breadth, in a cross line from Tunbridge Wells on the north to Beachy Head on the south, is twenty-seven miles. It contains 934,006 acres, and is inhabited by a population which, according to the census of 1881, amounted to 490,316; viz., East Sussex, 359,114; West Sussex, 131,202. In 1851 it amounted only to 336,844 for the whole county.

On the west, Sussex is bounded by Hampshire; on the north, north-east, and east, by Surrey and Kent; on the south, by the English Channel.

The whole district is divided into 6 rapes, 66 hundreds, and 324 parishes, containing 1 city and 21 market towns, viz. :—

	RAPES.	HUNDREDS.	PARISHES.
WEST SUSSEX...	Chichester.........	7	74
	Arundel............	5	56
	Bramber	11	40
EAST SUSSEX ...	Lewes	12	51
	Pevensey	18	52
	Hastings	13	51
	6	66	324

By the Distribution of Seats Bill (1884) the parliamentary representation of Sussex is divided among 9 members—6 from rural constituencies, 2 from the borough of Brighton, and 1 from that of Hastings.

Ecclesiastically it constitutes the Diocese of Chichester, and is subdivided into 2 archdeaconries and 11 rural deaneries, viz. :—

ARCHDEACONRY.	RURAL DEANERIES.	ARCHDEACONRY.	RURAL DEANERIES.
Chichester	Chichester.	Lewes	Dallington.
	Arundel.		Hastings.
	Boxgrove.		Lewes.
	Midhurst.		Pevensey.
	Storrington.		South Malling.
	Pagham.	Battle forms a deanery by itself.	

Sussex has preserved its Saxon and Norman divisions and local peculiarities more than almost any other county in England, and as a great body of curious information has of late years been published upon this subject, we make some extracts bearing upon it from a valuable work, Taylor's "Words and Places." Speaking of ancient county divisions, hundreds, rapes, &c., he says

"While the *hundred* seems to indicate the peaceful settlement of Saxon families, and the *wapentake* the defensive-military organisation of the Danish intruders, the *rape*, as it would appear, is a memorial of the violent transference of landed property by the Conqueror, the lands being plotted out for division by the *hrepp*, or *rope*, just as they had been by Rolf in Normandy.

"The districts of Iceland are called *Hreppar*. The *hyde* the Saxon unit of land, seems to have been a portion measured off with a thong. . . . The *hyde*, or *hide*, was a space of 100 or 120 acres, varying in different parts of the country. The *carrucate* was the fourth part of the hide, and was what one family could plough and cultivate in one year, being considered equivalent to their maintenance; hence it was also called a *ploughland*. Eight hides, or 800 acres, made one *knight's fee*, being considered as the land sufficient to maintain and furnish the king with one knight for his wars.

DIMENSIONS AND DIVISIONS.

" The *Hundred* is supposed to have been originally the settlement of 100 free families of Saxon colonists, just as the *canton* was a similar Celtic division (from the Welsh *cant*, a hundred). In rural districts the population must have increased at least tenfold—often in a much larger proportion—since the period of the formation of the present Hundreds. Many single agricultural *parishes* contain 100 families removed above the labouring class; and we may probably conclude that the population is equal to that of one of the Saxon Hundreds. The manner in which the island was gradually peopled, and the distribution and relative density of the Saxon population, are curiously indicated by the varying sizes of the Hundreds. In Kent, Sussex, and Dorset, which were among the earliest settlements, the small dimensions of the Hundreds prove the Saxon population was very dense; whereas when we approach the borders of Wales and Cumberland, where the Saxon tenure was one rather of conquest than of colonisation, and where a few free families probably held in check a considerable subject population, we find that the Hundreds include a much larger area. Thus the average number of square miles in each Hundred is—

In Sussex	28	In Kent............	24
Dorset	30	Wilts............	44
North Hants..	52	Surrey	58
Herts	79	Gloucester ...	97
Notts	105	Derby	162
Warwick	179	Lancaster ...	302

We arrive at similar conclusions from the proportions of the slaves to the rest of the population as returned in "Domesday." In the east of England we find no slaves returned, the Celtic population having become entirely assimilated. In Kent and Sussex the slaves constituted 10 per cent. of the population; in Cornwall and Devon, 20 per cent. ; in Gloucestershire, 33 per cent."—Taylor's " Words and Places."

With regard to Saxon names in Sussex, Mr. Taylor observes (p. 360) :—

" The vast tract in Kent and Sussex, which is now called the Weald (*Well* Street is the name of the Roman road which ran through the wooded district), is the remains of a Saxon forest called the *Andredesleah*, which with a breadth of thirty miles stretched for 120 miles along the northern frontier of the kingdom of the South Saxons. In the district of the Weald almost every local name, for miles and miles, terminates in *hurst, ley, den*, or *field*. The *hursts* and *horsts* were the denser portions of the forest ; the *leys* were the open forest glades, where the cattle love to lie; the *dens* were the deep wooded valleys ; and the *fields* were little patches of *felled* or cleared lands in the midst of the surrounding forest. From PETERS-FIELD and MIDHURST, by BILLINGHURST, CUCKFIELD, WADHURST, and LAMBERHURST, as far as HAWKHURST and TENTERDEN, these joint names stretch in an uninterrupted string. The *dens* (probably a Celtic word adopted by the Saxons) were the swine pastures ; and down to the seventeenth century the 'Court of Dens,' as it was called, was held at Addington, to determine disputes arising out of the rights of forest pasture. . . . An analysis of the forest names in the Weald gives the following results :—

	Hurst.	Den.	Ley.	Holt, hot.	Field.	Total.
Central Kent.......	33	42	22	1	19	117
Northern Sussex ...	40	16	21	4	28	109
Southern Surrey ...	1	0	8	11	2	22
Eastern Hants	26	1	15	8	6	51
	100	59	66	19	55	299

Much additional light has been thrown on this subject by a learned Sussex antiquary, Mr. W. Durrant Cooper, who has published an interesting paper on Sussex names in the 7th vol. of the "Sussex Archæological Collections." He observes that the names, syllables, or terminations, differ much in the two divisions of the county; and that in the eastern division *field*, *fold*, *leah*, or *ley*, and *hurst*, are to be found in fully one-half of all the names of places; while in the western division the same circumstance holds good for *den*, or *dean*, *ing*, *ton*, and *ham*. Saxon words, he says, are found entering into the composition of the names of at least 600 farms in Sussex, and he forms the following table of the chief words so compounded :—

Brook : as Kidbrook, Holbrook, &c.

Burn : as Glyndebourn, Hawks-bourne.

Bury : as Owlsbury, Chanctonbury, &c.

Camb (a valley with water) : as Duncombe, Combland, &c.

Croft : as Wivelscroft, Horncroft, &c.

Den : as Birchden, Highden, &c.

Field : as Freshfield, Oxfield, &c.

Fold : as Ashfold, Pensfold, &c.

Ford : as Blackford, Durnford, &c.

Ham : as Clapham, Wickham, &c.

Hoe : as Hoehouse, Hoefarm, The Hove, anciently The Hooe.

Holm : as Holmbush, Broomsholm, &c.

Holt : as Buckholt, Southholt, &c.

Hook : as Hookland, Hookfarm, &c.

Hurst : as Ashhurst, Ticehurst, &c.

Ig, or *Eye :* as Horsey, Thorney, &c.

Ing : as Angmering, Poleing, &c.

Knol : as Bigknowl, Woodknowl, &c.

Leah, or *Ley :* as Horleigh, Highleagh, Verdley, &c.

Ling : as Birling, Pelling, &c.

Low : as Burlow, Lowfield, &c.

Mere : as Duckmere, Radesmere, &c.

Mitchel : as Mitchelham, Mitchelgrove, &c.

Nap : as Nepcote, Napfarm, &c.

Slade : as Slade, Sladelands, &c.

Stan, or *Stone :* as Stamstreet, Stoneham, &c.

Stede : as Horstede, Stanstead, &c.

Streete : as Streetefarm.

Ton : as Preston, Houghton, &c.

Tye : as Brambletye, Tyehill, &c.

Wick : as Godenwick, Lutwick, &c.

Worth : as Atlingworth, Petworth, &c.

It may be added that a curious paper on Sussex provincialisms in dialect, &c., by Mr. M. A. Lower, is published in the thirteenth volume of the same " Collections."

II.—GENERAL ASPECT.

Sussex is a district of much picturesque beauty, although it has no high mountains, nor great valleys, nor wide rivers, nor leaping waterfalls, among its natural features. Its beauty consists in its well-wooded, well-cultivated lands; in the frequent occurrence of antique manors and castles; in the constant presence of village churches of every epoch of English architecture; and in its comfortable, well-stocked farms and cottages—every farm with its orchard; every cottage with its garden.

All along the south side of the county, from the neighbourhood of Chichester to Beachy Head, runs the hilly range of the South Downs, bare of trees, but famous for their white chalk cliffs and green sheep-walks: while the larger part of the county, to the northward and eastward, is a farming tract, broken up into small eminences, rising into the Forest Ridge on the north-east, and sinking into wide marshes on the south-east by the edge of the sea. Sussex abounds in small forests and woodlands, is exceedingly fertile and productive of all that is wanted in life, and is proverbially healthy in climate. A full account of the climate of Sussex, and of all the south coast of England, will be found in the Appendices to Horsfield: it contains tables of temperature and analyses of mineral water. The author was Dr. William King, a physician of eminence and scientific distinction living at Brighton.

At no very distant period the roads and means of communication were peculiarly bad; but during the present century they have been improving, and before the introduction of railways travelling had attained great excellence all over the county. At the present time Sussex is well off for railways, being traversed from north to south by the London and Brighton line, with its numerous branches; and from east to west, along the coast, by the Hastings and Folkestone branch of the South-Eastern line; and by the London and South Coast line running near and branching off to all the ports and watering-places.

Geology.—Dr. Mantell, in his account of the geology of Sussex, prefixed to Horsfield's "History," gives such a lucid sketch of the subject, that we cannot do better than quote many of his observations, and refer those readers who wish for further information to his works, as well as to papers by Lyell and other eminent geologists on the same subject.

Mantell says :—"The strata of Sussex belong to those secondary formations of England that are newer than, or, in other words, have been deposited subsequently to, the Purbeck limestone; comprising also outliers of the London clay or Isle of White basin; and accumulations of diluvial and alluvial *debris*. The principal regular deposits are the plastic and London clay of the tertiary formations; the chalk and the Wealden beds, comprehending the Weald clay and the sands and clays of Tilgate Forest and Hastings of the secondary. The physical characters of the district depend on the range and extent of these mineral masses. Along the southern division the chalk constitutes a magnificent chain of hills or downs, which extends through the county, in a direction nearly east and west, from Beachy Head to Hampshire. On the north of the Downs a valley of clay or marl appears, which is succeeded by a belt of sand that, in the west division, rises into hills of considerable elevation; a valley of clay, forming the Weald, runs parallel with the northern edge of the sand; and this vale is bounded by another ridge of sand and sandstone, which constitutes the northern limits of the county. . . . The agricultural features of the district vary, of course, with the nature of the subsoil. The chalk hills are principally reserved for pasturage, and support a breed of sheep which for fineness of wool and compactness of form are superior to any in the kingdom. The line of alluvial soil between the Downs and the sea, on the western side of the county, is equal to any for its richness and fertility; at the foot of the Downs, on the north side, where the marl emerges from below the chalk, the land is a very productive arable; the clay of the Weald produces a stiff soil, remarkably favourable for the growth of forest trees, particularly the oak; and the sand of the forest ridge constitutes the most picturesque, but barren, tract of the whole country."

The following table will give a succinct view of all the Sussex formations :—

FORMATION.	ORGANIC REMAINS.	LOCALITIES.
ALLUVIUM	Incrustation of tufts, trunks of trees, leaves, nuts, &c.; comminuted shells of existing species.	Springs; valleys of the Arun, Adur, Ouse, and Cuckmere; bogs at Amberley, Lewes, Pevensey, &c.
DILUVIUM	Bones and teeth of the elephant, &c.	Burton, Patcham, Hastings, &c.; summits and valleys of the Downs.
Tertiary Formations.		
CRAG	Bones, &c., of elephant, horse, deer, &c.; jaws of whale, &c.	Shoreham and Rottingdean; on summits and fissures of cliffs, &c.
PLASTIC CLAY	Ostreæ; cycladeæ; teeth of fishes; leaves of unknown plants, &c.	Castle Hill, Newhaven; Downs, near Seaford; Falmer, near Lewes.
LONDON CLAY	Septaria; teeth and palates of fishes, &c.	Bracklesham Bay, near Chichester; Bognor Rocks, &c.
Secondary Formations.		
CHALK, WITH FLINTS.	Nodules and veins of flint; pyrites; ammonitæ, echini, zoophytes, &c.	Upper portion of South Downs.
CHALK. WITHOUT FLINTS.	Pyrites, zoophytes, echini, shells, &c.	Lower division of South Downs.
CHALK MARL	Calcareous spar, turritellæ, crustacea.	Base of the Downs, Southbourne, Lewes, &c.

FORMATION.	ORGANIC REMAINS.	LOCALITIES.
UPPER GREEN SAND.	Ostrea, carinatæ, ammonitæ, &c.	Steyning, Bignor, New-sted, &c.
GAULT	Gypsum; ammonitæ, fishes, crustacea, &c.	Ringmer, Newtimber, Arundel, Bignor, &c.
SHANKLIN SAND ...	Trigoniæ; patellæ, veneri-cardiæ, &c.	Pevensey, Laughton, Ditchling, Pulborough, Petworth, &c.
WEALD CLAY	Paludinæ, saurians and fishes; limestone, with freshwater bivalves.	Laughton, Kirdford, West Grinstead, Cowfold, &c.
HASTINGS SANDS AND CLAYS.	Lignites, ferns, &c.	Bexhill, Horsted, &c.
TILGATE FOREST STRATA.	Teeth and bones of enormous reptiles; turtles, birds, fishes; shells of genera, renio, paludinæ, &c.; plants allied to palms, ferns, &c.	Hastings, Ore, Tilgate Forest, Horsham, Chaily, Rye, Winchelsea, Craw-ley, &c.
ASHBURNHAM BEDS.	Immense quantities of bi-valve shells, renio, and equiseta, &c.	Brightling, Hurst Green, Rotherfield, &c.

In the above series the chalk and the Tilgate Forest beds are the most remarkable; the former for their great thickness, and for the deposits of flint, &c.; the latter for the immense saurian remains, such as those of the iguanodon, an animal from 70 to 100 feet long, the megalosaurus, &c. &c.

Dr. Mantell, in commenting upon the Tilgate formations, observes—"The almost exclusive prevalence of land and fresh water exuviæ observable in these strata, warrants the conclusion that they were formed by a very different agent from that which effected the deposition of the Portland limestone below, and the sands and chalk above them. The seas, in the primitive ages of our planet, were inhabited by vast tribes of multilocular shells, which, however variable in their species, were not only of the same family, but also of the same genera, viz.: Belemnites, Ammonites, and Turrilites; and the presence of their remains in any considerable quantity in a formation affords a fair presumption that such a deposit is of marine origin.

"We cannot leave this subject," Mantell adds, "without offering a few remarks on the probable condition of the country through which the water flowed that deposited the strata of the Wealden ; and on the nature of its vegetable and animal productions. Whether it was an island or a continent may not be determined, but that it was diversified by hill and valley, and enjoyed a climate of a much higher temperature than any part of modern Europe, is more than probable. Several kinds of ferns appear to have constituted the vegetable clothing of the soil. The elegant *Sphænopteris*, which probably never attained a greater height than a few feet, and the beautiful *Lonicopteris* of still lesser growth, being abundant everywhere. It is easy to conceive what would be the appearance of the valleys and plains covered with these plants, from that presented by modern tracts where the common ferns so generally prevail. But the loftier vegetables were so entirely distinct from any that are now known to exist in European countries, that we search in vain for anything at all analogous without the tropics. The forests of *Clathariæ* and *Endogenitæ*, the plants of which, like some of the arborescent ferns, probably attained a height of thirty or forty feet, must have borne a much greater resemblance to those of tropical regions than to any that now occur in temperate climates. If we attempt to portray the animals of this ancient country, our description will possess more of the character of a romance than of a legitimate deduction from established facts. Turtles of various kinds must have been seen on the banks of its rivers and lakes, and groups of enormous crocodiles basking in the fens and shallows. The enormous *Megalosaurus*, and the yet more gigantic *Iguanodon*, to which the groves of palms and aborescent ferns would have been mere beds of reeds, must have been of such prodigious magnitude that the existing animal creation presents us with no fit objects of

comparison. . . . The sequence of the physical changes
that have taken place in this district is clearly established;
and it may be stated, not as an hypothesis, but as a necessary
deduction from known facts, that the part of the earth's surface, which is now the county of Sussex, has, within the
periods to which our researches refer, suffered the following
mutations :—

"1st. It was the delta of some mighty river, which flowed
through a country enjoying a tropical climate, and inhabited by
various reptiles, and clothed with palms and arborescent ferns.

"2ndly. This delta was covered by a profound ocean, and
formed the bottom of the deep for a period of sufficient duration
to admit of the deposition of several thousand feet of strata,
enclosing myriads of marine fishes, corals, and shells.

"3rdly. The oceanic deposit was broken up and elevated
above the waters, the higher summits forming groups of islands;
while in the hollows, which were covered by the sea, those strata
were deposited which geologists now term the tertiary formations.

"4thly. A further elevation took place; and the elephant,
the horse, the buffalo, and the deer lived on the hills and plains
and their remains became entombed in this superficial strata.

"Lastly. The surface assumed its present form, and man,
took possession of the soil, and destroyed many species of its
ancient inhabitants."

The opinion of Sir C. Lyell, and other recent geologists
who have worked at the Sussex district, may be briefly stated,
thus :—That after the deposition of the Wealden formations, that
of the chalk and its associated beds took place, beneath a very
deep ocean; that upheavals then took place, cracking and
breaking up the chalk, by forces acting, some from east to west,
some north and south, and that while the tertiary deposits were
being made amid an archipelago of islands, the chalk was being
gradually fetched out by the ocean from the surface of the

Wealden beds; and the downs north and south left in their present
general forms, with the transvere valleys of the present rivers
intersecting them; and that then diluvial and alluvial processes
took place during and after the great glacial epoch, and then
the subsequent approximation of the surface and its climatic
condition to what we now experience. To this it may be added
that within the historic period great changes have taken place
along the coastline of Sussex. Much cultivated land has been
washed away by the sea in the neighbourhood of Selsey,
Chichester Harbour, Bognor, &c. At Shoreham, the sea once
came further inland than it does now. At Aldrington, once at
the mouth of the Adur river, the habitations have disappeared,
and only the ruined church remains; yet the sea has subsequently retired, or rather has thrown up a long shingle bank,
changing the course of the river, and forming land on which
houses have again been built, as in the west portion of Hove
parish. At Brighton, towards the middle of the present town,
much land has been lost, and the dates of the marine encroachments are accurately known. All along the line of cliffs from
Brighton to Beachy Head a wasting process, by the action of
the sea, is going on. Beyond Beachy Head, however, at
Pevensey, the sea has retired; and, though it has gained on the
cliffs at Hastings, yet at St. Leonards it has shut itself out by
shingle. At Winchelsea, the sea, after destroying the old town,
has again retired; and at Rye great difficulty has been experienced in keeping the harbour navigable, even for small vessels,
though once it was one of the most flourishing ports of Sussex.
There is a perpetual drifting of shingle from the west all along
the coast, tending greatly to modify its outline. In general,
too, most of the Sussex rivers have suffered from gradual silting
up.

The subjoined table of the principal altitudes of the hills in
Sussex is taken from Mr. T. H. Cooper's "Account of the
Botany of the County" in the Appendices to Horsfield: —

Ditchling Beacon	858 feet above the sea.	
Firle Beacon	820 ,,	,,
Chanctonbury Hill	814 ,,	,,
Crowborough Beacon	804 ,,	,,
Rooks' Hill	702 ,,	,,
Bow Hill	702 ,,	,,
Brightling Hill	646 ,,	,,
Fairlight Down	599 ,,	,,
Beachy Head	575 ,,	,,

The average height, however, of the South Downs may be reckoned at about 500 feet above the level of the sea.

Rivers.—The Sussex rivers all flow ultimately into the English Channel, rising mostly in the northern parts of the county. The chief streams are :—

(1.) The Western Arun, rising near Petersfield, flowing eastward till it meets the Western Rother, at Selham.

(2.) The Western Rother, rising near Lurgeshall, joining the West Arun at Selham, and then flowing into the Arun, near Stopham.

(3.) The Arun, rising in St. Leonard's Forest, and falling into the sea at Littlehampton, below Arundel.

(4.) The Lavant, rising in Charlton Forest, and flowing into the sea near Chichester.

(5.) The Adur, rising near Nuthurst, and falling into the sea at Shoreham.

(6.) The Ouse, rising in St. Leonard's and Worth Forests, in two branches, and falling into the sea at Newhaven, below Lewes.

(7.) The Cuckmere, rising near Heathfield Park, and falling into the sea near Seaford.

(8.) The Ashburne, rising near Dallington, and falling into the sea near Pevensey.

(9.) The Asten, rising near Ashburnham, and falling into the sea near St. Leonards.

(10.) The Tillingham, rising at Beckley.

(11.) The Brede, rising near Battel.

(12.) The Tweed, rising near Playdon. These three small streams all fall into the East Rother.

(13.) The Eastern Rother, rising near Rotherfield, and falling into the sea at Rye.

The Kent Ditch is a branch of the East Rother, dividing Kent from Sussex.

There are two canals in West Sussex; one from Portsmouth to the Arun, but now dry, and one joining the rivers Arun and Rother with the Wey, and so with the Thames.

In East Sussex there is the military canal, a defensible work constructed during the great French war, running from near Hastings to Hythe in Kent, now disused.

Many meres, or small lakes, exist in the Weald of Sussex, as well as pools and ponds, formed for the iron-works which once flourished in that part of the county.

Besides the above, there are many small streams, serving as feeders to the principal ones. A full account of them all, compiled with great care, and accompanied by much admirable typographical detail, has been published by Mr. M. A. Lower, in the "Sussex Archæological Collections." It will well repay the trouble of consulting it.

Some names of Sussex rivers are evidently ancient British, such as the Arun, the Rother, the Adur, and the Ouse. One small stream is called the Esse, another the Tweed, a third the Limene (or Eastern Rother), and a fourth the Tyse or Tees.

Closely connected with the social habits and condition of any district and its historical changes, is the character of its architecture. The leading features of the principal buildings throughout the county, and the peculiarities of their styles, are recorded in this work according as the buildings themselves come to be mentioned. It is, however, desirable to state here that Sussex contains numerous specimens of almost all kinds of architecture ever produced in Britain. There is *Roman* work as at Pevensey castle, *Saxon* in some of the small churches in the western divisions, *Norman* throughout the whole county, and *Early English* closely associated with it in a large proportion of the parish churches. The later characteristics of English architecture, *Decorated, Perpendicular, Elizabethan,*

Carolinian, and the debased Dutch and Italian of more recent times, are all represented in Sussex buildings. The three leading peculiarities of the local architecture are to be looked for, first, in the fine old castles of Arundel, Bodiam, Hurstmonceux, &c. ; next, in the pile of Chichester Cathedral, and in all the little village churches for which the county is famous ; but, thirdly, and most remarkably, in the manor houses of the Elizabethan period which stud the district all over. Hardly a village is to be met with in which some remains of old manorial grandeur are not still to be found. They are nearly all specified in this work.

As a part of the *ecclesiology* of Sussex, it is proper to mention that antiquaries have of late been inquiring into the subject of its *church bells*, and have found it to be rich in the number of bells which it still possesses. The total number of church and public bells in the county is 1,013, of which 106 date from periods prior to the Reformation. There are 18 peals of eight bells, 39 of six, and 31 of five. The heaviest tenor is at St. Paul's, Brighton, weighing two tons. Some of these bells were cast by Sussex founders ; but the greater number, being old peals re-cast, have been made in London. Sussex villagers are peculiarly fond of bell-ringing. The inscriptions on some of the bells are very curious ; and a full account of them will be found in vol. xvi. of the "Sussex Archæological Collections."

LONDON & BRIGHTON & SOUTH-COAST RAILWAYS.
(LONDON TO BRIGHTON, PORTSMOUTH & HASTINGS.)

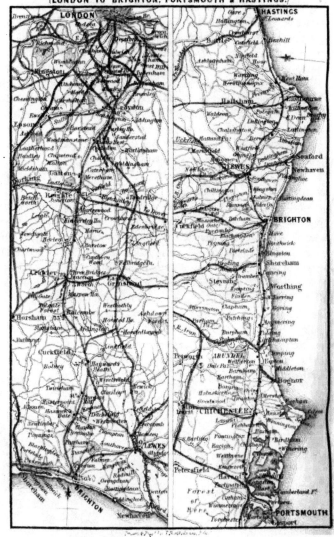

SUSSEX GUIDE.

HASTINGS and ST. LEONARDS.

[Population, 42,256. *Hotels:* Queen's ; Victoria ; Albion ; Royal Marine ; Castle ; Royal Saxon. London, 62 m. by L. and S.-E. R. Winchelsea, 8¼ m. Ramsgate, 23 m. Battle, 6 m. Rye, 11½ m. Eastbourne, 18 m.]

HASTINGS, forming with St. Leonards one borough, is the second town of the county as regards population, being next after Brighton, but it is one of the first in historical interest and importance, and certainly the chief in respect of beauty, whether of inland or coast scenery. In the famous Bayeaux Tapestry, which commemorates the Conqueror's expedition to England, and the battle that gave him the crown, we find Hastings named Hestenga-ceastra, showing that it was a fortified town at that period. It was a place of trade and strength in the Saxon times, and took its name from the family or tribe of the Hæstingas. In the reign of Edward the Confessor its ships and sailors were well known. It was chartered, and was afterwards placed at the head of the list of the *Cinque Ports.* Ship-building was carried on, but the trade was not equal to that of Rye or Winchelsea. The sea made encroachments, and destroyed its harbour, and the town gradually sank in importance till the latter part of the last century, when it was recommended by Dr. Baillie for invalids, and has since become one of the favourite watering-places of England.

" We have been," says Charles Lamb, " dull at Worthing one summer, duller at Brighton another, dullest at Eastbourne a

A

third, and are at this moment doing dreary penance at Hastings !
I love town or country, but this detestable Cinque Port is neither.
I hate these scrubbed shoots thrusting out their starved foliage
from between horrid fissures of dusty innutritious rocks, which
the amateur calls ' verdure to the edge of the sea.' I require
woods, and they show me stunted coppices. I cry out for the
water-brooks, and pant for fresh streams and inland murmurs. I
cannot stand all day on the naked beach, watching the capricious
hues of the sea, shifting like the colours of a dying mullet. I am
tired of looking out of the windows of this island prison. ' I
would fain retire into the interior of my cage." But the tourist
will err wofully if he accepts Charles Lamb's delightful badinage
for truthful description. Hastings is not only not a dull, but
it is even a romantic and picturesque town. It has, moreover,
good hotels and lodging-houses, excellent public-baths, a pier
900 feet in length, with a pavilion capable of seating 2000
persons, and a public park of 70 acres in extent.

Hastings and St. Leonards, although originally distinct and
separated from each other by about a mile, are now connected by
a line of terraces and parades, extending for nearly three miles
along the coast. St. Leonards is the more fashionable district
of the two, and has a separate station. Near the Saxon Hotel,
on the Grand Parade, an archway with the date 1828, marks the
eastern boundary of St. Leonards. Beyond this, to the west-
wards, are the Marina, where is situated the Victoria Hotel.
Near this are the Subscription Garden and Assembly Room.
St. Leonard's Green and the Archery Gardens are delightful
places of recreation as well as the Public Park which covers an
area of 70 acres. The pier extends 900 feet into the sea, and
the pavilion connected with it will accommodate 2000 persons.
Sea-bathing may be enjoyed at Hastings from machines, which
are stationed opposite the Marina, the Marine Parade, Eversfield,
and Stratford Place, and Robertson Terrace. There are also
baths in the town, and an aquarium.

The town of Hastings lies for the most part in a hollow,
snugly sheltered by hills, except where it slopes southward to the
sea. The original town is believed to have extended some distance
to the south, its site being now partly covered by the waves. There
has for the last 25 years been a continual effort to render every
part of the town as modern looking as possible, and any traces of
antiquity have now disappeared. Its industrial support is derived

HASTINGS.

from its fishery, boat-building, and lime burning ; its lime-kilns lying up at the valley, at some small distance from the sea. Messrs. Rock and Son have here a large and celebrated coach-factory. The principal thoroughfares are Pelham Crescent, Pelham Place, Wellington Street, the Marine Parade, and Robertson Street. Under the East Cliff, varying from 170 to 218 feet in height, Dutch fish-auctions are often held. The Town Hall is in High Street, and was built in 1823. It boasts of a shield taken from the French at the conquest of Quebec. To the west stretch the lofty and breezy terraces of St. Leonards, almost as far as Bulverhythe, or "the townsmen's haven." The Marina, a parade 600 feet in length, was designed in 1828 by Decimus Burton, the architect, and the Esplanade was also erected on his plans. Its new church was built in 1833.

Hastings, as may be supposed, has had its "distinguished visitors." Charles Lamb was here, as we have already shewn, and indulged his usual good-humoured vein of satire. Lord Byron was here in 1814, "swimming and eating turbot, and smuggling neat brandies and silk handkerchiefs, and walking on cliffs, and tumbling down hills." Here Campbell resided for five years, and wrote his beautiful "address to the Sea." Here the Rev. Charles Honeyman (vide "The Newcomes") displayed his white handkerchief and his lachrymose eloquence in Lady Whittlesea's chapel. Prout, the artist, lived at 53 George Street. Sir Cloudesley Shovel and Titus Oates—not exactly "Arcades ambo," though we class them together—were born in All Saints' Street. Louis Napoleon, the exile, resided at Pelham Cottage, in 1840, and Louis Philippe, ex-King of the French, at the Victoria Hotel, 1848.

The Climate in the higher parts of the town is vigorous and bracing ; in the lower range it is well adapted, from its mildness, to the most delicate pulmonary invalids. St. Leonards is, however, the healthiest and most genial quarter. According to Dr. Harwood, the average mean temperature, at 9 a.m., is, in November 45° ; December 47°, January and February 44° ; and out of 64 days the S.W. wind prevails 22, S. 11, N. 8, W. 8, S.E. 6, N.E. 4, N.W. 3, and E. 2.

The botanist will find in this vicinity—peppermint, catmint, calamint, wild cabbage, psamma arenaria, samphire, tamarisk, scorpion grass, henbane, wild celery, and pellitory. The kestrel, tern, bee-eater, phalarope, landrail, hobby, snipe, plover, and gull are met with along this coast from Hastings to Rye.—(*A. E. Knox.*)

Hastings, as the termination *ing* indicates, was a settlement of the Saxon Hæstingas, and cannot be connected with Hasten, the old Danish jarl. Edward the Conqueror erected it into a seaport, and its contingent to the Cinque Ports' fleet was estimated at 21 ships, each bearing 20 men and a boy. Its component limbs, or members, were—Pevensey, Seaford, Bekesbourne, and the Ville of Grange, Rochester. As late as the reign of Elizabeth it could boast of a wooden pier, now replaced by a handsome structure, which is a favourite resort of visitors. The harbour, however, is not considered a safe one for large vessels, and colliers after discharging their cargoes generally leave at next tide.

On this shore William the Conqueror landed on the 20th of September 1066, and, while his Knights stared at each other aghast, lost his footing as he leapt ashore. With the promptitude of a great mind he grappled the sands with his fingers, and exclaimed, "It is thus I take seisin of the land which shall shortly be ours." The table—a slab of rock—at which he is said to have taken his dinner, is now placed at the gateway of the old Subscription Gardens. His vessels, meanwhile, were moored in a line from Pevensey to Hastings. From this place he marched along the downs to Telham Hill. On the level, near the Railway Station, he formed his camp where his army passed the night in prayer and singing hymns.

HASTINGS CASTLE stands upon the brink of the cliff. Its principal entrance was necessarily on the land side, where the portcullis groove, and the hooks for the gate-hinges may yet be examined. The castle area occupied about an acre and a quarter. The south side was 400 feet long; the east side 300 feet long, with a fosse, and a massive wall strengthened by three semicircular towers whose fragments are still interesting. The northwest side was 400 feet in length. To the west, both a square and a circular tower are still standing, and a doorway which formerly opened into the chapel of St. Mary, a Transitional Norman structure, 110 feet long, with a nave, chancel, and aisles, now a mass of ruins.

The manor was bestowed by King William on the Count of Lee, who may have erected the castle. It remained in the hands of his descendants until the middle of the fourteenth century when, according to tradition, it was consumed by fire. In December

1093, William Rufus was detained here by contrary winds, and Archbishop Anselm consecrated—in the Castle Chapel—Robert Blovet as bishop of Lincoln. Adela, daughter of King William, presided here as Queen of Love and Beauty at the first tournament celebrated in England. The castle now belongs to the Earl of Chichester, and admittance may be gained at any time, except on Sundays, to see the ruins, fee 3d.

At the foot of East Hill stands the Perpendicular pile of ALL SAINTS' CHURCH, with a nave, chancel, south porch, and west tower, 73 feet high. Observe the sedilia in the south wall ; and the octangular font. It contains a brass to *T. Goodenough*. In the graveyard lies *George Mogridge*, d. 1854, better known as "Old Humphrey."

ST. CLEMENT'S CHURCH, in High Street, another Perpendicular building (1380), contains a chancel, nave, north and south aisles, and west tower. Two balls fixed to the tower commemorate the attack made by the Dutch fleet, under de Ruyter, in 1666. The font is Decorated and octagonal. There are brasses to *Thos. Weekes*, d. 1563, and *John Barley*, d. 1592.

ST. PAUL'S CHURCH, a handsome edifice, opened in 1868, is of the style of the early part of the fourteenth century. The roof is of deal varnished, and painted to resemble oak ; variegated stone and brick are used throughout in the paving of the chancel and tower. The apse is spacious, having fine windows of richly stained glass. The reredos in the centre is panelled, and the sides are lined with alabaster ; between the rail and the altar are five medallions let into the floors, representing

The Slaying of the Innocents ; the Stoning of St. Stephen ; the Beheading of St. Paul ; the Beheading of St. James ; the Crucifixion of St. Peter.

There are also five smaller medallions, representing the lash, ladder, nails, and other instruments of the sufferings of the Saviour. The reading ledge of the pulpit is upheld by an angel sculptured in pure marble, and the font is of sienna marble, its stand being of Emperor's red and Derbyshire fossil.

ST. MARY'S-IN-THE-CASTLE, a Grecian structure, in Pelham Crescent, built by Lord Chichester in 1828, has its altar in the middle of the south side. ST. MARY MAGDALENE'S was consecrated in 1852 ; ST. CLEMENT'S, Halton, in 1838 ; and the MARINERS' chapel in 1854. ST. LEONARD'S was erected in 1833.

A fragment of wall at the PRIORY FARM is the sole relic of
a house of Augustinian canons, founded by Sir W. C. Bricet, *temp.*
Richard I.

The climate of Hastings is salubrious, and in many respects
suitable for invalids, being generally cooler than London in
summer, and warmer in the spring months. The exposure varies
considerably ; but that portion of St. Leonards which lies beneath the cliffs which have been cut away for its erection, including Verulam and Eversham Place, the Grand Parade, and part of
the Marina, is almost completely sheltered from the north wind.

The view of Hastings from St. Leonards is one of exquisite
beauty. " The lofty and handsome range of Pelham Crescent, the
church of St. Mary-at-Cliff, and other modern buildings, occupy
a prominent place in the picture, and wear an imposing air as
they stand contrasted with the meaner houses at their base, and
are backed by the noble cliff which rises far above, and which
has been carved away to afford room for them. The houses of
the older part of the town running irregularly up the higher
grounds, and opposing to each other every variety of size, and
shape, and colour, prevent anything like formality, which the
preponderance of the newer buildings would otherwise produce ; while the gray fragments of the ancient castle, crowning
the summit of the lofty cliff, impart an air of dignity to the
humble dwellings beneath. And then, to complete the picture,
a large fleet of fishing smacks and boats, with numerous fishing-
boats moving about them, are seen on the beach."—(*Thorne*).

[HINTS FOR RAMBLES. 1. To Fairlight Down, and thence to Guestling. Cross
the country to Westfield. Keep northward, across the Rother, to Brede. Visit
Sedlescomb, and return by the main road. About 17 m. 2. Through Hollington
to Battle Abbey. Return by way of Catsfield and Crowhurst, 12 m. 3. Through St
Leonards and Bulverhythe to Bexhill. Strike across the country northward to
Crowhurst. Gain the high road by way of Crowhurst Park, and return *vid* Ore to
Hastings. 4. To Winchelsea by rail. Return, by the road, to Pett, and thence by
way of Fairlight Down, the Lovers' Seat, the Dripping Well, and Ecclesbourne
Cliffs to Hastings.]

We subjoin the distances from Hastings of the following
localities :—

To Belleport, 3 m. ; Crowhurst, 2¾ m. ; Dropping Well, 2 m. ;
Ecclesbourne Cliffs, 2 m. ; Fairlight Glen, 2¼ m. ; Glen Roar
Cascade, 2½ m. ; Hollington, 2 m. ; The Lovers' Seat, 1¾ m. ;
Old Roar Cascade, 2½ m. ; Ore, 1¾ m. ; Westfield, 5 m.

LOVERS' SEAT—FAIRLIGHT GLEN, NEAR HASTINGS.

FAIRLIGHT GLEN—LOVERS' SEAT—DRIPPING WELL.

This forms one of those numerous walks which render the neighbourhood of Hastings so attractive. The bold, bleak ascent of FAIRLIGHT DOWN is 600 feet above the sea, and commands the whole sweep of the coast from Beachy Head to the South Foreland. The inland views are of the most varied and interesting character. The village of FAIRLIGHT contains a population of some 500 inhabitants. Its pretty CHURCH, dedicated to St. Andrew, was consecrated in 1846. The vicarage is valued at £502 per annum. Passing the residence of FAIRLIGHT PLACE, we descend into the leafy and blossomy depths of FAIRLIGHT GLEN, and make our way to the DRIPPING WELL, where, in the shadow of a glorious beech-tree, plashes over the rock a bright shimmering streamlet. A path along the hill-side leads hence to the famous LOVERS' SEAT, where, to use a local rhyme,—

> " Youth, from sympathy, a visit pay,
> And age to pass the tedious hour away."

Here we may rest ourselves upon a rude oaken bench, and look out afar over a sea which seems lit with a thousand suns. This, we are told, was (at the close of the last century) the trysting-spot of two unfortunate true lovers—the heiress of the Bogs of Elford and Lieutenant Lamb, who commanded a revenue cutter stationed off this coast. Their stolen interviews led, in due time, to a clandestine marriage in Hollington Church. The lady, after presenting her husband with a daughter, sickened and died ; the widowed husband, while sailing up the Southampton river, was smitten overboard by the boom of his yacht.

We may now continue our stroll to the shingled beach of Covehurst Bay, and keep along to Ecclesbourne (or Eagle's Bourne) Glen, a picturesque gap in the cliffs, which are here 250 feet above the sea. Ascending the height we pass the coast-guard station, and afterwards, on the right, the grounds of ROCKLANDS, where Canning used occasionally to retire from the strife of St. Stephen's. We soon gain the elevation of the East Cliffs, where are visible enough the lines of a Norman entrenchment.

At Cliff End, below Pett, commences the low marshy ground

extending from the sandstone of the Hastings ridge to the chalk
of the Folkestone heights. The Hastings sand stretches from
this point over the whole valley of the Weald, bordered north
and south by the chalk ranges. The Forest Ridge, alternating
between sandstone and clay, includes Fairlight, Hastings, and
Bexhill, and gradually unites with the Wealden.

At this point we may turn aside to the village of PETT
(population, 364), where a church, dedicated to Sts. Mary and
Peter, is noticeable for its deformity. The rectory, valued at
£482, is in the gift of Mrs. Young.

Just beyond this the cliffs rise into something like grandeur
of elevation at HOOK POINT. The next headland is called GOLD-
BURY POINT.

ORE, HOLLINGTON, OLD ROAR, WESTFIELD, SEDDLES-
COMB, ROBERTSBRIDGE, SALEHURST, BODIAM,
ETCHINGHAM, TICEHURST, LAMBERTHURST.

Winding up the fair Hastings valley we turn to the right,
at (or near) the 62d milestone from London, and ascend the
hill to ORE (population, 2677,) facing the bold and abrupt elevation of Fairlight Down. Its Perpendicular CHURCH is dedicated to
St. Helen, and contains a brass to an unknown worthy, d. 1400.
The rectory, valued at £520, is in the hands of certain trustees.
ORE PLACE (Lady Elphinstone) retains, it is said, some portions
of the ancient house erected by John of Gaunt.

Another route which the tourist will find, perhaps, the most
picturesque, is by way of HOLLINGTON (population,1053),
about 2 miles north-west of Hastings. Its attraction is the
CHURCH (St. Leonard's), a quaint little Early English and partly
Late Norman structure, hidden away in a mass of leafiness, at
some distance from the village. Its steeple is a low pyramid,
sloping on the west side beyond the roof, and supported by a
massive but deformed buttress. It contains an old pentagonal
font, and some memorials of little interest. The tradition attached to it may be compared with that of Udimore. "When
a church was begun in the neighbouring village, the Evil One,

jealous of the encroachment on a spot which he had marked as his own, every night undid what the workmen had accomplished in the course of the day. Priests were summoned to lay the fiend, and they had prepared to commence their potent conjurements, when a voice was heard offering to desist from opposition if the building were erected on the spot *he* should indicate. The offer was accepted. The church was raised, and then sprung up all around it a thick wood, concealing it from the general gaze"—(*Thorne*).

The vicarage, valued at £259, is in the patronage of the Eversfield family.

The views from the Hollington hills are very beautiful—" charming reaches of down alternating with masses of rich foliage, with here and there a fine old farm-house, or old-fashioned Sussex cottage, and everywhere the ocean filling up the breaks in the distance."

We cross from Hollington to OLD ROAR (2 miles) by a pleasant path leading across fields and through hop-grounds. It lies in a leafy hollow, near Roar Farm, close by which is a blasted oak of bolder and more picturesque form than Salvator ever designed. It derives its name from " the tremendous noise made by a large body of water tumbling over a perpendicular rock, 40 feet high, which might be heard half a mile off." It won't roar now, not even for the gratification of a cockney enthusiast; but the nook is a romantic and sequestered one, and worth seeing. About a hundred yards higher up is GLEN ROAR, " a smaller edition of Old Roar," and only to be reached by the adventurer who makes light of brambles.

We now pursue the high road to Lamberhurst, and as we keep along the sandstone ridge, may see below us, on our right, 5 miles from Hastings, the pleasant village of WESTFIELD (population, 900), and its Early English church, a small but pleasant edifice, containing many memorials, but none which will induce us to turn aside to visit them. The vicarage, valued at £520, is in the patronage of the Bishop of Chichester.

[About two miles beyond, and across the Rother, lies BREDE (population, 1059), at a short distance south of the Winchelsea road. Here, on the slope of a gentle acclivity, stands the quaint old manor-house of BREDE PLACE, *temp.* fourteenth century, now made use of as a farm, but anciently the residence of the Attsfords, from whom it passed, early in the reign of Henry VI., to the Oxenbridges. Of these Sir Goddard, who about 1580 made considerable additions to the mansion, is traditionally reported to have lived upon human flesh, with a particular relish for that of infants. Neither bow and arrow, nor axe, nor sword, nor spear, could slay this redoubtable giant, but some of the country folk about here succeeded at length in making him drunk, and sawing him in half with a wooden saw! His house, about a century ago, was tenanted by a gang of smugglers, who, by inventing strange sights, and uttering unearthly noises, contrived very effectually to secure it to themselves, undisturbed by any over-curious hind. The hall, and a room beyond it, with their Caen stone-work and enriched windows, should be carefully examined.

The CHURCH is equally worthy of notice. The Brede chantry was enlarged and repaired by Sir Goddard Oxenbridge, who chiefly employed French workmen, and their skill and fancy may be admired in the window-traceries and the foliated decoration of the doorway. Observe the monument, and effigy in Caen stone, of Sir GODDARD OXENBRIDGE, d. 1537.

The patronage of the living, a rectory valued at £1023, is in the hands of T. Frewen, Esq.

A bridge which spans the rivulet, near Brede Place, is called the GROANING BRIDGE, in recollection, perhaps, of the noises artfully produced by the smugglers. On the left of the road, towards Udimore, is Great Sowden's Wood. It contains a large and well-known heronry.]

SEDLESCOMB (population, 714) straggles along the high road, at a distance of about seven miles from Hastings, in a pleasant valley, whose sides are not indifferently clothed with wood. Here the Romans had established an iron work, as appears from the Roman coins discovered in a recently opened cinder-bed, some of which were greatly corroded, and others had evidently been burnt—(*Lower*). The CHURCH, a noticeable old building, is Early English, with some Perpendicular insertions in the chancel. Its rectory, valued at £350, is included in the Lord Chancellor's patronage.

At Cripses' Corner we turn to the left, and regain the principal road, near Vine Hall. At Soins Cross the Battle road effects a junction with the Hastings one, and we soon reach the village of ROBERTSBRIDGE (population, 270), *i.e.*, Rother's-bridge—where there is a station on the Ashford and Hastings branch of the South-Eastern Railway ; an INN, The Old George ; and a cluster of old-fashioned, red-brick houses, intermingled with some bran-new villas. On the river bank, in one of those sweet, sequestered valleys, so dear to the Cistercian monks, moulder the scanty ruins of a Cistercian abbey, founded, in 1176, by Robert de St. Martin. The site of the chapel is still discernible, and there are materials for observation in a cone-roofed "oast-house," and a groined crypt. A volume preserved in the Bodleian Library contains a quaint inscription :—"This book belongs to ST. MARY of ROBERT's-

BRIDGE ; whoever shall steal or sell it, let him be anathema
maranatha." Underneath is the following commentary :—" I,
John Bishop of Exeter, know not where the aforesaid house is,
nor did I steal this book, but acquired it in a lawful way."
Despite of the Bishop's ignorance, the Abbey was one of some
importance, and its abbot was sent—in company with the Abbot
of Boxley, another Cistercian dignitary—to discover the place of
Cœur de Lion's detention in Germany

☞ The tourist should here turn aside to SALEHURST and
BODIAM. SALEHURST (population, 2191) lies at the foot of a
really bold ascent, SILVER HILL, whence the view over Kent and
Sussex is one to be enjoyed and remembered. When Walpole was
here in 1752, his dilettantéism warmed into an almost poetical
enthusiasm :—" It commands," he cries, " a whole horizon of the
richest blue prospect you ever saw." The landscape is not deteri-
orated by the occasional passage of a rapid train on the
neighbouring rail—a white rolling column of smoke marking its
swift transit through grove and over meadow. In this neighbourhood are IRIDGE PLACE (Sir S. Meiklethwaite), COURT LODGE
(J. Smee, Esq.), and HIGHAM (Mrs. Luxford). The hop-plantations
are of considerable extent. The Early English CHURCH, dedicated
to St. John the Baptist, is neat and picturesque. Its situation is
eminently agreeable. The font has an oaken cover. The vicarage,
valued at £550, is in the gift of J. Hardy, Esq.

Crossing the Rother at Bodiam Bridge, we see the CHURCH
on our left, and the Castle of BODIAM (population, 306) to the
right, on the river bank. A deep fosse, filled with water, and fed
by the Rother, encircles it. A round tower fortifies each angle
of the area (165 feet by 150); the great gateway, approached by
a causeway, is conspicuous on the north side ; and in the centre
of the other sides rise up stout, square towers. The central court
is 87 feet by 78 feet. Over the main gateway, observe the
armorial bearings of the Bodiams, Dalyngrugges, and Wardeuxs—
into whose hands the castle successively passed. The outer
portcullis may still be examined, and the tourist will find much
to interest him in the remains of the hall, chapel, and kitchen.

From the Dalyngrugges the manor and castle passed, by
marriage, into the Lewknor family. Sir Lewis Lewknor, its
representative, *temp.* Charles I., was a hot-headed cavalier, whose

stronghold was taken and dismantled by Sir William Waller's forces. It was built in 1386, by Sir Edward Dalyngrugge, one of the gallant knights who fought so brilliantly at Creçy and Poictiers.

BODIAM CHURCH, dedicated to St. Giles, at the other end of the village, is an Early English building, of some interest. Thomas Cubitt, Esq., is the patron of the vicarage, valued at £280 per annum.

From Bodiam we may cross the hill to the north of Salehurst, and regaining the high road, descend into ETCHINGHAM (population, 852). The village is one mile distant from the station. ETCHINGHAM CHURCH is one of the most interesting in the county. Its general character is Decorated, with a massive square tower, a staircase turret, a roof of unusual height, and windows ornamented with rich flamboyant tracery. The chancel is noticeable for its length—its south door—and Early English font. The founder of the church was one Sir *William de Etchingham*, d. 1387, to whom there is a brass in the chancel (much injured), and an inscription which may be compared with that on " the Black Prince's tomb at Canterbury." An enriched canopy overhangs a brass to a later Sir *William*, d. 1444, his wife, and son, and the south aisle is adorned with an Etchingham helmet. In the nave a monument, with a bust and a neat Latin inscription, commemorates *Henry Corbould*, the father of the brothers Corbould, the artists. The church has been recently and tastefully restored. A noble yew flourishes in the graveyard.

We now move northward, leaving altogether the line of the railway, and at Hurst Green cross the Lewes road. Near the 47th milestone a winding road leads off through a pleasantly undulating country (3 miles) to TICEHURST (population, 3148). This populous village is seated on an eminence, and surrounded by fertile hills and valleys, quite 3½ miles distant from the Ticehurst road Railway Station. The hop-grounds here are extensive; and a considerable amount of arable land is carefully cultivated. At Stonegate and Flimwell are two small churches of recent date. Much of the venerable wood which anciently gave name to this countryside, and which was haunted by the mischievous Saxon fairy *Tys*, to the great wonder of the woodmen and their households, still clothes the sides of the hills and involves their combes in heavy shadows.

The CHURCH, Perpendicular in style, and dedicated to St. Mary, was completely and carefully restored in 1856. The stained glass was then introduced. Both pulpit and font are curiously and elaborately carved. Observe the brass to *John Wybarne*, d. 1490, and his two wives—the figures evidently copied from an older brass, perhaps from that to Sir William de Etchingham, in Etchingham Church.

The Dean and Chapter of Canterbury have the presentation to this vicarage.

By way of Dane Hill and Fleniwell, we regain the high road, and cross the boundaries of Kent. A mile beyond Stone Crouch we again return into Sussex, and at 40 miles from London, and 23 miles from Hastings, reach LAMBERHURST (population, 1734), *i.e.*, the Lambs' wood. To the right of the Bayham road, a short distance from the village, are the remains of the once celebrated GLOUCESTER FURNACE, the largest of the Sussex iron-works, where the iron balustrade round St. Paul's, London, weighing 200 tons, and worth £11,202, was cast. At the time of its completion the foundry was visited by the Princess (afterwards Queen) Anne and the young Duke of Gloucester, whence the name. A cottage, formerly the counting-house, and the mill-pond, with some traces of the foundry walls, are the only *vestiges* of the once busy iron-works.

As we enter the village we pass, on our right, QUEEN VICTORIA'S OAK, planted by loyal hands on the Queen's marriage-day, February 10, 1840. A few paces farther and we reach the GEORGE INN. At the other end of the village, on the hill, stand the COURT LODGE (W. C. Morland, Esq.); the VICARAGE, a picturesque Elizabethan structure; and the CHURCH, an interesting building, with a fine Perpendicular window at the west end. The carved oaken pulpit, date 1630, should be examined. The chancel is separated from the Scotney chapel by an Early English arch, of earlier date than the rest of the church. A noble and venerable yew adorns the garth.

The vicarage, valued at £401, is in the patronage of the Dean and Chapter of Rochester.

HASTINGS to BATTLE.

There are two hotels at Battle—the *Railway* and the *George*
In proceeding northwards by railway on this excursion we pass CROWHURST PARK (2½ miles), the ancient demesne of the Sussex Pelhams. It extends as far as the Battle road. On our right, and near the line, stands CROWHURST (population 591), a pretty village in a well wooded valley, with clumps of dark green yews springing up at every point of vantage. The church, dedicated to St. George, was re-built (except the tower) by Teulon, in the Decorated style. There are fragments of painted glass in the tower window. In the tracery, and over the door-case, remark the celebrated device of the Pelhams; a *buckle*, adopted in commemoration of the capture of John of France at Poictiers—a "deed of derring-do," in which Sir John Pelham bore a conspicuous part. A wooden buckle was long suspended from the gallery front. A glorious old yew, 27 feet in girth at four feet from the ground, renders the churchyard memorable. The rectory, valued at £277, is in the gift of T. Papillon, Esq.

South of the church, notice the ancient COURT LODGE, 40 feet by 23 feet, and Early Decorated in character. It was a parallelogram in plan, but the only remains now extant are the east gable, and a porch at the south-east gable. Probably it had a hall on the south side, and was of greater importance than its present ruins indicate. Its erection is ascribed to a certain Walter de Scotney, of Crowhurst, Chief Steward of Clare, Earl of Gloucester, who was executed in 1259, on the charge of having poisoned his lord and his lord's brother.

[CATSFIELD lies beyond Crowhurst to the north-west. Its Church is small, and not peculiarly interesting. Normanhurst Court in this parish, built by Sir Thomas Brassey, is worth a visit. It is open to visitors on Tuesdays.]

At 6 miles from Hastings we reach the BATTLE STATION, where we quit the train, and proceed on a pilgrimage to the scene of the great fight which, in its mighty influence upon the destinies of England and the world, can never be over-estimated. A view of the abbey gateway—"one of the finest gate-houses belonging to a religious establishment that remain in England" —and of the leaf-encompassed church, may be obtained from the railway. Lord Harry Vane is the proprietor, and the property is only thrown open to the public on *Tuesdays*.

Before we enter into any minute examination, however, of
BATTLE ABBEY, it will be advisable to put together a few details
of the great victory which its founder designed it to commemorate.
Fuller particulars than we can here afford will be found in
Sharon Turner's History, and Thierry's Conquest of the Normans;
while an erudite and most interesting paper in Mr. M. A. Lower's
" Contributions to Literature" should be consulted by the tourist.
In our own sketch we shall be greatly indebted to it for topo-
graphical information. Our historical notes are principally drawn
from the old monastic chroniclers. The reader is also referred
to Freeman's " History of the Norman Conquest," vol. iii.

THE BATTLE OF HASTINGS.

[A.D. 1066. Duke William landed on the English shore, September 28th, 1066.
After resting his men, and fortifying the more important positions in the vicinity of
Hastings, where he had congregated his forces, he marched along the hills from
Fairlight to Battle, passing through Crowhurst Park to Hetheland (now called
Telham Hill, south of Battle, and distinguishable by a modern farmstead), which he
reached on the morning of October 14. Meanwhile, Harold's camp occupied the
ascent now crowned by Battle Abbey, was protected by deep trenches, and a breast-
work—or *chevaux de frise*—of osier hurdles. To the east extended broad morasses
and an almost impenetrable wood—to the west stretched the fastnesses and jungles
of the vast Andreds-leas. Victory was, therefore, imperative for the Normans. The
only alternative was—not simply defeat, but ruin.

The morning dawned all coldly and darkly upon Norman and Saxon. Then the
half brother of Duke William, Odo, bishop of Bayeux, celebrated a grand mass, and
afterwards mounting a large white steed, drew up the cavalry in line. William divided his army into three divisions or columns; in front were the light infantry, chiefly
armed with arrows; in the centre, the heavy armed foot; all the best and bravest
of the Norman chivalry, with the great duke at their head, formed the last division.
Then he addressed his soldiers in stirring words. " Remember," said he, " to fight
bravely, then shall we conquer and be rich. What I gain ye will gain, what I conquer ye will conquer; if I win this land ye shall have it." With a loud shout of
" God help us !" and singing the old Norman song of " Roland," and of " Ronces-
valles," the whole army moved impetuously forward.

The English, chiefly infantry, were drawn up by Harold in the form of a wedge.
Firm, motionless, impregnable as were their children at Waterloo and Inkermann,
their shields covered their bold hearts, their sturdy arms wielded the ponderous
battle-axe. Harold was amongst them, and on foot. His banner was planted near
him, and on its folds was blazoned in gold the device of a fighting warrior. When
the English saw their monarch in their midst, they burned for the battle, and
shouted enthusiastically " The Holy Cross ! the Cross of God !"

At length there comes a rush upon the startled air. The archers have discharged
their arrows, and they speed on their deadly way, like the bolts of heaven. Forward
press the Norman spearmen, forward up the grassy hills, forward to the very de-

fences of the Saxons; and then there are shouts, and groans, and loud outcries of rage, despair, exultation, and agony. From behind their ramparts the Saxons ply, with arms strengthened by patriotic fervour, their heavy battle-axes, and many a stout knight falls beneath the ponderous blow. In vain the Normans fill up the places of their slain, in vain they display the most heroic valour. Did the Saxons possess a reserve, or a body of cavalry, William's hopes of the English crown verily would be nought. As it is, his sixty thousand men find themselves unable to break through the noble Saxon phalanx, though they outnumber it by one-third. Great is their dismay, heavy are their hearts; and hark! there is a cry, uttered first by a few faint voices, but quickly taken up by many others, and soon swelling over the field—"The Duke is fallen! Duke William is dead!" A passion of terror seizes the Norman troops, and they fling down their arms, and take to flight. Then out from the *mêlée*, all maddened with indignation, sweeps Duke William! He rushes among the fugitives; he smites them with his spear. Throwing off his helmet, he turns his flashing brow and glowing eyes upon them, and he cries, "Behold! I live; and with God's help I will conquer! What madness makes ye fly? How will ye escape? Those whom, if ye willed, ye might slay like cattle, are destroying you. Ye fly from victory—from immortal glory! Ye rush upon your ruin!"

These fiery words reanimate the dispirited troops. And now the astute Norman, seeing that it is in vain his best soldiers charge that impenetrable wall, conceives a wary stratagem. His troops pretend to retreat—to fly in confusion; the Saxons, elate with the hope of victory, pursue them, and break for the first time, their firm array. Alas! it is their perdition. The main body of the Duke's army charges them in their flank with a horrible slaughter. Twice is the stratagem repeated, twice are the Saxons deceived. The great banner of the Fighting Warrior is seized by some daring Normans. The rival chiefs fight in the *mêlée* like the meanest soldiers. William's half brother, Odo of Bayeux, the warrior priest, in a fit of holy enthusiasm, wields his battle-axe with signal valour.

The sun is setting in the western seas, going downward in a sky as red as blood. Alas! it is the last sunset that shall shine on the eyes of Saxon Harold! Even while the issue of the dread fight is still uncertain, a random arrow flashes through the air, and smites the gallant monarch in the brain. He falls!—the ominous tidings of his death thrill through the Saxon ranks. Their leader dead; what is left them but despair? The Normans rush again to the attack; and, as the moon rises in silver light over the fatal field, it gleams upon William the Conqueror, and gilds the victorious banners of the Normans! Thus was the crown of England lost and won!

During the pretended flight of the Normans, and their impetuous pursuit by the Saxons, a terrible incident occurred. "In the plain," says Wace, "was a fosse. The English charged, and drove the Normans before them, till they made them fall back upon this fosse, overthrowing into it horses and men. Many were to be seen falling therein, rolling one over the other, with their faces to the earth, and unable to rise. Many of the English also, whom the Normans drew down along with them, died there. At no time in the day's battle did so many Normans die as perished in that fosse," which thenceforth was called MAL-FOSSE, and has been identified with the rill flowing at the foot of Caldbeck Hill, in the direction of Watlington. "This rivulet still occasionally overflows its banks, and the primitive condition of the adjacent levels was doubtless that of a morass, overgrown with flags, reeds, and similar bog vegetables."]

At the place now called Battle (and formerly Epiton), Mr. Lower believes that "no town, or even village, existed in Saxon

BATTLE ABBEY, NEAR HASTINGS, SEAT OF THE DUKE OF CLEVELAND.

times. It was probably a down covered with heath and furze,—a wild rough common, without houses, and almost without trees. The Saxon Chroniclers had no better mode of indicating the locality of the hostile meeting than by saying that it occurred at the HOARY APPLE TREE (at thære háran apuldran),—probably from some venerable tree of that species growing near at hand."

That portion of Battle town which now lies east of the church is called the Lake, and sometimes SANGUELAC, or Seulac, —i. e., "the lake of blood,"—so named it is said, by the Conqueror, "because of the vast sea of gore there spilt." It was called SANT LACHE, however, long before the battle of Hastings. In like manner, the springs of chalybeate water hereabouts, which form the sources of the Asten, derived their redness from the blood of the slaughtered Saxons.

"Asten, once distained with native English blood,
  Whose soil yet, when but wet with any little rain,
  Doth blush, as put in mind of those there sadly slain."
                              (DRAYTON—*The Polyolbion.*)

CALDBECK HILL was corrupted with "Call-back-Hill," because at that point the Duke "called back" his pursuing troops; "TELHAM" was made "Tellman," as the spot where the conqueror counted his forces; a large tree, on the London road, is named "Watch Oak;" and at *Standard Hill*, either William or Harold traditionally set up his standard. But Harold's banner, in truth, was first pitched at Battle, and there it remained until supplanted by the oriflamme of the conqueror; and there subsequently arose that majestic edifice "The Abbey of the Battle"—an expiatory offering for the terrible slaughter which had taken place.

THE ABBEY OF BATTLE.

The Abbey of St. Martin DE BELLI LOCO—"of the place of the battle"—was erected on the very spot where the Norman knights humbled the Saxon "Fighting Man," within ten years of that great event. Very nobly did William carry out the vow he uttered upon Telham Hill, and richly did he endow his new foundation. William Faber, a Norman knight who had heard the vow, and had assumed the cowl and robe in the Benedictine Abbey of Marmontier, had the superintendence of its erection. A circle of three miles diameter spreading around the Abbey was

B

set apart by William as a "lowy" or "leuca," over which it had
unlimited jurisdiction, and peculiar rights and privileges were
conferred upon its abbot. "Here William intended to place 140
Noman monks, for the full discharge of its pious services; but
he was prevented by death from executing the whole of his design.
He had endowed it with lands equal to the support of such a
number; and had bestowed on it the privileges of a sanctuary,
and a multitude of others usual in those days. He peopled it
with religious from the Benedictine monastery of Marmontier in
Normandy, and appointed one of them, Robert Blankard, first
abbot. He being drowned in his passage, was succeeded by
Gaubertus. William (Rufus?) honoured the church with his
presence, probably at its consecration, and offered at the altar his
sword and the robe he wore on his coronation"—(*Pennant*).

At the time of its dissolution this wealthy and "mitred"
Abbey had fallen into a most unsavoury condition, and the royal
commissioner, Layton, wrote of it as "the worst he had ever
seen," as inhabited by "the blake sort of dyvellyshe monks."
Its annual value was then returned at £880 : 14 : 7, according
to Dugdale, or £987 : 0 : 10, according to Speed. The site was
conferred upon Sir Anthony Browne, "the same who had the
courage to bring to his royal master the fatal message of death,"
and by his descendant, the fourth Lord Montacute, was sold to
Sir Thomas Webster.

Sir Anthony Browne converted the monastic buildings into
a stately mansion. Fronting the street still stands, in excellent
preservation, the GATE-HOUSE, late decorated in style, and probably erected by Abbot Bethynge, *temp.* Edward III. The house
nearest to it, on the west side, was the Pilgrims' HOSPITIUM, and
is called the ALMONRY; the range of buildings to the right, now in
ruins, was long made use of as the TOWN-HALL. Passing within
the entrance, we first inspect the HALL, 57 feet by 30 feet, very
lofty, and timber-roofed; the DORMITORY, now converted into a
corridor and bed-rooms; and the BEGGARS' HALL, a vaulted apartment underneath. Next we visit the terrace, traditionally reputed to have been the BANQUETING-ROOM, and overlooking the
scene of the great battle. Below it are eight vaults, each of them
29 feet by 14 feet, which had been "the magazines for provisions
and fuel in the flourishing days of this great foundation"—
(*Pennant*).

Viewing afterwards the east front of the splendid pile, we

remark its nine arches enriched with Perpendicular tracery. On the site of the flower-garden stood the conventual CHURCH, whose foundations were excavated in 1817, and the apse of whose crypt and the bases of its columns still remain uncovered. "Siste, viator; heroa calcas:"—it was here that Harold fell. "When William of Marmontier and his brethren, some time after the battle, engaged in the work of rearing the abbey, not liking the place on account of its lack of water, they proceeded to build on a more eligible site on the west side of the hill, at a place called HERST; but the Conqueror, hearing of what they had done, waxed wroth, 'and commanded them with all haste to lay the foundation of the temple on the very place where he had achieved the victory over his enemy.' The brethren suggested the inconvenience which would arise from the dryness of the site, when William gave utterance to the memorable promise that, if God would spare his life, he would so amply endow the establishment, that wine should be more abundant there than water in any other great abbey. The chronicler goes on to inform us that, 'in accordance with the King's desire, they wisely erected the high altar upon the precise spot where the ensign of Harold, which they call the Standard, was observed to fall'"—(*Lower*).

The Early English REFECTORY, with its lancet-windows and buttressed walls, and the vaulted rooms beneath it, must next be visited. One of the latter, the largest, has been called the SCRIPTORIUM, or LIBRARY, and among the books which Leland found here was Prior Clement of Llanthony's highly edifying treatise on "the Spiritual Wings and Feathers of the Cherubim."

The Battle Abbey roll of Norman knights, from which Duke William, it is said, called over his band of followers on the morning of the fight—but which, probably, was a later fiction, or, at least, compilation, of the Battle monks—was preserved in the monastery until the Dissolution, and afterwards removed to Cowdray, where it was destroyed in the great fire. Copies of it, but widely varying among themselves, may be consulted in Leland's Collectanea, in Holinshed, and the Normanni Scriptores.

On leaving this "hallowed ground"—this spot so sacred in the eyes of every intelligent Englishman—the visitor will join, we fancy, in the reprobation which has been pretty generally expressed of the mean and selfish restrictions here designed, as it would seem, to minister to his especial discomfort. Surely a place like this might be left for Englishmen to examine, unshackled by half a score of absurd conditions, and free from the constant supervision of a greedy janitor, whose cry, like the horse-leech's daughters', is—" Give! Give!"

BATTLE CHURCH is Transitional Norman in style, with a few Decorated additions. It contains a little stained glass ; and in the chancel stands the white marble tomb of Sir *Anthony Browne*, with recumbent effigies of that gallant knight and his wife *Alis*. Observe the brasses for a knight in armour, d. 1425 ; Sir *W. Arnold*, d. 1435 ; *Robert Clere*, d. 1440, and *John Wythines*, Deans of Battle, d. 1615.

The vicarage of Battle, valued at £500, is in the patronage of Sir A. F. Webster, who, as lay abbot, has the appointment of a dean ; and he, independent of the bishop, has complete sway over the ancient abbatical jurisdiction. The population of Battle is 3500.

Battle is famous for its gunpowder-mills, which are situated at some distance from the town beyond the woods. In the neighbourhood the lover of wild blossoms will meet with the field geranium, pansy, rue-leaved saxifrage, ivy crowfoot, corn-pheasant's eye, and cornwort.

On our way from Battle to Robertsbridge we pass SEDLES-COMB on the right, WHATLINGTON (population, 458), and MOUNTFIELD (population, 769), on the left. The latter is agreeably situated in a fair and leafy landscape, surrounded by low but pleasantly-verdurous hills.

At 62 miles from London we pass the Robertsbridge station ; 3 miles further and we reach ETCHINGHAM. About 3 miles to the right, on the hills, stands BURWASH (population, 2227), a large and busy village, with an interesting CHURCH, noticeable for containing " a curious specimen of the iron manufacture of the fourteenth century, and the oldest existing article produced by our Sussex foundries. It is a cast-iron slab, with an ornamental cross, and an inscription in relief. In the opinion of several eminent antiquaries, it may be regarded as unique for the style and period. The inscription is much injured by long exposure to the attrition of human feet. The letters are Longobardic, and the legend appears, on a careful examination to be —

'ORATE P. ANNEMA JHONE COLINE' (or COLINS).
' Pray for the soul of Joan Collins.'"

The living (a rectory and vicarage), valued at £1055, is in the patronage of the Rev. J. C. Egerton.

Either from Robertsbridge, Etchingham, or Ticehurst station (through Burwash) we may visit BRIGHTLING (population, 812), a spot assuredly not to be neglected by the tourist who has a brain and a heart to appreciate "the all-wondrous works of God." Here, as from the minaret of a mosque, one may look out upon the landscape sleeping all fair and serenely in the sunlight of heaven—upon broad reaches of meadow-land dotted by patient cattle—upon close-clinging branches hung with a myriad leaves —upon the shimmering and shining waters of the far-off sea— upon the silver trail of tiny rivulets—upon gray church-tower, and many-gabled manor-house, and quiet hamlet—upon hill and dale, and grove, and garden—a goodly picture, designed and coloured by a hand Divine! To the north and east spreads the Weald of Kent and Sussex, rich in a thousand changes of light and shade ; to the south-west rises the long bold line of the glorious Sussex downs ; to the south gleams and glitters the Channel, bounded in the distance by a low bank of clouds which denotes the position of the French coast. On the highest point of this elevation, and 646 feet above the sea-level, a neat Observatory stands—erected, some score of years ago, by S. Fuller, of Rose Hill Park. It is said to be visible from the neighbourhood of London, and the lofty columnar land-mark near it is necessarily of great service to the mariners of the Channel. The site of the ancient fire-beacon is curiously named "Browns Burgh."

In BRIGHTLING CHURCH there is nothing to interest the tourist. Its stained glass is not of special beauty. Its rectory, valued at £563, is in the patronage of the Mrs. B. Hayley.

In this neighbourhood, and sheltered in a gap of the downs, lies ROSE HILL PARK (A. E. Fuller, Esq.).

A pleasant road from Brightling leads into the valley of the Rother, and on crossing that stream, winds up the hills to the Ticehurst Road Station. BURWASH lies about 1½ mile to the right.

The rail now carries us through a fertile country-side—hop-grounds and corn fields smiling abundantly around us—to the WADHURST STATION, 1 mile from WADHURST (population, 2802), and 52 miles from London. Observe, as you enter the village—the natives, by the way, call it "a town."—WADHURST CASTLE (K. W. Smyth, Esq.), a pleasant house in pleasant grounds. About 1 mile to the left, on the road to Frant, stands KNOLE HOUSE, an Elizabethan pile of some pretensions. WADHURST CHURCH, dedicated to Sts. Peter and Paul, is partly Early English and partly Decorated. It has a lofty shingled spire, and contains no less than 30 grave slabs of Sussex iron. Notice the memorial to "*John Legas, Gentleman*." The vicarage, valued at £659, is in the patronage of Wadham College, Oxon.

WADHURST, or WADE-HURST, indicates by its name its position on a branch of the Rother, in a wooded country. The prefix WADE is identical with the Latin *vadum*, a ford.

Between Wadhurst and Frant we pass through a tolerably long tunnel. FRANT (population, 3263) is a large and busy town, with a handsome church, situated on an eminence which overlooks one of the most glorious landscapes in Kent and Sussex—from the Sevenoaks hills to the heights of Dover ; from Chatham on the north-east to Leith Hill, south-west. Frant Church, Dungeness, and Beachy Head form the three points of one of the triangles of the Ordnance Survey.

The present CHURCH, a quasi-Gothic edifice, was built in 1821-2. The windows contain some good modern painted glass. The rector of Rotherfield has the patronage of the living, a vicarage, valued at £800.

SPERNFOLD PLACE (Hon. P. Ashburnham) and SAXONBURY LODGE (R. Davidson, Esq.) are situated in this vicinity. ERIDGE PARK (Earl of Abergavenny) skirts the high road to the Wells. BAYHAM ABBEY is about 3 miles distant. TUNBRIDGE WELLS, 3 miles by rail.

A VISIT TO WINCHELSEA.

This forms one of the most favourite excursions from Hastings. On the way, either by rail or road, we may visit
GUESTLING (population, 860), to examine its CHURCH, dedicated to St. Andrew, a Transitional-Norman building, with
its tower surmounted by a low spire, standing about 300
yards from the road. The Ashburnham chantry is divided
from the south aisle by three pointed arches; the nave from
the north aisle by two Norman arches with chevron mouldings. In the vestry stands an old richly-carved " Flanders
chest." BROOMHAM HALL, a good stone house in a fair
demesne, has belonged to the Ashburnham family since the
days of Edward IV.

At Maxfield, in this parish—an old timbered farm-house—
was born Gregory Martin, the translator of the Rheims edition
of the Bible.

WINCHELSEA (population, 679)—*Inn:* the New Inn—
retains but few traces of its former importance; yet one may
discern the lines of its principal seats—ruins of groined vault and
crypt—a fragment of a shattered tower—the ivy-grown remains
of an ancient chapel—mute but eloquent witnesses to present
decay and bygone prosperity. But of all the impoverished old
towns along the coast, Winchelsea, as Mr. Thorne has observed,
is the best worth visiting. " It owns itself a wreck, and does
not try to get rid of the ruins, and put on an appearance of
smartness. The wide space which the town originally covered
helps now not a little to increase the reverend air it carries as
a ruin. You wander about its outskirts among pleasant bye-
ways, and are startled to come upon some fragment of a chapel
or an old house, when you thought yourself a long way beyond
the limits of the town." Let us, then, " go visit the reliques of
this city," and hear what they have to tell us of the brave and
palmy days that are gone,

Old Winchelsea occupied a site, about three miles south-east of the present town, upon land which the sea has long since claimed as its own. It was a complete peninsula, connected with the mainland on the west side, and defended by fortifications which were then considered of unusual strength. Like all the old sea-fortresses, it was continually suffering from the depredations of the lawless Norsemen, and its inhabitants, in their turn, became notorious pirates, and ravaged the narrow seas with their swift galleys.

Here William I. made his second landing from Normandy in 1067 ; here, in 1170, disembarked two of the knightly murderers of Thomas à Becket ; and such was its general prosperity that it furnished, in 1229, ten out of the fifty-seven vessels which formed the contingent of the Cinque Ports. A few years later, and its downfall began. In 1236, the waters, for the first time, broke beyond their ancient limits, and rolled in upon the doomed city. Again in 1250, on the eve of October 1st, when the cruel Winchelsea pirates had boarded a small bark freighted with pilgrims for the Canterbury shrine, and had foully murdered them, and the sea—as the old tradition runs—flooded the town in vengeance of the sacrilege. In 1264-5 it sided with De Montfort against Henry III.—an act of rebellion which Prince Edward terribly punished, when, on the 4th of August, he took it by assault, and put to the sword almost all its male inhabitants. From this severe blow it never recovered, and another disastrous inundation on the eve of St. Agatha, 1287, completed its ruin.

Edward I. now resolved to remove the town to a less exposed site, and the hill of Higham, now rising above the marshes like a natural watch-tower, was selected by the lord-treasurer, Kirkby, Bishop of Ely, despatched for that purpose. The sea bounded it on the east and north, on the south and west convenient roads struck inland to Robertsbridge and Hastings. The harbour was safe and commodious. So the town was laid out with the utmost regularity, and stout walls enclosed an area of 170 acres, sub-divided into thirty-nine squares or quarters. It had three gates, and on the west side a deep fosse or trench. On the south-west rose a castle, adjoining St. Leonard's Church ; in the centre, the stately tower of a church dedicated to St. Thomas à Becket. When completed, King Edward paid it a visit, and reviewed his fleet in its haven. As he rode onward near the Strand Gate, his horse, terrified by the sudden clangour of a windmill, leaped over the wall, and his attendants were in sore affright, believing he was killed. But the earth had been rendered soft by incessant rain, and the king re-entered the town uninjured by his fall.

Here, in 1350, King Edward the Third embarked on board his fleet, and in the offing defeated a Spanish fleet richly laden with Flemish goods on the 29th of August. Nine years later, and during the great Plantagenet's absence in France, 8000 Frenchmen landed, set fire to the town, and slew many of the townsmen who were assembled at mass in the great church. The spot where the unfortunate Winchelsea men were buried is still known as Dead Men's Lane. In 1359, it was assaulted by the French fleet of 120 sail, under the Comte St. Pol; and, in 1377 they again sailed along the coast, ravaged Rye, and would have taken Winchelsea, had not Haymo, abbot of Battle, drawn together his men-at-arms and made so gallant a show that the enemy withdrew discomfited. But in 1380 it was sacked by John de Vienne, and, for the last time, in 1449, was once more set on fire by the French.

From the assaults of its enemies it might, however, have recovered, and that its consequence was not inconsiderable may be inferred from the vast vaults and crypts built by the inhabitants for storehouses; but the rapid withdrawal of the sea, and destruction of its harbour, were not to be contended against. When, in 1573, it was visited by Queen Elizabeth, and its citizens and magistrates clothed themselves in scarlet, she was so pleased with its apparent prosperity that she christened it "Little London;" but, even then, not more than 60 families remained in the town, and it has never since held up its head. It is, as Wesley called it in 1790, when he preached his last sermon under a wide-spreading ash tree adjoining the west side of St. Thomas' Church, the "poor skeleton of ancient Winchelsea," and into its dead bones not even the Genius of the Steam Engine has been able to infuse any life.

The notable objects to be here examined are, however, many; first, there is the old STRAND GATE, an Early Decorated structure, which you pass under as you come from Rye—"a picturesque old pile, having a wide gateway between massive round towers. Looking through it from the inside, the town of Rye is seen seated on its hill, as though a picture, set in a heavy antique frame." LANDGATE, or PIPE WELL, or FERRY GATE, on the road to Udimore, is a mere shapeless mass of gray old stone,

near which a few dull houses straggle. It bears a shield with the
word *Helde* inscribed upon it, supposed to be the name of the
mayor during whose supremacy it was erected. NEW GATE, on
the Icklesham road, is a mile from any houses, and has no
architectural pretensions, but stands in a lovely nook, embowered
among trees, and opening into a lane whose banks, in the spring,
are flush with primroses. The foundations of the stout earthwork, and the line of the deep fosse, which defended the town,
may still be traced between the two latter gates.

In the centre of the town stands the CHURCH—or all that
remains of it—dedicated to St. Thomas à Becket. The nave
is said to have been destroyed by the French in 1380; the
chancel and side aisles are still extant. The style is Early
Decorated, and from its purity deserves particular examination.
Remark the exquisite fidelity of the sculptured foliage; the
curious corbel heads; the rich foreign tracery of the side windows; the piers of Bethersden marble and Caen stone; the
sedilia in the chancel (recently restored); the Perpendicular
English Windows; and the light and airy three-bayed choir.
In the south aisle is the ALARD CHANTRY, originally the Chapel
of St. Nicholas, where particularly observe the noble Alard
tombs—one to *Gervase Alard*, Admiral of the Cinque Ports, 1303
and 1306, with a recumbent cross-legged effigy—the hands
clasping a small heart—a lion at the feet, snarling, and half
rising as if to spring upon you—and over all a noble arched
canopy, adorned with heads of Edward I. and Queen Eleanor.
The other to *Stephen Alard*, grandson of the above, and Admiral
of the Cinque Ports, in 1324—with some fine foliaged ornamentation, and a canopy resembling that already alluded to. In
the north aisle is the CHANTRY of *John Godfrey*, d. 1441, and
Maline his wife. Remark the three canopied tombs, *temp.* Henry
III., with effigies of a mailed templar, a lady, and a young man,
robed. In the floor of the chancel is inserted a brass for a
priest, d. 1440.

The triple gable of the chancel, externally, is luxuriantly
shrouded in ivy, and connected with the ruined transept walls.
Observe over the porch, which is of later date, the arms of Win-
chelsea. (The town confers an earldom on the Finch family.)
The rectory, valued at £320, is in the patronage of the Rev. H,
Patch.

On the south side of the town lies the FRIARY PARK, or the FRIARS (R. Stileman, Esq.), to which admission is only obtainable on Mondays. The present house was erected in 1819, when the old Franciscan monastery was taken down. The exquisitely beautiful ruins of the CHAPEL OF THE VIRGIN have happily escaped profanation. It was founded in 1310. The apsidal choir is entered by a noble arch, 26 feet broad. "The Friars" was the residence, in 1780, of two daring robbers, George and Joseph Weston, one of whom was actually appointed church-warden of Winchelsea, and both brothers living here, under assumed names, on the plunder acquired in their daring excursions, were held in much repute. After robbing the Bristol mail they were detected, apprehended, and one of them was hung. James, the novelist, in one of his best romances, has made good use of these circumstances.

There are no ruins of the ancient Dominican Priory, founded by Edward II. The Court House and Gaol have Norman doorways, but are not peculiarly interesting. Of many old buildings there are vestiges, and the vaults are large and curious, but we have tarried as long as may be among the shards and débris of the ill-fated Winchelsea—twice grievously injured by the sea —and must resume our onward way. Up to the time of the Reform Bill it returned two members to parliament. Henry Lord Brougham represented it from 1815 to 1830. It is governed by a mayor and twelve jurats.

[About three miles north-west of the town is UDIMORE (population, 435), for whose name tradition supplies a curious etymology. While its church (a small and ancient building) was being built in a different situation, a spirit-voice, during the lonesome night-hours, came sighing across the wold, "O'er the mere! O'er the mere! O'er the mere!" and spirit-hands removed the stones. So the builders took the ghostly hint, erected the church on its present site, and named the village UDIMORE, a corrupted version of the spirit's cry. The perpetual curacy, valued at £100 per annum, is in the gift of T. C. Langford, Esq.]

One and a-half mile westward is ICKLESHAM (population, 728), which passed by marriage from the family of Alard to that of Finch. The CHURCH, dedicated to St. Nicholas, is mainly Norman in style. The north aisle is Early English; the east window, Early Decorated, and a good example. Observe the capitals of the pillars in the nave, and the round-headed windows of the south aisle. There is an altar-tomb for *Henry Finch*, d. 1498. The vicarage, valued at £715, is in the patronage of the Lord Chancellor.

From White Hart Hill, beyond the church, the view of sea and land is broad, magnificent, and constantly chequered with exquisite effects of light and shade.

RYE.

Hotels: The George ; Cinque Port Arms. Population, 4220.

About two miles to the east of Winchelsea is the ancient town and Cinque Port of RYE, supposed to have been the Portus Novus of the Romans. At one time the sea came up to its walls, but, owing to its gradual subsidence, the harbour is now about two miles off. The river Rother, after its junction with the Brede and the Tillingham, has its confluence with the sea here. The old town suffered much from attacks of the French in the 14th century, and also from pestilence. A great number of the Huguenots took refuge here in 1572 after the massacre of St. Bartholomew's day, and others resorted hither after the Revocation of the Edict of Nantes. The town is an old-fashioned place, and many old houses may still be seen in its narrow streets. The church of ST. MARY is a very fine building, partly Norman and partly of the 13th and 14th centuries. The altartable and clock are said to have been gifts of Queen Elizabeth. The YPRES TOWER, so called because built by William de Ypres, Earl of Kent, in the reign of King Stephen (1135-54), stands at the south-east angle of the walls, and is now used as a prison. The LANDGATE is at the opposite corner of the town, and in fair preservation. Rye was the birthplace (1579) of John Fletcher the celebrated dramatic writer, better known by his association with Beaumont in the annals of English literature. His father Richard was vicar of Rye, and was afterwards made Bishop of London. Here, too, were born Samuel Jeake the antiquary, 1623-1690, who published a work on the Charters of the Cinque Ports, and also his son Samuel, an ingenious but eccentric writer on astronomy and rhetoric. The Jeakes belonged to one of the families of French Refugees, their name being originally Jacques.

HASTINGS TO PEVENSEY AND EASTBOURNE.

At ST. LEONARD'S JUNCTION STATION we leave the South-Eastern Railway Company's carriages and jurisdiction, and commence our journeys upon that well-known system of lines which is included in the London, Brighton, and South Coast Railway. The first station (3¾ miles) is called BEXHILL (population, 2452), but the village is nearly 1½ mile distant; a quiet, breezy, summery watering-place, in a fertile country, and looking

out upon the waters of the Channel, which are here gradually
retiring from the shore, and have recently given up to the curiosity of the geologist a singular submarine forest. The village is
situated upon high ground. The CHURCH, dedicated to St Peter,
has a Norman nave and Early English chancel. An ancient
east window of painted glass, containing representations of
Henry III. and his Queen Eleanor, was removed from the building by Horace Walpole, through the agency of the Earl of Ashburnham, and became, for a time, one of the glories of Strawberry
Hill. A similar window, with figures of Edward III. and Philippa
of Hainault, may now be examined in the CHURCH of HOOE
(population, 574), dedicated to St. James, and about 5 miles north-
west. The vicarage of Bexhill, valued at £1291 per annum, is
in the gift of the Bishop of Winchester. Hooe vicarage, worth
£235 yearly, is the property of the present incumbent.

The railway now runs along the shore, which is flat and uninteresting, to Pevensey Station, 6¾ miles. The long range of the
Martello Towers, chiefly occupied as coast-guard posts, will be
duly noticed by the traveller. Inland rises the venerable pile of
PEVENSEY CASTLE. PEVENSEY HARBOUR curves boldly to the
south-west, and terminates at LANGLEY POINT, beyond which is
EASTBOURNE BAY, bounded, in its turn, by the lofty chalk-heights
of BEACHY HEAD.

PEVENSEY.

[Population, 412—*Inn :* The Royal Oak. 65 m. from London, by rail.; 60 m. by
road; 11½ m. from Hastings.]

ANDERIDA, the modern PEVENSEY (*an* not, and *tred*, inhabited
—the uninhabited), was one of the great Roman strongholds which,
under the government of the *Comes Saxonici Littoris,* defended the
south-eastern coast ; and derived its name from its position on
the borders of the vast ANDREDES-WEALD, or " uninhabited forest."
The Romans chose for the position of their camp one of the in-
sulated hills which then rose above the watery morasses, and
strengthened it with all the appliances suggested by their military
knowledge. In 477, Ælla and his Saxons effected a settlement
upon the coast near Chichester, and a few years later (A.D. 491)
attacked Anderida, captured it, and " slew all that dwelt therein,
nor was there one Briton left "—a simple but significant passage

(in the Saxon Chronicle), which Gibbon has commended for its impressive terseness.   Anderida afterwards became an important Saxon settlement, and its area was considerably enlarged.   The sea, now a mile distant, then beat against its cliffs on the south and east.

After the Conquest, Pevensey was bestowed by King William (who had chosen its bay for the disembarkation of his forces) upon Robert, Earl of Mortaigne and Cornwall, his half-brother, and one of the most potent of the Norman Barons.   Recognizing the importance of its position "for one whose interests lay between England and Normandy," he founded here a Castle, at the southeast angle of the ancient town.   From this point the conqueror embarked, in 1067, for his Norman dominions.

During his brief revolt (in 1089) against William Rufus, Pevensey castle was held by Odo of Bayeux, but famine threatening the besieged, and no succour arriving from Duke Robert, the warrior-priest was compelled to surrender.   About 1104, Henry I. granted the manor and barony to Gilbert de Aquila, whence it acquired the name of the "Honour of the Eagle."   It remained with his respresentatives about a century.   Gilbert Earl of Clare, in 1144, defended it with extraordinary resolution against King Stephen, who was forced, after a wearisome siege, to withdraw his forces.   It next passed into the hands of the Earls de Warrenne; was granted in 1269, to Prince Edward (afterwards Edward I.) and his heirs; remained with the Crown until Edward III. settled it on John of Gaunt, who conferred the governorship upon the Pelhams; was threatened with destruction in the reign of Elizabeth; sold, in 1650, by the Parliamentary Commissioners to John Warr, for £40; escaped these dangers, and partly survived the assaults of time; and is now a venerable memorial of a long and chequered history, secure in the reverent care of the Duke of Devonshire.

Besides the sieges we have enumerated, the old castle was attacked, in 1265, by Simon de Montfort; and, in 1399, by Richard the Second's forces, who were gallantly repulsed by the garrison under the command of the heroic Lady Pelham—her husband at the time serving under the flag of Bolingbroke. Edmund, Duke of York, found here a prison; and at a later period, Queen Joanna of Navarre was confined within its walls for four wearisome years, on a charge of having subtilely plotted against the life of her step-son, Henry the Fifth.

PEVENSEY CASTLE, AND THE OLD ROMAN WALLS, NEAR EASTBOURNE.

With these few historical notes to assist us, let us turn to a survey of the ruined stronghold, adopting the results of the patient investigations of Mr. Lower ("Chronicles of Pevensey"), and Mr. Wright ("Wanderings of an Antiquary.")

The Castle is situated on gently rising ground, on the edge of Pevensey Level. Its walls are conspicuous from the railway station, whence a bye-lane leads into the road which leads up to the stately entrance towers, the "Decuman Gate" of the ancient Anderida. The width of the opening between them is now 27 feet. Probably, it was an approach to the narrower gateway of the town. The Roman masonry is still in wonderful preservation; although it has been exposed to the changes of a great part of 2000 years, the mark of the trowel is still visible on the mortar, and many of the facing stones look as fresh as if they had been cut yesterday." The walls are generally 12 feet in thickness, and between 24 and 30 feet in height; they enclosed an area of about 8½ acres, and on the southern and eastern sides "occupied a sort of low cliff, washed at every tide by the waters of the ocean, or at least a considerable arm of the sea."—(Lower.)

Taking the road to the left, outside the northern wall and its massive towers, and passing a modern house of no picturesque design, we reach a fine Roman tower, bearing on its summit a Norman superstructure, which appears to have been intended as a watch tower, and commands an extensive view of the principal approaches to this important fortress. "There is a striking contrast between the rough masonry of the Norman superstructure and the workmanlike finish of the Roman building below. The latter is here extremely well defined. It consists of a regular facing of squared stones, with the usual banding courses of bricks (a very peculiar characteristic of Roman masonry in this country). The interior is filled up with irregular materials, among which liquid mortar was thrown, and the latter (in which we observe at once the mixture of pounded tile so peculiar to the Roman mortar) has become harder than the stone itself." In one of the towers a large breach in the Roman masonry has been filled up with the usual Norman "herring-bone work."

At the south-east corner the Norman castle stands on what seems to have been an artificial mound, occupying an area of nearly an acre and a half, and forming an irregular pentagon round a large mound, so that the small interior court is much higher than the ground outside. The gateway, flanked by two towers, nearly faces the Decuman gate, and have evidently been imitated by the mediæval architect from the Roman models before him. The east tower formed the Keep ; the north-west may nave been the governor's residence. Two sides were defended by a moat, over which was thrown a drawbridge. The ancient Chapel, excavated in 1852, stood within the court, to the right of the north-west tower. A rude Norman font, and three skeletons were found here. The castle well is 50 feet deep.

Some portions of Robert of Mortaigne's Castle may plainly be detected ; but most of the ruins exhibit the characteristics of the Transition Norman and Early English styles.

From the Castle we descend to PEVENSEY CHURCH (dedicated to St. Nicholas, the favourite Norman Saint), an Early English building, with a nave of Decorated character (restored). The tower stands at the east end of the north aisle. There is a noble chancel-arch, and the clustered columns have richly foliated capitals, but the interior has been disfigured by modern innovations, and is in a somewhat mutilated condition. It contains a monument and effigy for *John Wheatley, temp.* James I.

The vicarage, valued at £780, is in the patronage of the Bishop of Chichester.

PEVENSEY HARBOUR was formed by the estuary of the river Ashbourne, navigable for small vessels as high as Pevensey Bridge in 1720, but, in Pennant's time " quite choked a mile distant from the shore, and nothing left but a narrow drain, the receptacle of a few boats." Here the landing of Julius Cæsar has been fixed by Professor Airey, who has supported his theory by ingenious but unsatisfactory arguments. Here the disembarcation of William and his Normans *did* take place, his six hundred vessels filling all the coast from Pevensey to Hastings ; and he himself stumbling forward as he set his foot upon the shore. With what curious eyes must the bold adventurers have looked upon the glittering cliffs, the undulating downs, the vigorous woods, the already venerable walls of the ancient Anderida, as with glancing spear and glittering axe they prest forward towards that memorable plain where a nation's destiny was to be sealed in blood !

Pevensey was, and still is, a member of the Cinque Ports, and its corporation seal bears the usual Cinque Ports' escocheon. Here was born, or, at least, for some years resided, and practised as a physician, *Andrew Borde*, the original " Merry Andrew," and author of the famous " Tales of the Wise Men of Gotham." We owe to him the anecdotes of the humble-minded magistrate, who protested that " though Mayor of Pevensey he was but a man ;" of the " freemen of the port" who *drowned an eel* as a mode of capital punishment calculated to be highly effectual ; and sundry other " merrie jestes" which our space forbids us to recapitulate.

Near the Pevensey railway station, and, as its name indicates, west of the castle, is situated WESTHAM (population, 761), with a church, dedicated to St. Mary. The south wall of the nave has Norman characteristics, and the south transept is entered through a Norman arch. The rest of the building is Perpendicular. Some portion of the rood-loft remains, and the upper portions of the east and north-east windows contain old stained glass. The vicarage, valued at £347, is in the patronage of the Duke of Devonshire.

At LANGNEY, 1½ mile south, moulder the desolate ruins of a grange-chapel formerly belonging to Lewes Priory. Two small forts have been erected at Langley Point.

The next station we reach is at POLEGATE, whence diverge short branches to Hailsham, on the north, and Eastbourne, south.

WILLINGDON (population, 678) is about 1 mile south of Polegate. The CHURCH is small and uninteresting. Beyond it, even to the very line of the rail, stretches the PARK.

EASTBOURNE.

Hotels : The Cavendish, Grand, Queen's (near the pier), Albion, Anchor, Burlington, Marine, Sussex, South Down, Gilbert Arms, and Terminus.

THIS elegant and modern watering - place consists, first, of SOUTHBOURNE, a part lying back, away from the shore, containing the chief shops, some good villas, the theatre, and other buildings ; and, secondly, SEA-HOUSES, the principal and most fashionable portion, facing the beach, where are the baths, chief hotels, and lodging-houses. These form an extremely neat and clean assemblage of houses in rows and terraces, with a fine esplanade ; the whole looking out upon a truly magnificent view

C

of the ocean, including Beachy Head, in the immediate vicinity.
The Eastbourne sands are at low tide dry and extensive, the
water is clear, and there are plenty of bathing-machines. The
climate of the place is exceedingly healthy, a proof of which
may be gathered from the Registrar-General's Report which
shows that the rate of mortality for each thousand of the population here is 15, or 10 less than the general average of London
(25), and 1 lower than the lowest of all our other watering-places.
The drainage is on the most approved plan, and the water supply
excellent.

The GRAND PARADE, which is a beautiful marine treble-
terraced walk, forms an agreeable and fashionable promenade.
It consists of an upper and lower promenade, connected at intervals by flights of steps, and the intervening slopes are planted
with shrubs and evergreens. From the Anchor Hotel on
the N.E., it stretches for 1¼ mile south-westwards to the
Wish Tower Gardens, and extends inland to the village of
Meade, the whole course measuring 2½ miles. Wish Tower
an old Martello, is situate on a hill laid out in pleasure-grounds,
affording a delightful view, and in its immediate vicinity is
Devonshire Park, the gift of the Duke, covering an area of 12
acres.

The pier 1000 feet long, forms an agreeable resort. Eastbourne once noted for its quiet, and the absence of hackneyed
watering-place gaieties, has assumed larger proportions of recent
years. The assembly-rooms and ball-room, a theatre, library,
and reading-rooms, are the chief sources of amusement. There
is also a literary institute. In 1851 the population amounted
to 5795, while in 1881 it was 21,977.

EASTBOURNE CHURCH (St. Mary's) is a Transition-Norman and
Early English structure, measuring 124 feet by 50. The lofty
tower contains a peal of six bells, of Sussex metal, cast at Chiddingly in 1651. There are three Perpendicular sedilia in the
chancel, an Easter sepulchre (also Perpendicular), and a brass to
J. Hyng, d. 1445. The chancel-arch is round with Norman
mouldings. The north chancel is divided from the south by
Transition-Norman piers and arches. In the former stands a
monument to Gilbert Davies, President of the Royal Society, who
long resided at Eastbourne Place.

ST. SAVIOUR'S CHURCH, designed by Street, is a prominent

BEACHY HEAD, NEAR EASTBOURNE.—Height 575 Feet.

Gothic edifice of red brick and Bath stone, surmounted by a spire 175 feet high. St. Gregory's Chapel, the old Parsonage House, the curious vaulted room, believed to be the remains of an alien priory that was situate here, and subterranean passage at the Lamb Inn, are objects worthy of note by the tourist. A circular redoubt, erected in 1804, near the barracks on St. Anthony's Hill, mounts twelve guns, and can accommodate 400 men.

Mortimer, the painter, was born at Eastbourne in 1741, and passed his early years in consorting with the bold smugglers and studying the wild scenery of this picturesque coast, the haunt of numerous sea-birds, and where the crambe maritima, dropwort, and dwarf orchis flourish in vigorous growth. The ring-dotterel, too, deposits her three eggs, scarcely to be distinguished from the surrounding pebbles.

Eastbourne Bay has witnessed an unwonted spectacle—a naval battle between the English and Dutch fleets, as allies, against the French, and the defeat of the former. This was in 1690. The Pevensey plain, as far as Hastings, is full of interesting associations connected with the Conquest.

Delightful excursions may be made to the ruins of Pevensey Castle, where William the Conqueror landed, September 28, 1066, 4 miles distant; Hurstmonceux Castle, 9 miles; Lewes, the county town, with the ruins of its old castle and priory, about 17 miles by train. At Holywell, a short distance, there are chalybeate springs, possessing somewhat similar qualities to those at Clifton.

In the neighbourhood of Eastbourne the Romans had a settlement. On the road to Pevensey, 1½ mile east, a tesselated pavement and bath were discovered towards the close of the last century. South-east of Trinity Church the foundations of a Roman villa were excavated in 1858. The remains of numerous tumuli and of circular encampments may be traced on the Downs.

Beachy Head (575 feet above sea level) raises its glowing block of chalk about 3 miles south-west of Eastbourne, and is a favourite excursion-point of the Eastbourne tourists. The prospect is sublime: eastward it extends to Hastings and Dungeness, westward to Brighton and Worthing. Selsea Bill may also be seen, it is said, on a cloudless day. But not for the mariner

does this precipitous cliff wear so goodly an aspect. It is
associated in his mind with tales of fearful wrecks—not so
frequent now that our charts are more skilfully constructed, and
the science of navigation is better understood, but still numerous
enough to render Beachy Head "a word of fear." The Dalhousie,
a fine East Indiaman, was lost here, October 24, 1853, and only
one life was saved.

Off Beachy Head, June 30, 1690, was fought the great fight
between the combined English and Dutch fleets of 56 sail, under
Arthur, Earl of Torrington, and the French, of 82, under the
Comte de Tourville. The Dutch behaved with great valour, and
were only saved from annihilation by Torrington's manœuvres,
who contrived to interpose his fleet between them and the French.
The combined fleets then took shelter in the mouth of the
Thames. Torrington was tried by court-martial, but acquitted,
and, hoisting his flag in his barge, went up the Medway in
triumph. He was, however, deprived of his commission by King
William,—wroth at the loss which his beloved Dutch had sus-
tained,—and was never again employed.

A throng of wings immediately starts out of the chinks and
crannies of this great ocean-wall at the sound of a bugle or mus-
ket. Guillemots, razor-bills, choughs, puffins, and other sea-
fowl resort in vast numbers to this lonesome headland. Samphire grows here in profusion.

At BELLE-TOUTE, 1 mile west—a lofty promontory flung
farther out into the sea than Beachy Head—stands a lighthouse,
erected in 1831. Beneath the brink of the cliff are a staircase
and a cavern, in two compartments, hollowed out of the solid rock,
as a means of escape for shipwrecked seamen, by Jonathan Darby,
a former vicar of East Dean (1715-28), who also found them, it
is said, a convenient refuge for himself from the tongue of a
shrewish wife. On one occasion a hurricane drove a Dutch
galliot against this point, and fixed her bows in the mouth of one
of the caverns (now known as "Parson Darby's Hole"). Twelve
sailors were rescued by the intrepid pastor.

BIRLING GAP, 1½ mile west, was formerly defended by an
arch and portcullis. Near this point Duguay Trouin, the bold
French privateer, with 9 sail of the line, and some smaller vessels,
captured the Hampton Court and Grafton men-of-war, and their
convoy, and drove ashore the Royal Oak. At this "gate" or
opening in the cliffs, the tourist may ascend to the high land.

The beautiful Sussex downs stretch from Beachy Head to the Hampshire border in an undulating line, 53 miles in length.

[Just beyond Beachy Head, in a deep quiet valley, which is reputed to have been the scene of the first interview between King Alfred and the learned Asser, lies EAST DEAN (population, including Friston, 446). "Ibique illum," says Asser, "in villa regia, qua dicitur DENE, primitus vidi;" but some authorities place the meeting-place at East Dean, near Chichester. The Old Church is surmounted by a tower, and has a heavy round chancel arch; its pulpit dates from 1623.

FRISTON PLACE is a picturesque Tudor mansion. The cliffs beyond this point are broken into several conspicuous eminences, known as The Seven Sisters, haunted by the peregrine falcon, the raven, and the kestrel.

WEST DEAN (population, 129) is a pretty village at the head of a narrow chalk valley, which opens out upon the river Cuckmere. Its CHURCH is Norman, with Perpendicular windows; there is a fine tomb in the chancel. The PARSONAGE HOUSE, a fourteenth century building, now divided into several small tenements, is partly built of stone and partly of timber. A newel staircase leads to the upper story, where an ancient fire-place is built into the wall. The rectory is valued at £102, and is in the Duke of Devonshire's patronage.

At JEVINGTON (population, 325) a Norman Church, dedicated to St. Andrew, has a noble and massive square west tower. The rectory, valued at £309, is presented to by the Duke of Devonshire.]

From the POLEGATE STATION, a branch line, 3 miles to the north, conducts the tourist to the quiet market-town of HAILSHAM (population, 1825), one of the largest cattle-markets in Sussex. Its CHURCH is dedicated to St. Mary, is mainly Perpendicular in style, and has a low pinnacled tower of more than ordinary interest. The vicarage is valued at £356. Hailsham is a place of considerable activity on Wednesday, the market-day, and can boast of three decent inns—the TERMINUS, the GEORGE, and the CROWN. The tourist will find it a convenient point from which to visit HELLINGLY, MICHELHAM, and HURSTMONCEUX.

☞ MICHELHAM, 2 miles west, is interesting from its ruined PRIORY,—a house of Augustinian canons founded by Gilbert de Aquila, *temp.* Henry III. It formed a stately quadrangle, which was encircled by a broad deep moat, fed by the river Cuckmere, and noted as a favourite resort of the stealthy otter. Three fish-stews, supplied by the moat, are still in good condition. A drawbridge, now replaced by a permanent bridge, was the only approach to the priory.

The remains of most importance are the square three-storied GATEWAY TOWER, the CRYPT, now made use of as a dairy, and the CANON's ROOM, or, as it is usually called, the Prior's chamber. Observe in the latter a curious stone fire-place, with its projecting funnel, and a pair of andirons, of Sussex iron, terminating in human heads, *temp.* Henry VII. Near the back door of the present farm-house, some Early English arches seem to indicate the position of the Priory Chapel. The large parlour is Elizabethan. An arched passage, running parallel with the crypt—called ISAAC'S HOLE—may have been the monastic LATERNA, or place of punishment.

We may commend to the sketcher the old Priory-mill, with its background of venerable trees, as an exquisite "bit." The farmstead is abundantly favoured by the residence of a complete colony of the birds of Minerva.

☞ HELLINGLY (population, 1501), 2 miles to the north, on the left of the Mayfield road, is a pleasantly situated village, with a gray old church, and many picturesque cottages. The vicarage, valued at £420, is in the patronage of the Earl of Chichester.

HELLINGLY PARK, formerly in the possession of the Pelhams, was the scene of a hunting fray in the reign of Henry VIII., unhappily attended with fatal consequences. Holinshed relates the incident with his usual graphic simplicity :—" There was executed at St. Thomas Waterings three gentlemen—John Mantel, John Frowde, and George Roydon. They died for a murther committed in Sussex in company of Thomas Fiennes, Lord Dacre of the South ; the truth whereof was this. The said Lord Dacre, through the lewd persuasion of them, as hath been reported, meaning to hunt in the park of Nicholas Pelham, Esq. of Laughton, in the same county of Sussex, being accompanied with the said Mantel, Frowde, and Roydon, John Cheney and Thomas Isley, gentlemen, Richard Middleton and John Goldwell, yeomen, passed from his house of Hurstmonceux the last of April, in the night season, toward the same park, where they intended so to hunt ; and coming into a place called Pikehay in the parish of Hellingly, they found one John Busbrig, James Busbrig, and Richard Sumner standing together ; and as it fell out, through quarrelling, there ensued a fray betwixt the said Lord Dacre and his company on the one part, and the said John and James Busbrig and Richard Sumner on the other, insomuch that the said John Busbrig received such hurt that he died thereof the second of May next ensuing. Whereupon as well the said Lord Dacre as those that were with them, and divers others likewise that were appointed to go another way to meet them at the said park, were indicted of murther ; and the seven and twentieth of June the Lord Dacre himself was arraigned before the Lord Audley of Walden, then Lord Chancellor, sitting that day as High Steward of England, with other peers of the realm about him, who then and there condemned the said Lord Dacre to die for that transgression." He was executed at Tyburn June 29th, " sore lamented by many," and not without suspicion that "his great estate, which the greedy courtiers gaped after, caused them to hasten his destruction"—(*Camden*). The estates, however, were so closely entailed that they did not fall into the hands of these rapacious cormorants.

An ancient boundary-stone, near Hellingly Park, is known as the Amber-stone. " As *amber* is a word often found connected with Druidical remains, this stone may have been held sacred by our Celtic ancestors"—(*Lower*).

A pleasant walk of about 4 miles will take the tourist from Hailsham to HURSTMONCEUX (population, 1292), whose verdurous hill looks out upon a rich and fertile valley, while away to the north and east sweep the glorious rounded Downs. Its CHURCH, dedicated to All Saints, is Early English, and consists of a nave, aisles, chancel, and north-western tower surmounted by a shingled spire. Its principal memorials are—a fine brass to Sir *William Fiennes*, d. 1402 ; a canopied tomb of Caen stone and Petworth marble, finely sculptured, with recumbent effigies to *Thomas Fiennes*, second Lord Dacre, d. 1534. The east window, picturing scenes in the life of our Saviour, is a memorial to the late learned and virtuous Archdeacon *Hare*, d. 1855, rector of Hurstmonceux for many years, of active benevolence and unaffected piety. A monument by Kessels, a young Belgian sculptor, commemorates Mrs. *Naylor* of Hurstmonceux Place, the mother of Archdeacon Hare. The font is Decorated.

In the quiet shadowy churchyard sleep, under the dark-green branches of a magnificent yew, Archdeacon Hare, his estimable brother Marcus, and others of their kith and kin. Here the tourist will do well to pause, and survey the glorious landscape of dale, and down, and valley, and meadow, of lofty cliffs and bright shimmering sea which spreads around and beneath him.

Here John Sterling was Archdeacon Hare's curate, in the earlier years of his incumbency. Sterling died, and was buried, at Bonchurch, in the Isle of Wight.

A fine avenue, which no longer exists, formerly connected the church with HURSTMONCEUX CASTLE. The present path, however, is a sufficiently pleasant one, and as the pedestrian pursues it, he may prepare himself for his visit by turning over Horace Walpole's lively account of a pilgrimage to Hurstmonceux in his correspondence with Mr. Bentley (vol. ii. p. 300, of Cunningham's edition).

HURSTMONCEUX derives its name from Waleran de *Monceux*, its first Norman proprietor, from whose representative it passed by marriage into the hands of Sir John de Fiennes. Sir Roger de Fiennes, one of the heroes of Agincourt, and treasurer to Henry II., built the castle in a quiet leafy hollow on the site of a camp formed here in 1162 by Henry II. It remained with the Dacres of the south until 1593 ; and passed from the Lennards early in the eighteenth century, to the Naylors, allied (by marriage) to the Hares. Having fallen into considerable decay, the Rev. Richard Hare, in 1777, called in that destructive architectural doctor, Mr Wyatt, who advised the demolition of the interior, and employed its materials in the repair and enlargement of the present mansion, situated on the west side of the Park, and known as HURSTMONCEUX PLACE (H. M. Curteis Esq.)

The position of Hurstmonceux is remarkable for its quiet beauty. It lies in a coombe or valley, from which, on every side, rise up low wooded hills. A dry moat surrounds it, and beyond flourishes a grand old grove of vigorous chesnuts. Everywhere a soft and fresh green sward springs, as it were, beneath the visitor's feet ; a luxuriant growth of ivy and hazel-bush lends to the gray walls an effective colouring. The building itself—one of the very first English edifices constructed of brick—is of singular interest. It retains the general form of a castle, with the battlemented towers, machicolations, drawbridges, moat, and other offensive and defensive appliances proper to one ; but having also something of comfort, and even ornament, combined with due regard to its belligerent character. It is, in fact, the intermediate link between the ancient castle and the modern manorhouse. It belonged to a transition state of society. It was strong enough, probably, to have withstood the casual attack of a wandering band of marauders, but would have been utterly incapable of enduring a regular siege—(*Thorne*). It encloses three courts ; a large, and two small ones. In the south front rises the MAIN-GATEWAY, a noble feature ; above it is sculptured the

HURSTMONCEAUX CASTLE, NEAR PEVENSEY,
ANCIENT SEAT OF THE FIENNESES, LORDS DACRE.

Fiennes *escocheon*, and their device, the ALAUNE, or wolf-dog.
At each angle stands an octagonal tower, 84 feet high, surmounted by beacon-turrets, which command a fine view of the
distant channel. On the right side of the south front, beyond the
gateway, stretches a LONG ROOM, which Grose represents as intended for a stable in case of a siege. The Hall measures 54 feet
by 28 feet. The KITCHEN was placed on the west; the great
oven in the bake-house is 14 feet in diameter. The south-
east front contained a small CHAPEL, whose stone-pillared oriel
still remains. None of the coloured glass which Walpole saw is
now in existence. The south-east tower was used as the
DUNGEON, giving " one a delightful idea of living in the days of
soccage, and under such goodly tenures"—(*Walpole*). The ancient
drawbridge has been replaced by a rude wooden bridge. In a
room over the PORTER'S LODGE, called " the Drummer's Hall,"
flourishes " the violet of a legend ; " shewing how, at midnight,
the roll of a drum echoed through the silent ruins, and how that
an invisible drummer guarded an invisible chest which was laden
with an invisible treasure. The drum roll was, in fact, a rascally
gardener's signal to certain smugglers who had made the castle
their favourite haunt. Addison founded his indifferent comedy
of " the Drummer" upon this tradition.

The plan of the castle is nearly a square, 200 feet on the north
and south, and 214 feet on the east and west sides. Both hall
and kitchen are lofty, and there is no upper storey above them.

The visitor to Hurstmonceux, desirous of fuller details than
we have here afforded, may consult with advantage the interesting monograph by the Rev. E. Venables,—" Hurstmonceux and
its Lords."

Some exquisite wood-carvings by Grinling Gibbons are preserved at HURSTMONCEUX PLACE. They were removed from the
Castle, where they were seen and admired by Walpole.

POLEGATE STATION TO LEWES.

The railway now runs along a fertile country, with the noble
heights of the Downs terminating the prospect to the south. Upon
their slopes, at 3½ miles from the Polegate station, and conspicuous from it, stand the gray old church and quiet village of
WILMINGTON (population, 288). Upon the hills beyond are
traces of the fosse and vallum of a semicircular camp, enclosing

an area of about 12 acres. On the south-east side of the Downs may be traced the outline of a rude gigantic figure, popularly known as "the Long Man of Wilmington," 240 feet long, and holding in each hand a pole of the same length. "It appears that the outline was originally incised through the turf, leaving the chalk bare, but as it has not been kept *scoured*, like the famous White Horse in Berkshire, the depression has become so slight as to be invisible upon the spot, and it is only when the light falls upon it, at a particular angle, that it can be seen from a distance. At Cerne Abbas, in Dorsetshire, there is a similar figure, 180 feet long"—(*Lower*). As both these figures occupy a slope on a chalky down, immediately opposite a religious house, they have been supposed to be the work of the monks, but more probably their origin may be traced further back. The long man has been recently *scoured.*

WILMINGTON PRIORY was founded by Robert, Earl of Cornwall, lord of Pevensey, and bestowed upon the Benedictine Abbey of Grestein, near Honfleur. Its remains have been converted into a farm-house. The timbered roof is probably ancient ; the chapel has been secularized into a sitting-room ; the cellar is still supported by its old hexagonal pillar. At WELL HOLES, about 400 yards distant, is the monastic fish-pond.

The CHURCH is mainly Norman, and cruciform in plan. The arches and pillars of the south transept, and many of the windows, are fashioned out of the chalk of the district. A goodly yew, 20 feet in girth, adorns the churchyard. The vicarage, valued at £111, is in the patronage of the Duke of Devonshire.

[In the valley beyond Wilmington, and on the banks of the Cuckmere, is a complete cluster of villages, with gray old churches, and neatly ordered cottages,— FOLKINGTON (population, 191); LULLINGTON (population, 26); and LITTLINGTON (population, 105), ancient Saxon settlements, which may probably afford the tourist much gratification.]

☞ From the BERWICK STATION, 3½ miles beyond Polegate, we can best visit ALFRISTON and SEAFORD.

ALFRISTON (population, 576)—*i.e.,* Aluricestone, or *Aluric's town*—is about 3¼ miles from the Berwick Station, and lies at the foot of the Downs, on the west bank of the small stream of the Cuckmere. Its ancient church is dedicated to St. Andrew. The Star Inn dates from the early part of the sixteenth century, and may have been resorted to by the devout on their way to the shrine of St. Richard of Chichester. Mitred figures of St.

Giles, with a hind, and St. Julian, the patron saint of wayfarers, are supported by wooden brackets on each side of the entrance. Other rude figures will reward the industrious investigation of the curious. A beam in the parlour bears a shield, lettered I.H.S.

The vicarage, valued at £175, is in the patronage of the Lord Chancellor.

SEAFORD (population, 1357), a member of the Cinque Port of Hastings, is, probably, the ancient *Mercredesburn* (Mœr-cryd, the sea-ford), the site of Saxon Ella's victory in 485. It stands on the right bank of the Cuckmere. The old town was placed on the marge of the haven—formed by the junction of the Ouse with the Channel—which has been long filled up. The position, however, of the modern hamlet, with a bold sweep of sea before it, and lofty hills rearing their rounded crests behind it, is so picturesque that we may anticipate for it a long and prosperous career.

The last Martello-tower, No. 74, stands on the neighbouring shore, and one of Henry the Eighth's circular forts is placed under the cliff. Collins has made the scene the subject of one of his finest sea-scapes.

The history of Seaford is easily summed up : it was often attacked by the French, *temp.* Edward III., and was almost depopulated by "the black death." Claude d'Annebault, and his fleet, attempted to surprise it in 1545, but were repulsed by Sir Nicholas Pelham :—

"What time the French sought to have sackt Sea-ford
This Pelham did *repel 'em* back aboord."

On December 7, 1809, seven merchantmen and their convoy, H. M. Brig Harlequin, were wrecked upon this shore with a fearful loss of life.

The men of Seaford and the neighbouring villages were, in the bad old times, daring wreckers, and the unfortunates who escaped from the perils of the sea fell into a far more terrible danger. Congreve has alluded to their rapacity in bitter lines :—

"The Sussex men that dwell upon the shore
Look out when storms arise and billows roar,
Devoutly praying with uplifted hands,
That some well-laden ships may strike the sands,
To whose rich cargo they may make pretence,
And fatten on the spoils of Providence."

SEAFORD CHURCH is dedicated to St. Leonard, and is mainly Norman and Earl English in its architectural character. The central column of the south aisle is carved with a representation of the crucifixion, and above it stands a rude sculpture of St. Michael and the Serpent, found in the churchyard some years ago. A tombstone, graven with a cross, is inserted both in the north and south walls. The vicarage, worth £167, is in the patronage of the Bishop of Oxford.

A paper in the first volume of the "Sussex Archæological Collections" embodies a quaint story of a certain monk, Balger, of the priory of Bergue St. Winox, whose vessel having been forced by stress of weather into Seaford Harbour, he contrived to rifle the neighbouring monastery of St. Andrew of the bones of St. Lewuina, one the early Sussex apostles. The chronicler enthusiastically and antithetically extols him as "fidelis fur et latro bonus"—a faithful rogue and an honest thief!

PUCK CHURCH PARLOUR (from the popular Sussex "pharisee," the fairy Puck), a curious ledge of rock, jutting out beneath the brink of the cliff, east of the town, can only be reached by a dangerous path from above, and is now the sheltering-place of some wise old Reynards, who here have little reason to dread the huntsman or his hounds.

☞ From Seaford the tourist may keep along the coast to Newhaven, 2 miles, and thence, by the cliffs, proceed to Brighton.

The next station is at GLYNDE (population 323), lying, as its name—GLYN, Celtic—indicates, in a *vale* at the foot of the chalk-downs. The CHURCH was rebuilt, 1765, by Trevor, bishop of Durham, and in its frigid classicism is to be regarded as a warning by young architects. An obelisk in the churchyard is adorned with an inscription, from the pen of Mrs Hemans, to the two sons of Wedderburn, the great lawyer. The vicarage, worth £132, is in the patronage of the Dean and Chapter of Chichester.

On the left of the line, 1 mile north, spreads the fair estate of GLYNDE PLACE (Lord Hampden), and to the right, 1 mile south-east, stretches the woodland scenery of FIRLE PLACE (Viscount Gage). Both are picturesque Elizabethan houses, seated at the base of the Downs, which at Firle Beacon rise to an elevation of 820 feet. WEST FIRLE (population, 701) has a good sized church, on the left of the road to Alfriston. The vicarage is

annexed to that of BEDDINGHAM (population, 321), is worth
£345, and in the patronage, alternately, of the Bishop, and the
Dean and Chapter of Chichester.

Passing swiftly through the valley which lies between the
two walls of chalk-hills, separated by the Ouse—

> " Here Ouse, slow-winding through a level plain
> Of spacious meads, with cattle sprinkled o'er,
> Conducts the eye along his ruinous course,
> Delighted "—

we are borne onward to the beautiful and ever memorable town of

LEWES.

[Population, 6017. — *Hotels :* The White Hart, the Star, the Bear, the Crown.
51 miles from London, by road ; 50 miles by rail.—26 miles, by rail, from Hastings ;
7 miles from Brighton ; 7 miles from Newhaven.]

☞ Communication with Brighton, Newhaven, Uckfield, Eastbourne, and
Hastings by rail. With Ringmer by omnibus. There are also conveyances between
the town and railway station.

LEWES is the county town of Sussex, though Chichester may
be regarded as the capital of the western division. It lies chiefly
on the right bank of the small river Ouse, on the slope of a chalk-
hill, one of the glorious south downs, and others of that famous
range are raised around it so as to shelter it, on almost every side.
Its hilly uneven site gives to it a peculiarly picturesque appearance ; it seems an old town, though without many very old
edifices, and is distinguished by an air of decorous respectability
and sombre importance. Around its castle and priory it clusters,
as if it felt that all its consequence was due to them ; and whether
viewed from the Cliff, from the high ground of Southover, or from
its own High Street, it presents a singular and romantic character,
not, to our thinking, equalled by that of any other English town
save Durham.

It principally consists of one street—the HIGH STREET—
winding from St. Anne's Church, east, to the foot of Cliffe Hill,
west, about three-quarters of a mile, where it throws out two
branches. One, named SOUTH STREET, leads to Glynde, Firle,
Alfriston, and Eastbourne ; the other, MALLING STREET, to Uckfield, East Grinstead, and so to London. Some smaller thoroughfares diverge from the High Street on each side. Of these we

need only notice MARKET STREET, leading from the brow of
School Hill into EAST STREET, which runs parallel to SCHOOL
HILL, but with an easier descent, and is better adapted for
equestrians and carriage-folk.

Quitting the railway terminus—the focus of trains from London, Hastings, Tunbridge, and Newhaven—and turning to the
right, we see the bold ascent of Cliffe Hill before us, forming the
eastern boundary of the Ouse valley. The suburb of the Cliffe
extends over the marshy plain on the opposite side of the river,
and is connected with the High Street by a neat bridge of stone.
Looking to the left, we notice School Hill connected with the
central part of the High Street, " which is built on a nearly level
terrace of inconsiderable breadth." Here are situated the Crown,
Star, and White Hart inns ; the County Hall ; the Markets ; the
Castle Gateway and Keep ; and St. Michael's Church. At the
foot of School Hill formerly stood the east gate of the town, commemorated in a street to the right called EAST GATE STREET ;
while that to the left, leading to Southover, is named FRIAR'S
WALK, " in reference to the monastery of Grey Friars that
anciently occupied the adjacent meadow."

Before we enter upon an examination of the notable antiquities that " do renown this city," let us, in accordance with our
custom, glance rapidly at its interesting annals.

There is abundant proof of its early importance. The localities in its neighbourhood have chiefly British names. Roman
urns and coins have been found here ; numerous earthworks
and encampments ; and some antiquarians have supposed it to
be the site of the mysterious *Mutuantonis* of the geographer
Ravennas.

It was strongly fortified during the reign of Alfred, and in
Athelstane's time possessed two mints. Specimens of Lewes
coinage have been dug up at Milton Court 9 miles from Lewes.
This place formed one of the royal demesnes. From Domesday
Book we learn that the king's rent and tolls in Lewes amounted
yearly to £6 : 13 : 1½, and he had 127 burgesses who were his
immediate vassals ; and from the same authority we gather the
following customs of the borough eight centuries agone :—

" The seller of a horse within the borough pays 1d. to the
mayor, and the purchaser another ; if an ox, ½d. ; if a man, 4d.,
in whatever place he may be bought within the rape.

" A murderer forfeits 7s. 4d. ; a ravisher, 8s. 4d. ; an adulterer,

8s. 4d.; an adulteress, the same. The king receives the adulterer's fine, the bishop the adulteress's.

"A runaway, or vagabond, that is recovered pays 8s. 4d."

After the Conquest, Lewes and numerous other estates belonging to the dead Harold—the "Last of the Saxon Kings," and not the unworthiest—were bestowed by the Conqueror upon Earl William de Warrenne, who had married his daughter Gundrada, and was potent in the royal councils. This famous earl built the Castle of Lewes (or largely repaired the old Saxon fortress), and, in conjunction with his wife, erected and endowed the Priory of St. Pancras. The fair Countess died in 1085, the wealthy baron in 1087.

With the De Warrennes this noble inheritance continued until the failure of the male line in 1347. The seventh Earl of Warrenne and Surrey joined the royal party against Simon de Montfort and the Barons, and was the stout noble who, when interrogated by the commissioners of Edward the First as to the titles by which he held his vast estates, drew forth his sword, and exclaimed, " By this instrument do I hold my lands, and by the same do I intend to protect them !"

The BATTLE OF LEWES was fought on Wednesday the 14th of May 1264. King Henry, accompanied by his son Prince Edward, and Richard, king of the Romans, arrived at Southover on Sunday, May 11, 1264, where he was sumptuously entertained by the Prior of St. Pancras, Prince Edward and his *suite* becoming the guests of Earl John de Warrenne in the Castle. The royal forces united with the earl's contingent, and encamped outside of the town.

De Montfort followed quickly in their footsteps. At Fletching Common, about 9 miles from Lewes, he halted his troops, and despatched the Bishops of London and Worcester with the view of effecting, if possible, an amicable arrangement. They reached Lewes on the 13th, and were received by the king in the Refectory of the Priory ; but their mission was utterly fruitless, and the barons found that there was no resource but the sword.

By break of day on the 14th the barons' army was in motion, and winding through the narrow glades of the leafy Weald, advanced towards the Downs by Newick and Hamsey, and ascended the hill by the road which winds along the steep northern escarpment overhanging Coombe Place (about two miles north-west of Lewes). "They arrived on the Downs at so early an hour that the king's army was unsuspicious of their approach, and would have fallen an easy prey had not '*such villanie*,' as the old chronicler indignantly terms it, been inconsistent with the chivalrous spirit of those times. De Montfort immediately drew up his forces on the plain [just beyond the Lewes race-course], and having addressed them on the righteousness of their cause, and exhorted them to be valiant and steadfast in the glorious struggle in which they were about to engage, he alighted from his horse, and prostrating himself on the ground, again implored Heaven to bless them with victory. He then conferred knighthood on several of his chiefs, and advanced towards the town, which was seen at about a mile and a half distant, reposing in the balmy dews of a bright May morning. A foraging party of the royalists was soon descried and intercepted ; and some of them escaping, fled to Lewes with intelligence of its approach."

The ridges, divided by three deep coombes, jut out from Mount Harry (so called, it is said, in remembrance of Henry the Third) across the country to Lewes, a distance of 3 miles. Along these ridges pressed forward the barons' army in three divisions, —the right wing commanded by De Montfort's sons, Hugh and Guido ; the left, chiefly composed of London volunteers, led by Nicholas de Segrave ; and the van by the Earl of Gloucester. The reserve was under the immediate command of Leicester. "The centre of the army was therefore posted on that ridge of the hill which descends with a gradual and uninterrupted slope to St. Anne's ; the left wing occupied the north branch of the Downs, that extends to the WALLENDS ; and the right wing was on the southern slope, which stretches towards Squthover"— (*Mantell*).

The royal forces were also divided into three bodies : the centre commanded by the king, the right wing by Prince Edward, and the left by the king of the Romans. Bearing down upon De Montfort's army they hoisted the royal standard, the "dragon full austere," and King Henry, elate with hope of an easy triumph, exclaimed, as he neared his rebellious subjects, "Simon, je vous defie !" And so the great fight began.

Prince Edward was speedily assaulted by Segrave's division, but he repulsed them immediately, and pursued them for four miles without ever checking the speed of his horsemen. This was much to the discomfort of the barons' host ; "but the

barons," says Grafton the chronicler, " encouraged and comforted
their men in such wise, that not all onely the fresh and lustye
knights fought eagerly, but also such as before were discomfited
gathered a newe courage unto them, and fought without feare,
insomuch that the king's vaward lost their places. Then was the
field covered with dead bodyes, and gasping and groning was
heard on every syde ; for eyther of them was desyrous to bring
others out of lyfe. And the father spared not the sonne, neyther
yet the sonne spared the father ! Alliance at that time was
bound to defiaunce, and Christian blood that day was shed without pitie. Lastly the, victory fell to the barons ; so that there
was taken the king, and the king of Romaynes, Sir Edward, the
king's sonne, with many other noblemen, to the number of fifteen
barons and bannerets ; and of the common people that were slain,
about twenty thousand. For their safe keeping the prisoners
were sent unto dyverse castellis and prisons, except the king, his
brother the king of Almayne, and Sir Edwarde, his sonne ; the
which the barons helde with them vntill they came to London."

A dreadful slaughter took place south of the town, where a
bridge crossed the river Ouse. Numbers were drowned, and
others were suffocated in the mud. "From the swampy nature
of the ground, many knights who perished there were discovered
after the battle, still sitting on their horses in complete armour,
and with drawn swords in their lifeless hands." The king of the
Romans at first took shelter in a windmill which then stood on
the site of the present Black Horse Inn—

> " The Kyng of Alemaigne wende do full well ;
> He saisede the mulne for a castèl,"

but he was soon compelled to surrender. Prince Edward retired
to the Priory, and was hotly beset by the barons, who set fire to
the magnificent church. Fortunately, the monks succeeded in
extinguishing the flames ; and Prince Edward gave himself up to
the victorious Leicester.

The immediate consequence of this great triumph was the
treaty of peace, historically known as " the Mise of Lewes." Its
grander effects our limits will not permit us to trace. He who
with earnest eye looks around England as it is, will easily re-
cognize them, and in that recognition will see sufficient cause
for grateful recollection of the genius and wisdom of Simon de
Montfort !

D

There is little else of historical interest associated with Lewes, which, indeed, may be well content to rest its claims to remembrance as an English shrine upon the memorable battle which we have so briefly recorded. John, eighth Earl de Warrenne, married Joan, the grand-daughter of Edward I., and figures as the hero of a mediæval romance. He had found, it appears, "one fairer and dearer, who occupied all his thoughts, and for whose sake he braved the anger of royalty, and the thunders of the church. It might have been that he had formed a contract with the beautiful *Maud de Nerford* before his fate was sealed to Joan. Such he asserted to be the case ; and in spite of all remonstrances he persisted in keeping her near him, and openly acknowledging her children ; while his wife sought, with an indignant mien, counsel from the ecclesiastics, who taking up her cause and that of morality, excommunicated the noble lover of Maud"—(*Costello*). Edward I. and his Queen Eleanor were entertained by the monks of Lewes for four days, in January 1276, on their way from Chichester—where they had been present at the translation of the body of the holy St. Richard de la Wych—to Canterbury.

LEWES CASTLE is gained from the High Street by a lane which turns off below St. Michael's Church. The GATEWAY, a fine old structure of great strength, in the early Edwardian style, is about 50 feet high, with machicolated battlements, and a circular tower at each angle. The staples for the hinges of the gates, and the grooves for a double portcullis still remain. The front wall is of squared flints, with fire-stone facings. Within, the old Norman gateway and plain semicircular arch will attract observation.

We now enter the outer BALLIUM, or BASE-COURT, irregular oval in shape, extending north-east and south-west for nearly 300 yards, and 130 yards in diameter. An artificial mound has been raised at each extremity, and surmounted by a keep. Of one of these the remains are considerable ; of the other, which crowned the Brack Mount, there exists but some slight traces of the foundations.

We reach the existing KEEP by a narrow winding path, closely overshadowed by trees. It was originally quadrangular, and strengthened by four hexagonal towers, about 54 feet in height from the base. The south and west towers alone remain, and time has adorned them with its wonted garniture of glossy foliage. The principal tower is occupied by the MUSEUM of the

SUSSEX ARCHÆOLOGICAL SOCIETY, and a fee of sixpence is required for the privilege of admission—a sixpence well bestowed, since it enables the visitor who mounts to "the leads" to enjoy an extensive and magnificent view of Lewes and the surrounding country. The picturesque old town, with its roofs, and spires, and winding columns of smoke, lies immediately beneath us, and away to the north and south stretches the deep river-valley—the Ouse trailing its somewhat sluggish current through a gap in the chalk-hills to join the gleaming waters of the Channel at New-haven. Northward, the eye ranges over the leafy groves and tree-encompassed meadows of the Weald, to the blue line of the Surrey-downs. From the terrace, known as the CASTLE BANKS, there is also a charming prospect which includes a portion of the river-valley, the chalk-pits of Offham, the villages of Malling and Barcombe.

We now descend the hill to examine the interesting ruins of the PRIORY of ST. PANCRAS, which, in their desolate solitude excited the regret of the poet Bowles. " All," he exclaims,

> " All, all is silent now ; silent the bell,
> Which, heard from yonder ivied turret high,
> Warned the cowled brother from his midnight cell ;
> Silent the vesper chants, the litany,
> Responsive to the organ ; scattered lie
> The wrecks of the proud pile, mid arches gray,
> Whilst hollow winds through mantling foliage sigh,
> And e'en the mouldering shrine is rent away,
> Where, in his Warrior-weeds, the Norman founder lay."

The ruins are private property, and there is some difficulty in procuring permission to view them, but from MOUNT CALVARY a sufficiently good position can be obtained. Over the site of the once magnificent PRIORY CHURCH the railway passes, and it was during the excavations here necessitated that the discovery was made of the coffins of William de Warrenne and his wife Gundrada.

Lewes Priory was erected by the great Norman baron on the site of a small wooden chapel, dedicated to St. Pancras, and colonized with Benedictine monks from Clugni, where the founder and his Countess had been splendidly entertained on their route to Italy in 1070. The edifice was completed in 1078, and was the first Cluniac priory in England, and the *only one* for a period

of nearly 150 years. It rapidly rose into importance, and gained
in wealth, and was esteemed one of "the five chief daughters"
of the mother-abbey of Clugni. Thirty-two priors ruled over it
from the time of its foundation to its dissolution in 1537. Hugh,
the second prior, became Archbishop of Rouen ; John de Courtenay resigned an earldom for the abbot's mitre ; and John
de Cariloco, in 1377, led his retainers and vassals against the
French at Rottingdean, and was taken prisoner. Here were interred the founder and his Countess, Peter de Warrenne, John de
Braose of Bramber Castle, many of the Earls and Countesses de
Warrenne, and other notable personages, whose names are recorded
in Mr. Horsfield's History of Lewes. The magnificent church of
St. Pancras was founded in the reign of Henry II., and at the
time of the Dissolution was rich in gold and purple, in stately
turrets, in gorgeous shrines, in windows glowing with the figures
of saints, apostles, priests, and barons. The revenues of the
priory were then estimated at a sum equal to £20,000 of the
present currency. The pigeon-house, which, until about 60 years
ago, stood south-west of the present ruins, "equalled in magnitude many a parish church, and contained 3228 pigeon-holes.
The fish-ponds, of which some traces are still discernible, were on
a corresponding scale of grandeur. The refectory was worthy of
so splendid an establishment. The garden probably occupied the
large hollow area called "the Dripping Pan," and the Mount
Calvary was perhaps the artificial mound near the cricket-field,
where the tourist is now supposed to be standing. The "lantern,"
or prison of the priory, a circular building underground, stands in
a private garden.

Some notion of the general extent and splendour of the priory
buildings may be gathered from a letter addressed to Cromwell—
on whom, at the Dissolution, its demesnes were conferred—by
his agent, John Portmari. It is curious enough to deserve a
place in these pages :—

"My Lord—I humbly commend me to your Lordship. The
last I wrote to your Lordship was the 20th instant (March), by
the hands of Mr. Williamson, by which I advertised your Lordship of the length and greatness of this church, and the sale, how
we had begun to pull down the whole to the ground, and what
manner of fashion they used in pulling down. I told your
Lordship of a vault on the right of the altar that was borne with
four pillars, having about it five chapels, which were compassed

with the vaults, 70 steps in length, that is, 210 feet. All this is down Thursday and Friday last. Now we are pulling down a higher vault, borne up by four thick and lofty pillars, 14 feet from side to side, and in circumference 45 feet, this shall be done for our second work; as it goes forward I will advertise your Lordship from time to time. And that your Lordship may know with how many men we have done this, we brought from London 17 men,—3 carpenters, 2 smiths, 2 plumbers, and 1 that keeps the furnace,—every one of these keeps to his own office. Ten of them hew the walls, among which are 3 carpenters; these make props to underset, where the others cut away. The others cut the walls. These are men exercised much better than the men we find here in the country, wherefore we must have men, and other things also that we have need of, the which I shall in a few days show your Lordship by mouth. They began to cast the lead, and it shall be done with such diligence and saving as may be. So, as our trust is that your Lordship will be much satisfied with what we do, when I must most heartily commend myself, much desiring God to maintain your health, and your heart's ease,

" Your Lordship's servant,

" JOHN PORTMARI.

" *At Lewes,* March 24, 1538.

"Underneath, your Lordship shall see a just measure of the wide abbey.

"Length of the church, 150 feet; height, 63 feet; the circumference, 1558 feet.

"The wall of the front, 10 feet thick.

"Thickness of the steeple-wall, 10 feet.

"There be in the church 32 pillars standing equally from the walls; a high roof made for the bells; 8 pillars very high, 13 feet thick, and 45 feet about. The height of the greatest sort is 43 feet; of the other, 28 feet.

"The height of the roof before the great altar is 93 feet; in the middle of the church where the bells did hang, 105 feet; the height of the steeple in the front is 90 feet."

Some of the monastic buildings, however, were converted into a stately residence for Gregory Cromwell, the great statesman's son, who had married Elizabeth Seymour, sister to the Lady Jane, Queen of Henry VIII., and the king meditated paying them a

visit, but was dissuaded by the younger Cromwell because the
plague was raging terribly at Lewes.

The monastic lands afterwards reverted to the Crown ; were
bestowed on Sackville, Earl of Dorset ; and have since undergone
more mutations of proprietorship than it would interest the
tourist to recount.

In the cloister school, attached to the priory in its palmy
days, were educated Archbishop Peckham, and Edmund Dudley,
Henry the Seventh's unscrupulous agent, whose father was, it is
said, the monastic carpenter-in-chief.

The coffins of William de Warrenne and his Countess were
discovered in October 1845, during the works carried on for the
construction of the London and Brighton Railway. A cutting
40 feet wide, and 12 feet deep was required, and this cutting was
made across the site, as it proved, of part of the ancient Priory
church, and the adjoining Chapter-house. Here, about 2 feet
beneath the turf, were discovered the coffins of the Earl and
Countess, now preserved at Southover Church ; and other remains of considerable interest, to which we shall hereafter more
particularly allude.

Close to the principal entrance of the Priory stands SOUTH-
OVER CHURCH, dedicated to St. John the Baptist, a curious composition of many styles, repaired and improved some fifteen years
ago. The chancel (at one time much larger than it is now), is
Perpendicular ; the nave is Early Norman ; and there are also
Early English insertions. The Norman chapel which encloses
the remains of William de Warrenne and Gundrada was erected
by subscription in 1847, from the designs of a local architect.
The material employed is Caen stone. Figures of the Count and
Countess, and the patron saint St. Pancras, are emblazoned on
the richly painted windows. The floor is paved with tiles which
glow with the escocheons of many a potent baron. Arcades
relieve the monotony of the walls. The leaden coffins of the
Count and Countess, respectively lettered " GUNDRADA" and
" WILLELM," are preserved in two deep arched recesses in the
south wall. The great Baron's coffin is 2 feet 11 inches in length,
that of the Countess, 2 feet 9 inches. " From their small size it
is clear that they were constructed to receive the bones long after
their first interment, in consequence of the decay of the original
coffins ; and it is probable that this took place in the time of
Henry II., when the remains of William and Gundrada were

transferred from their tombs in the original church of the Priory,
to the chapter house of the new and more splendid edifice, styled
by the old chronicler the 'great church of St. Pancras ;' the building of which was begun on the anniversary of the founder's death,
in 1243"—(*Mantell*).

Of these coffins Mr. Lower supplies some interesting particulars :—" The lids do not appear to have been soldered or otherwise fastened to the coffins, but merely flanged over the edges.
The ornamentation of both is very singular, though simple. The
plates composing them are evidently cast. A cord of loose tex-
ture seems to have been impressed in the sand at regular intervals,
and then crossed in the opposite direction, so as to produce on
the plates a lozengy or network pattern, *in relievo*, with interstices
averaging 5 inches by 3." From measurements made by Mr.
Pickford, Earl William's stature was probably 6 feet 2 inches ;
Gundrada's, 5 feet 8 inches.

Nearly seven centuries after the death of Gundrada, a slab of
black Norman marble, richly sculptured, was discovered by Dr.
Clarke, rector of Buxted, in the Shirley chancel of Isfield church,
where it formed the table part of the mural monument of Edward
Shirley, cofferer to Henry VIII., who appears to have rescued it
from the ruins of the Priory, and converted it into a memorial
for himself. At the expense of Sir William Burrell it was removed to Southover church, where, curiously enough, after so many
changes, it has been restored to its original destination. The
English version of the inscription is here adopted from one by
Dr. Mantell :—

> " Gundrad, a noble branch of ducal race,
> Pour'd out on English shrines balsamic grace;
> Like Mary holy, and like Martha kind,
> In her were truth and charity combin'd.
> Though death the part of Martha now receives,
> The better part of Mary ever lives,
> Then, holy Pancras, whom she made her heir,
> Still genial listen to our mother's prayer!
> On June's sixth kalend, nature's struggle came,
> And chill'd the life-blood in her tender frame;
> Her spirit burst its marble shrine and gave
> The fragrance of her virtues to her grave."

In a recess in the north wall is placed an effigy, *temp.* Henry
III., which, from some dim outlines of the Braose armorial bear-

ings on the surcoat, has been supposed to personate *John de Braose*, lord of Bramber, d. 1232. Over the altar is a picture of the Last Supper by Mortimer.

The rectory of St. John's, Southover, is only valued at £35 per annum, and is in the patronage of the Lord Chancellor. It is generally held in conjunction with the rectory of All Saints.

The other churches of Lewes are St. Michael's, St. Anne's, St. John's (*sub castro*), All Saints', and St. Thomas-at-Cliffe.

ST. MICHAEL'S IN FORO stands in the High Street—conspicuous enough with its circular tower surmounted by a picturesque shingle spire. The body of the church was rebuilt in 1755, with the usual Georgian characteristics of plainness and deformity. There are two fine brasses, however, to afford the tourist some slight compensation ; one to *John Braydforde*, rector, d. 1457, and another to a nameless knight, *temp.* 1380-1400, apparently a member of the proud race of the De Warrennes. The tomb underneath was opened in 1828, and a leaden coffin discovered, enclosing " a tall slender corpse."

A fine mural monument on the north wall represents a knight and his lady in the costume of the sixteenth century, with figures of their ten children. A helmet hangs above it. The following inscription will interest the reader :—

" Hereunder lye buried the bodies of Sir Nicholas Pelham, Knt. (son of Sir Wm. Pelham of Laughton), and Dame Anne his wife, daughter of John Sackvile, Esq., grandfather of the Right Hon'ble Thomas (late) Earl of Dorset. They had issue six sonnes and four daughters.

" His valrs. proofe, his manlie vertues prayse,
Cannot be marshall'd in this narrow roome ;
His brave exploit in great King Henry's days,
Among the worthye hath a worthier tombe ;
What time the French sought to have sack't Sea-Foord
This Pelham did repel 'em back aboord.
" Obiit 15 Decembris anno Dno. 1559.
Ætatis suæ 44."

The rectory, valued at £177, is in the Lord Chancellor's patronage.

ST. ANNE'S CHURCH, a neat Early English edifice, stands on the summit of the hill to which it gives its name. It consists of a nave, chancel, and tower, surmounted by a shingled spire. The porch doorway is enriched with the usual Norman zigzag moulding. A cylindrical font, richly ornamented, is ancient. A small brass affixed to the east wall of the chancel, bears a Latin epitaph to *Dr. Twyne*, a famous physician, d. 1613, who is extolled as " the flower and ornament of his age," and posterity is warned that it must not hope to produce " so great a physician and so renowned a man."

To the west of the church, in the old days, stood the ill-omened PEST HOUSE, and an hospital dedicated to St. Nicholas.

The Lord Chancellor presents to the rectory, which is valued at £230 per annum.

ST. JOHN'S SUB-CASTRO is a modern building, which was reconstructed on the site of a Saxon church of more than usual interest. The arch of one doorway has, however, been preserved, and a curious Latin inscription, of four hexameters, divided into two rhyming hemistichs, " deeply and rudely cut on blocks of limestone," may easily be read. Dr. Mantell thus translates it,—

> " Here, lies a knight of royal Danish birth,
> Magnus his name, and great alike his worth;
> Who, contrite for his sins, and spurning fame,
> A lowly, lamb-like Anchorite became."

The Magnus so highly extolled, and whose name has beer misspelt by his panegyrist, was, according to tradition, a son of King Harold by his second wife Githa, sister of the Dane-King Sweyn.

The site of the churchyard is remarkable; it occupies the brink of an abrupt cliff of chalk, on the south side of the river-valley, and was originally an oblong encampment, enclosing two conical mounds, one at the west angle, the other at the east. A deep vallum surrounded it on three sides. East of the church stands the tomb of Mr. *Thomas Blount*, " an eminent Lewes barber," d. 1611, who bequeathed a silver cup to the dignitaries, and certain sums of money to the charities of the town which he adorned.

The rectory of St. John Sub-Castro, valued at £244, is in the gift of H. P. Crofts, Esq.

ALL SAINTS' CHURCH, in the Friars' Walk, at a short distance beyond the spring called PINWELL, has a fine Perpendicular tower, with a curious and many-windowed excrescence, built by Wylde, in 1807. It contains a memorial to *John Stanfield*, and a good painting of St John the Baptist in prison, presented by the Earl of Chichester, who purchased it in Italy.

Among the incumbents of the rectory of St. Thomas-at-Cliffe, referred to below, should be mentioned Richard Cecil, the eminent divine ; and Thomas Aquila Dale, father of the late Rev. Canon Dale.

ST. THOMAS-AT-CLIFFE, dedicated to St. Thomas the Martyr, stands in the High Street of the Cliffe,—a venerable Perpendicular building, which occupies the site of a religious house established in honour of Thomas à Becket, shortly after the Archbishop's murder. The altar-piece is a picture of the Ascension, by Van der Gucht. The organ is said to be the instrument with which Handel delighted the lordly owner of Canons.

The rectory, valued at £185, is in the patronage of the Lord Chancellor.

Let us now proceed to summarize, as briefly as may be, the principal objects of interest in Lewes, since the limits to which we are necessarily confined will not permit us to luxuriate, as we could wish, among the historical and legendary details connected with them. We may commend the tourist who desires to dwell at greater length upon the history and romance of Lewes to Mr. Dunran's, and Mr. Horsfield's elaborate histories ; to Mr. M. C. Lower's excellent handbook ; to Mr. Blauuw's valuable essay on " the Barons' War ;" Dr. Mantell's " Day's Ramble in and about Lewes ;" and, finally, to Miss Costello's " Legendary Towns."

[MEMORABLE PLACES and NOTABLE HOUSES.—The STAR INN contains a fine old staircase of carved oak, removed from Slaugham Place, the family seat of the Coverts ; and an ancient vaulted cellar which, it is said, in the days of the Marian persecution served as a prison for the martyrs, many of whom were burnt at the stake in the street opposite the house.

The OLD HOUSE, near Southover Church, is traditionally reputed to have been the residence of that much-wandering Queen, Anne of Cleves. The great gate of the Priory formerly stood near the east end of the church, but was pulled down, we believe, in 1832. The side portal, however, still remains at the end of Southover Crescent.

The COUNTY HALL, in High Street, built in 1812 at a cost of £10,000, contains a Shaksperian picture by Northcote, and a portrait of General Elliot, Lord Heathfield, the gallant defender of Gibraltar.

JIREH CHAPEL, in the Cliffe, was erected by a fanatic, S. Jenkins, who distinguished himself as W.A.—or Welsh Ambassador—and its graveyard contains the tomb of William Huntington, S.S., or "Sinner Saved," a religious enthusiast of remarkable character. His epitaph, written by himself, runs as follows :—" Here lies the COAL-HEAVER ; beloved of God, but abhorred of men : the omniscient Judge at the grand assize shall ratify and confirm this to the confusion of many thousands ; for England and its metropolis shall know that there hath been a prophet among them. W. H. S. S."

On the Downs, between the windmill and the great chalk-pit on Offham Hill, are the *mounds* of those who fell in the sanguinary battle of Lewes.

The BULL LANE MEETING-HOUSE was built by the Gorings, *temp.* King Henry VIII. In the house adjoining, Tom Paine for a time resided, while acting as a Lewes exciseman.

SOUTHOVER HOUSE was erected, in the sixteenth century, by a Mr. Newton, a steward of Lord Buckhurst's, out of the ruins of the desecrated priory. It contains some curiously inlaid doors. In a neighbouring field are the scanty ruins—a gothic window, and a fragment of a chancel-wall—of an ancient Alms House, or Hospital for thirteen poor brethren and sisters, dedicated to St. James.

The deep abrupt valley, known as THE COOMBE, should certainly be visited for the sake of the marvellous effects of light and shade which it presents at sunrise.

POINTS OF VIEW.—From Plumpton Plain, Mount Harry, St. Anne's Church-yard, and Lewes Race Course, on the west; from Baldy's Garden, Cliffe Hill, Mount Caburn, Malling Hill, and Southerham Corner, on the east; from Offham-road, Malling Deanery, and Malling Mill, on the west; from Mount Calvary, Winterbourne Bridge, and road near Southover Church on the north.

GEOLOGICAL LOCALITIES (as pointed out by Dr. Mantell):—The Chalk-pits at Offham; Malling Hill, Bridgwick, on the Ringmer road; in South Street; Southerham Corner; Marlpits on the Glynde road, Chalk Cliffs on each side of the Coombe, and the Coombe itself.

DISTANCES OF PLACES.—East Hoathly, 7 m.; East Tarring, 4 m.; Glynde, 4 m.; Mount Caburn, 2 m.; Offham, 2 m.; Ringmer, 3 m.; South Malling, 1 m.; Stanmer Park, 5 m.; Wilmington, 10 m.; and West Firle, 3½ m.

HINTS FOR RAMBLES.—1. Through the Friars' Walk, so named from a House of Grey Friars, fl. *temp.* Henry III., and thence to Southover. Visit the Church, and proceed to the Priory ruins. Observe the view from Mount Calvary. Return to South-over, and cross to the hills west of Lewes. Visit St. Anne's Church, and afterwards the Castle.—2. Through Malling Street to Ringmer. Take the road to Glyndbourne, and cross the Downs, by the base of Mount Caburn, to Glynde. Return by Rans-combe to Southerham, and thence to Lewes by road.—3. Through Iford, Rodmill and Southease to Newhaven. Cross the Ouse, and return by Denton, East Tarring, and Beddingham, about 14 m.—4. Through Ringmer to Laughton, and thence to East Hoathly. Cross to Little Horsted and return by the road, leaving Ifield, Barcombe and Hamsey, on the right; or from Little Horsted proceed to Uckfield, and return by rail.—5. From Lewes to Charby. Cross to Wivelsfield. Keep southward to Ditch-ling, and return along the Downs by way of Plumpton, entering Lewes through Offham.—6. To Brighton by rail, and return by road.—7. Or to Brighton by rail, and then by the cliffs to Rottingdean and Newhaven. Return to Lewes by rail, or by way of Rodmill, Southease, and Iford.]

BRANCH ROUTE FROM LEWES TO BATTLE.

We leave Lewes by way of MALLING (population, 730)— an ancient settlement of the Saxon *Mallingas*—and pause to ex-amine the CHURCH, founded in 1628 by John Evelyn, the author of "Sylva," who was educated at Southover school. The site of an old collegiate church, called the "Deanery of Malling," lies at

an inconsiderable distance west. Having been founded by Cead-
walla, King of Wessex, about 680, it must be regarded as one of
the earliest Christian churches in Sussex. It was attached to the
see of Canterbury, whose Bishop had here an archiepiscopal
palace. It was to South Malling the four knightly murderers of
Thomas à Becket rode with whip and spur, after their dreadful
deed. " On entering the house, they threw off their arms and
trappings on the large dining-table which stood in the hall, and
after supper gathered round the blazing hearth ; suddenly the
table started back, and threw its burden on the ground. The
attendants, roused by the crash, rushed in with lights and replaced
the arms. But soon a second still louder crash was heard, and
the various articles were thrown still further off. Soldiers and
servants with torches searched in vain under the solid table to
find the cause of its convulsions, till one of the conscience-stricken
knights suggested that it was indignantly refusing to bear the
sacrilegious burden of their arms. So ran the popular story ;
and as late as the fourteenth century it was still shewn in the
same place—the earliest and most memorable instance of a ' rap-
ping,' ' leaping,' and ' turning table ' "—(*Stanley*). All that now
remains to recall to the tourist " the stormy days of yore " is
a foliated capital in the farm-house kitchen, and a " bit " of Early
Norman wall in the garden.

The perpetual curacy of South Malling, valued at £200, is
in Mr. Courthope's patronage.

About 2 miles beyond Malling we arrive at RINGMER (population, 1374), a village rendered interesting by its associations
with White of Selbourne, who was accustomed from this point
to pursue his delightful labours in the grand laboratory of
nature. Though he had travelled the Sussex downs for upwards
of 30 years, yet he could still investigate " that chain of majestic
mountains with fresh admiration year by year." Ringmer lies at
the base of Mount Caburn, whose entrenched summit and verdurous slopes are things of fame all round this countryside.
Here the soft green sward, and the deep shadowy coombes, and
the patches of fragrant thyme, will fill the soul of the spectator
with delight. The green paths that wind across these downs are
called " Borstalls "—from BEORH-STEGELE, hill-paths, according
to Kemble. From every point is commanded a breadth of glorious
scenery of the richest and most varied character

RINGMER CHURCH is a low but venerable building, with a tower, nave, chancel, and north and south chapels, containing numerous monuments and inscriptions of the seventeenth century.

The vicarage of Ringmer, valued at £400, is in the patronage of the Archbishop of Canterbury.

LAUGHTON (population, 812) is a pleasant, breezy village, interesting from its association with the knightly Pelhams, who had here a large moated mansion, built about 1534. The ruins are of no great importance, but a tower of brick, now rising out of the shapeless mass of a modern farm-house, and a gabled building at the south angle, may interest the tourist. The Pelham buckle is frequently introduced among the ornaments.

The vicarage, valued at £224, is in the patronage of the Earl of Chichester.

Our route now takes us through a romantic and, generally, a well-wooded country, with broad patches of heath, wide sweeps of cornfield, and fresh green reaches of meadow land. Just beyond the eighth milestone, a road on the left leads to CHIDDINGLY (population, 1053), where there are some ruins of the picturesque Elizabethan mansion of the Jefferays, and a goodly Early English church, with a tower surmounted by a tall stone spire. Observe here the remarkable memorial, with recumbent effigies, to Sir *John Jefferay*, Chief Baron of the Exchequer, *temp.* Elizabeth. In niches on either side are placed the figures of Sir Edward Montague and his wife, a daughter of Sir John.

Lord Sackville has the patronage of the vicarage, which is valued at £229 per annum.

Our road to Battle passes through other villages of little interest to the tourist. At 12 miles from Lewes he reaches HELLINGLY, already described (see p. 38), while, 4 miles to the south, lies HURSTMONCEUX (see p. 39). After crossing Boreham Bridge (18 miles), he will observe a turning on the left,—a green and leafy lane—a true Kentish lane, tree-shadowed, and meadow-bordered,—which leads to ASHBURNHAM PLACE (Earl of Ashburnham), a tabooed locality to the tourist, for whom neither gold nor silver key will unlock the magic gates. The causes of this illiberal seclusion we have been unable to ascertain, but such is the fact; into Ashburnham Place there is no admission for the archæological inquirer or historical student.

The family mansion of the Ashburnhams is a towered and gabled structure of red brick, situated on a gentle ascent which swells out of a broad deep hollow, and reposes in the shadow of a background of dense and venerable woods. The park is full of beauty ; there are sudden ascents, and wide stretches of springy turf, and clusters of dark brown trees, and dells of romantic loveliness. A path, open to the public, crosses the demesne, and opens up some rare rich prospects of the distant cliffs and the ever-changeful sea.

Here is preserved a remarkable collection of rare MSS. and valuable printed books, chiefly Latin, French, and Flemish, with some exquisite specimens of the burins of the early German artists. Armour of the knights of old ; a mass of antique and valuable plate ; and some fine specimens of Cuyp, Teniers, Rembrandt, and Rubens, are among the Ashburnham treasures. Scarcely less interesting, perhaps, are the Carolian relics ;—Charles the First's watch, his white silk drawers, the blood-spotted shirt which he wore upon the scaffold, and the sheet flung over his corpse after the cruel axe had done its worst,—relics treasured up by the pious devotion of John Ashburnham, the king's faithful attendant. " For some years they were carefully preserved at Wick-Rising-ton, near Stow-on-the-Wold, Gloucestershire. In 1743, they were bequeathed to the clerk of the parish of Ashburnham, Sussex, and his successors for ever, to be kept in the church," whence they have been removed, on what grounds we know not, to Ashburnham Place.

The Ashburnhams trace their descent from Bertram de Ash-burnham, Vice-comes of Kent and Sussex under Harold, the last of the Saxon kings. Fuller's panegyric of them, therefore, is not undeserved, as " a family of stupendous antiquity, wherein the eminency hath equalled the antiquity."

ASHBURNHAM CHURCH stands in the park, at no great distance from the house. It was rebuilt by John Ashburnham, d. 1671, gentleman of the bed-chamber to Charles I. and Charles II., and contains a memorial to that worthy and his wives, and to his brother, Sir William Ashburnham. There are some other monuments of an interesting character. The vicarage of Ashburnham (population, 865), valued at £307, and in the patronage of the Earl of Ashburnham, is associated with the rectory of Penhurst. PENHURST (population, 120)—i. e., the wooded hill—lies a short distance beyond Ashburnham Place.

From this point the road leads, through a fair and open country, to Battle and its historic ruins.

BRANCH ROUTE—LEWES TO FRANT.

After passing Ringmer, and its pleasant coppices, the first place of any interest on the road to Frant is EAST HOATHLY (population, 667), a picturesque village, situated on the borders of HOLLAND PARK, a former residence of the Pelhams. There are some remains of the Tudor mansion. The CHURCH is a Perpendicular structure, with a fine old tower, ornamented with the Pelham device of "the buckle." The rectory, valued at £261, is in the patronage of the Earl of Abergavenny.

WALDRON (1106), is a large and populous village, in a luxuriantly wooded country. The rectory, valued at £455, is attached to the patronage of Exeter College, Oxon.

Our road now runs along a branch of the great Forest Ridge of the Hastings sand, climbing short steep hills, descending into shadowy valleys, passing under the interweaving branches of ash and elm, skirting smiling meadows which are rich in blossom and verdure, running through clusters of quaint old cottages, crossing "brawling brooks," and plunging deep into leafy hollows; winding, in fact, through landscapes of the most marvellous and unexpected beauty. Here and there we meet with a rustic inn, where we may obtain the homely refreshment of home-brewed ale, and bread and cheese, or, haply, of eggs and bacon, or we come to a sequestered farmstead, reposing under its ancestral trees, and seeing itself unchanged, and apparently unchangeable, in the pond which glimmers somewhat fitfully before it. The highest point of the ridge is at CROSS-IN-HAND (where there is a tolerable "hostel"), the point of divergence of the Mayfield road.

[About 4 miles beyond lies HEATHFIELD (population, 2200), with its pretty little church recently restored, and its noble PARK, the residence for many years of General Elliot, the Gibraltar hero, who obtained his barony from this place. The grounds, and *not* the house, will obtain the visitor's approval. HEATHFIELD TOWER, 590 feet above the sea level, was erected as a memorial to the gallant Elliot by Francis Newbery, Esq., to whom the estate was sold by that hero's successor. The view from the tower is of great extent, and includes a circle of some 30 miles in diameter.

The neighbourhood of Heathfield presents a free and open aspect, the village taking its name from the heath which once extended far and wide on its sandy soil.

A very fine view is obtained from the INDEPENDENT CHAPEL, reaching to Eastbourne and the sea, vessels being plainly visible on a clear day.

About half-a-mile from this point, on the roadside, is a monument commemorating the death of Jack Cade.   It is a square stone erection about five feet square by ten high.   The inscription runs :—

"Near this spot was killed the notorious rebel Jack Cade."

Three miles south is situated WARBLETON (population, 1509), where the remains of a house of Augustinian canons, removed from Hastings by Sir John Pelham, *temp.* Henry IV., are, as was apparently usual in Sussex, embodied in a farm-house. The CHURCH contains a fine brass to *William Prestwick,* d. 1436, prior of Battle Abbey.   The pelican crest of the canopy, and the inscription on the priestly apparel —"Credo quod redemptor meus vivit"—should be remarked.   A loft in the church, tower was used as a prison for heretics during Queen Mary's reign, and here Richard Woodman was confined previous to his auto-da-fé at Lewes.

MAYFIELD (population, 2300), situate on the Tunbridge Wells and Eastbourne line, is a very picturesque little town, and from the station a delightful view may be obtained of the surrounding country.   There is a good deal to interest both the antiquary and the artist here.   There are several old-fashioned cottages and gable roofs ; and the large "Middle House" is a fine specimen of Elizabethan domestic architecture.   The massive remnants of the old wall of the archiepiscopal palace, the church of St. Dunstan, and the recently erected conventual establishment, in which the ruins of the abbey are incorporated, add further to the attractions of the place.   Visitors can gain admittance to the convent, and are shown round the chapel with its old arches.   The verger of St. Dunstan's church will also gladly admit visitors into that building, where there are some interesting tablets and iron slabs with inscriptions, telling of the days when the iron-masters flourished in these parts.   A pretty walk from here through the meadows into the woods leads to the old "furnace-house."

St. Dunstan is said to have founded here an archiepiscopal palace, but the present ruins are evidently of no greater antiquity than the fourteenth century.   Archbishop Islip erected the principal portion in the Decorated style, and cut down so much of the Weald timber as to incur censure for his rapacity, and to bring down upon himself "a signal judgment."   While riding from Sevenoaks to Tunbridge he was thrown by his horse, repaired to Mayfield, and after dinner was seized with paralysis

—a warning to all sacrilegious meddlers with the sacred oak! Archbishops Stratford and Islip also died at Mayfield. A great council was held here by the former in 1332, for the regulation of the feasts and fasts of the church. Cranmer exchanged Mayfield with Henry the Eighth for other estates, and it afterwards passed through a long succession of proprietors. Sir Thomas Gresham resided here, and splendidly received under his roof the great Gloriana. Towards the end of the eighteenth century the despoiler, as usual, stepped in, and despoiled and shattered into ruins the stately pile hallowed by so many interesting associations.

The principal, and the most ancient portion of the ruins, is the GREAT HALL, 70 feet long, 39 feet wide, and 50 feet high, erected by Archbishop Islip about the middle of the fourteenth century. The three arches which formerly supported the open roof remain entire. They are turned above the windows and between the buttresses, so as to sustain a longitudinal as well as an outward pressure. The tracery of the windows is beautiful, and of that kind which is known as " Kentish." It is to be lamented that the timber roof should have been destroyed, for " it was probably unique." A niche formed of roses, carved in stone, at the upper end of the hall, indicates the position of the archiepiscopal chair.

The GREAT DINING-ROOM occupies one side of the quadrangle. Observe its hooded chimney-piece of stone, and the iron chimney-back, dated " 1663." The GRAND STAIRCASE now leads into a large wainscoted room, the receptacle of the St. Dunstan relics— his anvil, hammer, and tongs. The iron handled hammer is ancient, but the tongs and anvil cannot boast of a very great age. An old sword is also said to be St. Dunstan's. The iron rail of the staircase, and these notable relics, were all manufactured at the Mayfield furnaces—formerly of great repute.

On each side of the door of the ante-room are obliterated armorial bearings, probably those of the See of Canterbury. North of the hall some steps descend to a doorway, which opens upon a subterranean passage to Mayfield Church. The kitchen and buttery were at the lower end of the hall, and the servants' apartments in a projecting square tower—[See the description of Mayfield in Parker's Domestic Architecture."] The gate-house still remains entire. St. Dunstan's Well, reputed to be 300 feet in depth, adjoins the kitchen apartments, and has been walled round.

x

Thomas May, the eloquent historian of the great deeds of the Long Parliament, was born at Mayfield Palace in 1595.

MAYFIELD CHURCH, dedicated to St. Dunstan, occupies the site of an ancient wooden structure, which was totally destroyed by fire in 1389. It is a building in the Early English style of architecture, recently restored. As stated above, the verger will gladly afford admittance to the church ; and its interior is not without interest.

About 4 miles to the north-east lies ROTHERFIELD (population, 4149), the ancient "Ville of Redrefeld," where the ealdorman Berhtwald, having been restored from a severe illness by a visit to the shrine of St. Denis, built a church in honour of that saint, and deposited in it the precious relics he had brought back from the Norman abbey. He afterwards bestowed the church on its monks (A.D. 792), who founded here a small cell. The present structure is principally Early English, with a tall, tapering spire of much elegance. Its arched roof is of chestnut-wood. The rectory, one of the wealthiest in Sussex, is valued at £1354, and is in the patronage of the Earl of Abergavenny.

The old manor-house of WALSHES, with its original porch and two or three antique windows, is about 2 miles east of the church.

Hence the tourist will proceed, by way of Mark's Cross and Sockbury, to FRANT.

BRANCH ROUTE—LEWES, *viâ* UCKFIELD, TO TUNBRIDGE WELLS.

We shall avail ourselves, on our way to "the Wells," of the branch railway to Tunbridge, which, at about 2 miles from Lewes, passes to the west of HAMSEY (population, 529), a village bordering on "the sad-coloured Ouse," with a Perpendicular church, (not used), picturesquely situated on a considerable ascent. In the north wall is placed a richly sculptured Easter sepulchre. The rectory, valued at £650, is in the patronage of Sir George Shiffner, Bart.

Still speeding through the fertile river-valley, we reach, at 2 miles farther north, BARCOMBE (population, 1182), a busy and populous hamlet in a good agricultural district. The rectory, valued at £960, is included in the Lord Chancellor's patronage.

ISFIELD (population, 508), is the next station, but the village itself stretches away along the road to Baresfield for some distance, with its CHURCH at its northern extremity, on the right bank of a small offshoot of the Ouse. This is a building in the Decorated style, with some Perpendicular insertions. The SHIRLEY or SHURLEY CHAPEL, on the south side, contains some memorials of interest; a stately altar-tomb, with recumbent effigies to Sir *John Shurley*, d. 1631, and his two wives, and small kneeling figures of their children. The brasses commemorate *Edward Shurley*, d. 1558, and his wife, and *Thomas Shurley*, d. 1571. The rectory, worth £340, is in the Archbishop of Canterbury's patronage.

ISFIELD PLACE still retains some traces of its ancient splendour, and over the entrance are preserved the escocheons and mottoes of the Shurleys. A high and massive wall, strengthened at each angle by a watch-tower, formerly encircled it, and is still in tolerable repair. The mansion has been *diminished* into a farm-house.

[On the north bank of a tributary of the Ouse, and to the right of the Tunbridge road—about 2 m. east of Isfield—is seated LITTLE HORSTED (population, 283), a picturesque village, with a Norman church, which the tourist should examine. It consists of a nave, chancel, and turret. The rectory, valued at £356, is in the patronage of J. Barchard, Esq.]

At 8 miles (by road) from Lewes we reach UCKFIELD (population, 2146), from whence the line proceeds by Pound Green, Rotherfield, and Groombridge. The town mainly consists of one long street, lining the high road to Tunbridge Wells, and on "market day" presents a lively and attractive scene—Sussex lasses, fresh and blooming, Sussex farmers, many of them retaining the traditional top-boots and "cut-away coats" of the Georgian era, London contractors, and staring villagers gathering here on their divers errands. The neighbourhood is rich in attractive landscapes—woodland, and meadow, and cornfield, and brown ridges of heathy hills—combining in pictorial effects of great interest and beauty.

The church is modern, and contains nothing worthy of special notice. The living is a perpetual curacy, valued at £340, of which the Archbishop of Canterbury has the patronage.

At THE ROCKS (R. J. Streatfield), on the margin of a fine sheet of water, lie some masses of rock of similar character to those which are scattered in the neighbourhood of Tunbridge Wells.

Proceeding through a country of unusual interest, enjoying a succession of bold and varied landscapes, but thinly populated, we arrive at the station for

BUXTED (population, 840),—a pleasant village with a conspicuous CHURCH, in the Early English style, standing on an ascent, with a low shingled spire, a decorated chancel, nave, and aisles—an interesting and, indeed, a handsome building. Here is a brass to *Butellus Avenel*, rector, d. 1375, with the figure of a priest ; *Christopher Savage*, " both flesh and bone," lies interred in the chancel. The figure of a female holding in her hands a large churn—a rebus for the name of Alchurn, Alchorn, or Allchorn—and flanked by warriors, each with a shield on his breast, should be noticed over the north porch. She was possibly a benefactor to the church or village. The rectory is in the patronage of the Archbishop of Canterbury.

At the north-east angle of the chancel of the church the visitor cannot fail to observe a remarkable yew tree which measures 23 feet in circumference. Buxted Rocks and Caves are well worth inspection by persons interested in these phenomena of nature. The caverns have been considered to bear a resemblance to the caves which exist in the rocks at St. Andrews in Scotland, between the castle there and the harbour. The Rev. Edward Clarke, father of Dr. Samuel Clarke, the adventurous traveller, held this quiet Sussex incumbency for some years. George Watson, the Sussex calculator, was born here. His dexterity in arithmetical operations and his powers of memory were extraordinary ; in other respects he was almost imbecile. Richard Woodman, one of the ten protestant martyrs burnt at Lewes in 1557, was a native of Buxted.

BUXTED PLACE (Colonel Vernon Harcourt) was the seat of the late Earl of Liverpool, whose daughter brought it by marriage to its present proprietor—formerly M.P. for the Isle of Wight, and the third son of the late Archbishop of York. The house is commodious and pleasantly situated. The park is of considerable extent, and rendered specially attractive by its rich masses of vigorous foliage.

Buxted was one of the great " iron-towns " of the Weald whose noble trees—

"Jove's oak, the warlike ash, veined elm, the softer beech,
Short hazel, maple, plane, light asp, the bending wych,
Tough holly, and smooth birch, must altogether burn,"—

to supply its famous furnaces, before the introduction of coal for
manufacturing purposes, removed them to the busy northern
counties. An interesting relic of the iron-times is still extant at
HOWBOURNE, in this parish—an old hammer-post, on the marge
of the once extensive but now drained pond. It is formed of an
oak tree, and in excellent preservation. Its height above ground is
9½ feet.

The first iron cannons cast in England were manufactured
at Buxted, in 1543, by Ralph Hoge, or Hogge, assisted by Peter
Baude, a Frenchman, and Peter Van Collet, a Flemish gunsmith.
Bombs, fawconets, fawcons, nimions, and sakers, and other kinds
of ordnance, were here produced. Hogge's house is still standing,
near Buxted Church, and from their rebus, or "name-device,"
a hog, carved over the doorway, is called the Hog-house. "The
name of Hogge or Hoggé seems to have been confounded with
that of Huggett; and there is a place on the confines of Buxted
and Mayfield, called Huggett's furnace, where, according to tradition, the first iron ordnance was cast. The traditionary distich that

'Master Huggett and his man John,
They did cast the first can-non,'

is firmly believed in the locality"—(Lower). Many persons of the
name of Huggett still carry on the trade of blacksmith in east
Sussex.

The decline of the Sussex iron-manufacture dates from the production of iron in the northern coal-fields. In 1740 there were
59 furnaces in England, and 10 of these were in Sussex; in 1788,
there were 77, but only 2 in Sussex; and in 1796, while England
possessed 104, Sussex had but one! Many of the great Sussex
families owed their prosperity to this now extinct staple. "In
the days of Elizabeth, the Ashburnhams, the Pelhams, the Montagues, the Nevilles, the Sidneys, the Sackvilles, the Dacres, the
Stanleys, the Finches, the Gages, and even the Percys and the
Howards, did not disdain such lucre, but pursued it to the destruction of old ancestral oak and beech, and with all the apparent
ardour of Birmingham and Wolverhampton men of these times.
We may add after these the Culpepers, the Dykes, the Darrels,
the Apsleys, the Coverts, the Merleys, the Shirleys, the Burrells.

the Greshams, the Bullens (kinsmen of royalty), the Grativekes, the Bakers, and the Fullers. Concerning the last mentioned, there is a foolish tradition that the first of the name and family in Sussex gained his wealth by hawking nails about the country on the backs of donkeys. This is absurd; but at the same time it is generally understood that the family were greatly enriched by the manufacture—a fact which is indeed frankly avowed in their singular motto ; ' *Carbone et forcipibus.*' "

Returning into the high road, we see to our left the populous village of MARESFIELD (population, 1805), where, through the researches of the rector, the Rev. Edward Turner, have been discovered the remains of extensive Roman iron-works. Some Roman coins, a considerable quantity of pottery, fragments of glass, pieces of sheet-lead, a stylus, and several skeletons, have here at various times been excavated.

MARESFIELD PARK (J. V. Shelley, Esq.), is a demesne of goodly proportions and picturesque beauty. It lies between the East Grimstead and Tunbridge roads. MARESFIELD CHURCH is a small Decorated structure, containing some good ancient woodwork. The rectory, valued at £680, is in the patronage of Rev. J. B. Butler. There is a small district church at Nutley Green, 3 miles north, on the East Grimstead road.

The road now winds through "the tufty friths" and "mossy fells" of the Weald country,—still rich in masses of leafy shadow, though the glorious old forest has been shorn of almost all its ancient grandeur,—and ascends a steep ridge of the Hastings sand to CROWBOROUGH, 804 feet above the level of the sea, which may be discerned from this lofty elevation, though distant from it some five and twenty miles. The prospects enjoyable on every side are such as can barely be realized in words. Especially so towards the south, where the Downs rear their magnificent crests like crowned giants, and now glow in the golden sunshine, now loom all grandly and solemnly through the passing shadows.

Crowborough was one of the beacon-stations of Sussex, where the ball-fire was lighted on all occasions of impending peril, and shot up its warning flames to the awakening of the entire Weald. The place where it stood may be seen at a short distance from the wayside inn, on the opposite side of the road.

The road now skirts the remains of Ashdown Forest as far as

BOAR'S HEAD STREET,—a name* which has a veritable woodland
flavour,—and, passing through the romantic charms of ERIDGE
PARK, again ascends the rising ground before it reaches TUN-
BRIDGE WELLS, at 22 miles from Lewes.

☞ From Crowborough the tourist may descend by a most
picturesque and delectable route to WITHYHAM (population,
1692), a route which, if his time will permit, he must not fail
to undertake, as it traverses a country side of extraordinary and
romantic interest. Whether he be a sketcher, intent on trans-
ferring to his tablets the outlines of a magnificent landscape ; a
botanist, eager to investigate the treasures of the Sussex flora ;
a geologist, learned in strata ; or an idler, in search of the
picturesque,—he will do well to adopt our recommendation.

Withyham itself is a village of more than ordinary interest,
and the tourist may provide himself with the Hon. and Rev.
Sackville West's " *Historical Notices of the Parish of Withyham,*"
if he care for fuller details than our plan permits us to afford.
The CHURCH, dedicated to St. Michael, is situated upon rising
ground, near the rectory,—where application must be made for
permission to view the chancel and Sackville Chapel,—and is a
large and goodly Early English building, with additions made in
the seventeenth century, after it had severely suffered in a terrible storm of lightning and thunder (June 16th, 1663). The
repairs were not completed until 1672, the date now upon the
porch, where it was replaced after some careful restorations made
about 20 years ago. In the chancel windows there is some good
stained glass, and the north windows of the nave are emblazoned
with armorial bearings. The Dorset chancel, or Sackville Chapel,
was rebuilt in 1624. The south aisle is a modern addition, and
the Sackville Chapel itself has been thoroughly restored by the
present incumbent of Withyham. The ceiling is a reproduction
of the Tudor style. A genealogical emblazonment of the Sackvilles, from the time of the Norman William, in richly coloured
glass, and several interesting memorials, including two fine
sculptures by Flaxman and Nollekens, will repay the visitor's
careful examination. In the vaults beneath lie many of the
famous Sackvilles—knights, poets, statesmen—the " true men of

* Some authorities pretend that the village is named from a curious
rock placed in a garden on the right of the road, in which they see a
resemblance to " a monstrous head."

old," whose names are among the cherished memories of our
glorious England, and among them the great *Thomas Lord Buckhurst*, Lord High Treasurer to Gloriana and her successor, the
pedant James, and the author of " Gorboduc." His monument
was destroyed in the fire of 1663.

The chapel is decorated with the Sackville banners. Observe
the white marble altar-tomb to *Richard Earl of Dorset*, d. 1677,
representing his infant son, recumbent, between the standing
figures of his countess and himself. It was originally designed
for the infant, but the Earl died before its completion. Observe,
too, the monuments already referred to, by Nollekens and Flaxman respectively, to the first *Duke of Dorset*, d. 1749, and the second
Duke of Dorset, killed by a fall from his horse in 1815. The
Earl of Dorset, d. 1705, commemorated by Pope as

" Dorset, the grace of courts, the muse's pride,"

is buried in this church, but the monument on which the poet's
panegyric was to have been engraved has never been erected.

Both church and churchyard are maintained in admirable
order, and the tourist will find no difficulty in obtaining admission.

The rectory, valued at £600, is in the patronage of Earl
Delawarr, the proprietor of BUCKHURST PARK, which passed to
him upon his marriage with the Countess,—a lineal descendant
of the Sackvilles.

Of BUCKHURST, the ancient seat of this ancient family, situated
at a short distance south-east of the church, only the gate-tower remains. It was originally a pile of unusual magnificence, and
appears—from the ground-plan preserved in Horace Walpole's
" Anecdotes of Painters,"—to have occupied an area of 260 feet
by 200. The HALL was 55 feet long and 40 feet wide, the
TENNIS COURT was 55 feet in length, and the other apartments
were constructed on the same scale of grandeur. There were
eight towers besides the gate-tower, and the surrounding park
was of noble dimensions and admirable beauty. But such were
the " extreme bad ways" and miry roads by which the Sackvilles
alone could reach their Sussex-palace, that they represented their
miserable condition to the Crown, and obtained, about 1630, a
grant of Knole, near Sevenoaks, and removing thither, permitted
Buckhurst to fall into ruins. Some portion of it was broken up,
and made use of in the erection of Sackville College, at East
Grinstead.

The present house, a noble Tudor building, stands at a short distance from the old tower, in a park of great extent, famous for its rich masses of beech-trees. On the death of John Frederick, third Duke of Dorset, it fell to the share of one of his daughters and co-heiresses, Elizabeth, who married the Earl Delawarr.

One mile beyond Withyham, on the north boundary of the once famous Ashdown Forest, is situated HARTFIELD (population, 1573), a pleasant village, with some leafy copses round about it. The CHURCH, dedicated to St. Mary, stands on rising ground. It is partly Early English and partly Decorated. The rectory, valued at £900, is in the nomination of Earl Delawarr, who is one of the largest land proprietors in this part of Sussex. BOLEBROOK, an old house of the Sackvilles, which passed to them, by marriage, from the Dalyngrugges, about 1400, is now included in the Buckhurst estates. It was built in the fifteenth century, and was one of the earliest brick-built houses in England. A gate-tower is the principal portion extant.

[4 m. north of Hartfield, and across the Kentish boundary—here formed by the river Medway, is situated COWDEN (population, 712), with its old church on the brink of a hill, overlooking a wide and varied landscape. The pulpit bears the date of 1628, and one of those old hour-glasses which were a warning to prolix preachers and a comfort to inattentive congregations. The present incumbent holds the advowson of the rectory, valued at £347.

A pleasant walk may be taken from this starting-point passing HOLLY HOUSE (R. M. Whatley, Esq.), and thence, by way of Holt Common, across Blackham Common, and through Ashurst to Tunbridge Wells.]

The tourist may penetrate from Hartfield or Withyham into the depths of the romantic district still known as ASHDOWN FOREST. It lies within the manor of Maresfield, and was included in the Honour of the Eagle of Pevensey. The Earl Delawarr is, at present, lord of this extensive chase. About 13,000 acres were formerly enclosed within a fence, and well stocked with deer ; but during the troublous times of the Civil Wars, the fences were uprooted, and the deer slain. The thick woods which were once the boast of this sylvan country side, are now represented by clumps of trees crowning the higher ground. The north-west extremity is FOREST Row, a pretty village, built, it is said, for the accommodation of those nobles and their retainers who pursued the chase in the adjoining forest. Near it is KIDBROOK, the seat of Lord Colchester. A new district-church. Early English in style, was erected at Forest Row in 1836.

Its south boundary was formed by the Downs, which extend from Uckfield to Etchingham. Withyham was its north-east point, and Crowborough, on the east, overlooked the entire tract of rank and luxuriant woodland.

BRANCH ROUTE—LEWES TO EAST GRINSTEAD.

The direct East Grinstead road, at about 3 miles from Lewes, leaves the COOK'S BRIDGE STATION on the left, and CONEYBAR-ROW PARK on the right. About 5 miles further, after passing the village of CHAILEY, it is crossed by the road from Cuckfield to Etchingham. Following the latter for 2½ miles we should reach NEWICK, and crossing the Ouse at Gold Bridge, and turn-ing to the left at Pitt Down, visit FLETCHING, and, by way of SHEFFIELD PARK, regain the high road near the 39th milestone. From this point the route lies through a thinly populated and romantic country, skirting Ashdown Forest, crossing Dane Hill, and by way of Chelwood, Kidbrook, and BRAMBLETYE PLACE, entering East Grinstead.

If at the cross road already alluded to we took a westerly direction, we should proceed by Pelling Bridge to LINDFIELD, and thence, by the main road, with HORSTED-KEYNES and WEST HOATHLY on the right, and Ardingley on the left. At Sidles-field Common a road branches off to East Grinstead—the main road continuing by way of Godstone and Croydon to London. For the convenience of the tourist, we notice the places particu-larized in capitals in the order in which we have named them :—

CHAILEY (population, 1268) is a large agricultural district. The rectory, valued at £505, is in the hands of the Blencowe and Hepburn families as patrons. The church is not a very interest-ing building. NEWICK has a population of 1083. The Rev. J. Powell holds the advowson of the rectory, which is valued at £327. FLETCHING (population, 2132) is an extensive and populous parish. The village lies to the south-east of SHEFFIELD PARK (Earl of Sheffield), a noble and well-wooded demesne. The stately mansion was greatly enlarged and completely renovated by the late Earl. The walls are decorated with carvings of the armorial bearings of the different lords of the manor, from the days of William the Norman. A fine portrait, by Sir Joshua

Reynolds, of Gibbon, who spent many years at Sheffield Place, then in the hands of his friend, John Holroyd, first Earl of Sheffield, is preserved here.

FLETCHING CHURCH, dedicated to St. Mary and St. Andrew, is a large Early English building, with a nave, chancel, aisles, transepts, and tower surmounted by a spire. The tower is Norman, and the double windows are divided by Norman balusters. An altar-tomb in the south transept bears a brass for a Sir *Walter Dalyngrugge*, d. 1395, and his wife. Observe, also, the altar-tomb, with figures, of *Richard Leche*, d. 1596.

Gibbon lies interred in the Sheffield mausoleum. The inscription, in sonorous Latin, is from the pen of Dr. Parr.

The vicarage of Fletching, valued at £300 per annum, is in the patronage of the Earl of Sheffield.

Sir S. Maryon Wilson, Bart. of Charlton, has a pleasant house and grounds at SEILES, adjoining Sheffield Park.

The reader will remember that the night before the battle of Lewes, May 13, 1264, Simon de Montfort and the Barons' army encamped in the woods of Fletching, then a dense and almost impenetrable mass ; and it was from this point he moved forward to Mount Harry, after the failure of his attempt to negotiate with the king.

Regaining the high road beyond Sheffield Park, we proceed through a hilly and sparsely cultivated country, by way of Kidbrook and Forest Row, to East Grinstead (9½ miles). Just beyond Forest Row, a turning on the left leads to the ruins of BRAMBLETYE HOUSE, associated in the memory of veteran novel-readers with the scenes of Horace Smith's best romance. It was built, *temp.* James I., by Sir Henry Compton, whose armorial bearings quartered with those of his second wife, Mary Browne, are sculptured over the entrance. It was captured by the Roundheads during the Civil War, and in 1683, while its then owner, Sir James Rickards, was rousing the deer in the great forest-depths of Ashdown, it was searched by the royal messengers, and considerable quantities of arms and ammunition were found. Sir James fortunately obtained information of the movements of his foes in time to make his escape and retire to Spain. The house was thus left without a lord, and speedily fell into decay. The existing ruins consist of the chief gateway, one square turret, and portion of another. Underneath the building are the domestic offices and vaulted cellars, displaying some good pointed arches.

The valley where Brambletye House is situated is of great beauty and is still clothed with a fresh and vigorous verdure. It is watered by the infant stream of the Medway, which has its source at Turner's Hill, west of East Grinstead Church, and about 4 miles distant.

Returning to Chailey, and taking the Cuckfield road instead of the route we have just described, we first arrive (7 miles) at LINDFIELD (population, 866), a village romantically situated in a luxuriantly wooded, " deep-bowered and happy-meadowed " country-side. Its CHURCH, dedicated to St. Michael, has an Early English tower—a nave, chancel, and aisles, Perpendicular. The wall of the aisle is enriched with a curious fresco of great antiquity, dating from, perhaps, the fourteenth century. The Virgin is pictured with a glittering nimbus round her head—a small figure kneeling at her feet—and with a staff in her hand which she aims at a six-headed dragon, whose heads, however, have already been severed by her companion, St. Michael. The robes of the archangel are spotted with the letter M.; he stands upon the conquered dragon, and weighs souls in a pair of scales.

Observe, too, the remarkable effigy engraved upon three glazed tiles which each measure 15 inches square—2 feet 9 inches in all. The date is 1520.

The Archbishop of Canterbury holds the right of presentation to the perpetual curacy of Lindfield.

In the neighbourhood of this quaint, old-fashioned, and secluded village—secluded, though it is scarcely 2 miles from the Hayward's Heath Station on the London and Brighton railway, and about 5 miles from Cuckfield—are some most delectable bits of scenery, some nooks and corners of enchanting beauty, which the tourist should leisurely explore. There are some old houses, too, which deserve examination ; old Elizabethan mansions, with many gables, and twisted chimneys, and curious effects of light and shade :—PAX HILL, EAST MAXALLS (the ancient seat of the Newtons), KENWARDS (of the Challoners), and LUNT (of the Hamlyns).

A pleasantly leafy road, by way of Pax Hill, leads to HORSTED-KEYNES (population, 715), lying in a picturesque hollow brightened by the waters of the Ouse. Its small Early English church should be visited for the sake of its effigy, 27 inches in length, of a knight templar—possibly one of the *Keynes* or *Chey-ney* (from Cahaignes in Normandy) family, who may have fought against the Saracens under the banner of Edward I. Archbishop *Leighton*, d. 1684, the virtuous primate of Glasgow, who resided for ten years—after his resignation of his mitre—at Broadhurst in this parish, and preached constantly by word and example in the neighbouring villages, lies interred in the south chancel.

The rectory, valued at £342, is in the patronage of Thomas Davis, Esq.

Some curious illustrations of Sussex life will be found in the DIARY of Giles Moore, rector of this parish from 1655 to 1679, printed in the first volume of the "Sussex Archæological Collections." For a companion-picture the reader may turn to the JOURNAL kept by one Timothy Burrell, Esq. of Ockendon House, near Cuckfield, from 1683 to 1714, and preserved in the third volume of the same work.

A road which passes the church of Horsted-Keynes, crosses a branch of the Ouse, and soon ascends to higher ground, conducts us (4 miles) to WEST HOATHLY (population, 1068). Its Early English CHURCH is large and interesting, and consists of a Perpendicular tower, nave, chancel, and aisles. At the entrance lie two iron slabs, memorials to members of the Infield family. The fort is ancient. The Lord Chancellor presents to this vicarage, valued at £198 per annum.

To the left of the church, about ½ mile distant, and on the very brink of a sandstone cliff, are placed two rocks—one, a mass of about 350 tons weight, being exactly poised on the other, which is a much smaller rock. The villagers expressively call them "Great-upon-Little." According to some authorities they are connected with the old Druidic rites, but the grounds for this opinion seem very unsatisfactory.

[ARDINGLEY (population, 1095) lies about 3 miles south-west of Hoathly, on the eastern slope of a sandstone-ridge of picturesque character. The landscapes here are reproductions, in their general outlines, of the Tunbridge Wells scenery. The CHURCH, chiefly decorated, has an ancient wooden porch, a good oaken screen, stone effigies of an unknown knight and a nameless lady, and several *brasses*, memorials of the Culpepers of Wakehurst, a branch of the Great Kentish family. Observe the altar-tomb and brass to *Richard Wakehurst*, d. 1464, and his wife *Elisabeth*, with their figures in the costume of the period.—The rectory, valued at £596, is in the gift of Trustees.

WAKEHURST PLACE, which is a handsome mansion, lies in the bosom of much agreeable leafiness, about 1 mile north of Ardingley village, and near the East Grinstead road. It was formerly the seat of a family of the same name, and afterwards passed to the Culpepers, one of whom, in 1590, erected the present house—a quaint, old-fashioned, and goodly pile.]

From West Hoathly we cross the high ground of SIDLES-FIELD or SILSFIELD COMMON—one of the ancient beacon-stations, and overlooking an extensive prospect—to

EAST GRINSTEAD (population of the parish, 5250—*Inn :* Dorset Arms), an irregularly-built, but pleasant market-town, situated on an ascent which commands a good view of Kent, Surrey, and Sussex. It contains some old timbered houses, and some modern ones of tolerable pretensions, and may probably become the great agricultural depot of northern Sussex.

The CHURCH, dedicated to St. Swithin, is, from its lofty position, a conspicuous object from many points in the surrounding landscape. It is the third that has existed in the short space of a century and a half. The spire of the old building was struck by lightning in 1685, and the tower of the second fell in 1758 and demolished a portion of the church. The present tower is of great height, and adorned with pinnacles. The nave, aisles, and chancel are all of good dimensions. Observe the brass (from the ancient building) of *Catherine Lewkner*, of Brambletye, d. 1505, and the stately monument to the first Lord *Colchester* (better known as "Speaker Abbott"), d. 1829. A brass, and monument of Sussex marble, commemorate Dame *Elizabeth Gray*, and her two husbands. She was one of the ladies in attendance upon the Queen of Henry VII., and, in conjunction with her second husband, "founded, indued, inorned this present church to the lawde and honore of God with dyvers ornaments, and an almshouse for three persons." Lord *Abergavenny*, d. 1744, is commemorated by a tablet in the south aisle.

Lord Sackville has the patronage of the vicarage, which is valued at £468 per annum.

East Grinstead formerly returned two members to Parliament, and is now one of the polling-places for the electors of East Sussex. It is 29 miles from London by road ; and connected with the London and Brighton railway by a branch line, 7 miles in length, from the Three Bridges' station. The neighbourhood is rich in scenery of a somewhat wild and picturesque character.

BRANCH ROUTE, BY RAILWAY, FROM LEWES TO BURGESS HILL.

At first we are rapidly borne through the fertile valley of the Ouse—the lofty crests of the South Downs looming magnificently to the south west, against the distant and misty skies. At about 3 miles from Lewes we pass on the right, Coneybarrow Park, and reach the COOK'S BRIDGE STATION, on a branch of the Ouse. PLUMPTON (population, 383), a pretty village built upon a pleasant green, lies nearly 3 miles west. There are here a small, and not peculiarly interesting CHURCH, and an old moated house, PLUMPTON PLACE, the ancient residence of the Maxalls—one of whom, Leonard Maxall, *temp.* Henry VIII., first introduced carp, it is said, into this country by domesticating some *Cyprinidæ* of the Danube in the moat which encircled his house. He is also reputed to have brought "the Golden Pippin" into Sussex, but some authorities pronounce it indigenous to the county.

The rectory (worth £337 yearly) is in the patronage of the present incumbent.

[STREET PLACE is another interesting old house, 1½ mile north of Plumpton. It was the seat of the Dobells, and dates from *temp.* James I. The library, now converted to "baser uses," is adorned with carved pilasters, and with a cornice which is elaborately lettered with quaint Latin mottoes. Behind the great chimney-place of the hall was a deep recess, used for purposes of concealment, and there exists a tradition that a cavalier horseman, hotly pursued by some "malignant" troopers, broke into the hall, spurred his horse into the recess, and disappeared for ever. STREET (population, 170) has a small Early English church. The rectory, valued at £172, is in the gift of H. C. Lane, Esq.]

PLUMPTON GREEN now lies on our right, and DITCHLING on our left. We soon cross the main road, *via* Lancefield, to London, and through a hilly and undulating country, reach the BURGESS HILL STATION, 41½ m. from London, and 9 m. from Lewes. Here the main line diverges to Brighton, and passes through a country which we shall hereafter describe [See Route XI.]

LEWES to BRIGHTON.

[Lewes to Falmer, 5 m.; Brighton, 8 m.; New Shoreham, 6 m.; Worthing, 4½ m.; Angmering, 5 m.; Arundel, 8 m.; Barnham Junction (for Bognor, see p. 141), 5 m.; Chichester, 5 m.]

" That palace or China shop, Brighton which is it ?
With lanterns, and dragons, and things round the dome."—MOORE.

We leave Lewes for Brighton by the branch line which runs through an open country to FALMER (population, 537), a small and pleasant village where we need not linger, and underneath which we are carried, by means of a tunnel 285 yards in length. Shortly afterwards we skirt the fair demesne of STANMER PARK (Earl of Chichester), a well-wooded and pleasantly-diversified estate, some 1500 acres in extent—and enter a deep cutting three quarters of a mile in length. We next pass through two short tunnels, and enter Brighton over the PRESTON VIADUCT—a noble structure of 27 arches, elevated 67 feet above the Preston road (observe, on the right, the cavalry barracks.) We here obtain a good view of the north-eastern suburb of Brighton—pleasant, populous, agreeable Brighton. The monster " watering-place " of England—indeed, the largest in the world—to which we shall be constrained to devote a considerable number of our pages.

BRIGHTON.

[Population, municipal borough, 107,523.—Average number of visitors, 80,000.—
Hotels : Bedford, Grand, Old Ship, Sussex, Royal Crescent, Royal Albion, Norfolk,
German Place : Royal York.—*Boarding-houses :* Cavendish Mansion, Connaught
House, Silwood Place, Dudley Mansion, etc.—*Restaurants :* Mutton's, King's Road ;
Aquarium, etc.—*Rinks :* at King's Road, West Street, and Hove.

50½ m. from London, by rail ; 53 m. by road ; 8 m. from Lewes ; 9 m. from Newhaven ; 6 m. from Shoreham ; 4½ m. from Rottingdean ; 5½ m. from the Devil's
Dyke ; 9½ m. from Bramber ; 28 m. from Chichester.

⌨ *Omnibuses,* to meet the trains, between Hove, Brighton, and the Railway
Station (on the north of the town). *Conveyances,* daily, to Lewes and Shoreham.
Flys, 1s. per mile. *Post-Offices ;* 3 arrivals and 5 departures daily. *Baths :* Brill's,
Hobden's, and the Turkish. *Bathing-Machines,* 6d. and 9d. each person. Railway
Journey to London 1 hour 15 minutes by express.

"Brighton," says Hazlitt, " stands facing the sea, on the bare cliffs, with glazed windows to reflect the glaring sun, and black pitchy bricks shining like the scales of fishes. The town is, however gay with the influx of London visitors—happy as the conscious abode of its sovereign ! everything here appears in motion— coming or going. People at a watering place may be compared to the flies of a summer ; or to fashionable dresses, or suits of clothes, walking about the streets. The only idea you gain is, of finery and motion." Thackeray, in THE NEWCOMES, writes of it more eulogistically :—" It is the fashion," he says, " to run down George IV. ; but what myriads of Londoners ought to thank him for inventing Brighton ! One of the best physicians our city has ever known. is kind, cheerful, merry doctor Brighton. Hail thou

BRIGHTON

Scale of ⅛ a Mile.

Furlongs

purveyor of shrimps, and honest prescriber of South Down
mutton ; no fly so pleasant as Brighton flys ; nor any cliffs so
pleasant to ride on ; no shops so beautiful to look at as the Brighton gimcrack shops, and the fruit shops, and the market. " Mr
Thorne's graphic description will interest the reader :—" If some
daring engineer were to lift the line of houses facing Park Lane,
place them upon the south-coast railway, convey them to the sea-
side, and plant them directly alongside the beach, he would
make an almost exact resemblance to Brighton as viewed from
the sea. So much does the line of houses facing the cliff resemble some parts of the West-end, that the spectator who has
been shot down from town in an hour by the express-train, finds
a difficulty in believing that he is far away removed from his old
haunts, until he turns to the bright sea, which lies before him
like a flat and polished mirror, and champing and frothing upon
the pebbly beach below. The western extremity of the town,
which is bounded by Adelaide Crescent and Brunswick Terrace
and Square, lies comparatively low : and from this point to
Kemp Town, which is fully 3 miles to the east, runs a splendid
promenade. The life and variety which everywhere meet the eye
along this pleasant walk, is perhaps unequalled." The great draw-
back of Brighton, however, is its *want of shade*. It has no
trees to afford a coolsome shadow—no obscure groves, no romantic bowers—though, indeed, Hood has protested " that of all
the trees he ever saw, none could be mentioned in the same breath
with the magnificent BEACH at Brighton."

But now a-days everybody goes to Brighton. It is brought
so near to London by the agency of the rail ; the excursion fares
are so moderate ; there is such a *reality of sea* about it—not like
that shrimp-abounding town—yclept Gravesend, which is simply
brackish—that we marvel not the eager Londoner starts away,
fifteen minutes before eight, to enjoy " six hours" at this city of
chalk. There are grand, lofty cliffs, glittering like ramparts of
silver or walls of pearl. There is a glorious expanse of ocean-
waters, ever varying from blue to green, and green to purple, as
they surge and seethe in sunshine or in shadow ; aye, ocean waters,
only bounded by the dim circle of the distant sky. And there
is a pebbly beach, with huge clusters of dank seaweed, and trim
fishing boats hauled up above the tide-mark, and—yes, we must
proclaim it—most loveable groups of dark eyes and blue eyes,
bent, apparently, upon their sketch-books, or the pages of the

last new novel. "A day out," if spent at Brighton, is a day to be remembered. We once heard a mechanic, in an excursion train, describe this favourite town in language quaint, but not elegant : "It's a stunning sight," said our emphatic friend ; "for all the world like Piccadilly gone out to sea !"

Certainly, there is little sign of antiquity about the good town at present, and yet its annals begin at a period not within the memory of even "the oldest inhabitant." It was, probably, a British settlement, for in its vicinity are numerous traces of the rude fortifications or "earthworks" of our ancestors. That it existed during the Saxon period of English history is indisputable. Its name is Saxon, derived, it is said from Brihthelm, a Bishop of Selsay, and we know that it paid a rent, or " gablum," to Earl Godwin, the great Saxon noble. In 1081, this rental was paid in herrings (4000 halices) yearly—equivalent, in our money, to something like £300. There were then two distinct settlements here—one upon the heights, "a colony of landsmen ; " one upon the shore, a village of *jugs* or fishermen. It was then called Brighthelmstone, a name it retained until very recently ; and was numbered among the rich manors bestowed by William the Conqueror on his loyal adherent, Earl de Warrenne, who exercised almost a sovereign sway over the fair county of Sussex.

The French attacked the town, and burnt it, in the reign of Richard II. In 1513, they again made a descent upon the coast, under "Prior Jehan," but were compelled to retreat, with considerable loss. During the war between Henry VIII. and Francis I., in 1545, they harassed the whole southern coast, under their high admiral, Claude d'Annebault, who, says the old chronicler, Holinshed, "hoisted up sails, and with his whole navie came foorth into the seas, and arrived on the coast of Sussex before Bright-Hamsted (Brighton), and set certain of his soldiers on land to burne and spoile the countrie ; but the beacons were fired, and the inhabitants thereabouts came down so thick, that the Frenchmen were driven to flie, with losse of diverse of their numbers, so that they did little hurt there."

Shortly after this event, considerable fortifications were erected. There was a circular fort, called the Block House, and a battery called the Gun Garden, and a flint wall, 400 feet long, "from the east gate westward, where the cliff was lowest ; and from that point a parapet three feet high, with embrasures for cannon, was continued to the west gate." These no longer exist.

There was, also, a small battery at the verge of the cliff, on the King's Road, which mounted six forty-two pounders ; but Brighton's present defences are England's " wooden walls," well manned by " hearts of oak."

Amongst the interesting events of Brighton history, we must not omit to record the escape of Charles II. from Cromwell's troopers. After the fatal battle of Worcester—which Cromwell might well speak of as his " crowning mercy," for it placed the English sceptre virtually in his hands—the unfortunate king made his way, in disguise, to Brighton, where he arrived on the 14th of October. He passed the night at an inn (*The King's Head*) in West Street ; and the following morning moved to Shoreham, whence he immediately departed for the French coast, in a small boat belonging to a gallant loyalist, named Tattersall. After the restoration, the Brighton mariner, perceiving that the king's memory was very treacherous, sailed in his little craft to the River Thames, and moored it opposite Whitehall. Charles ordered it to be entered in the Royal Navy as the " Royal Escape," settled upon the gallant mariner and his heirs an annuity of £100, and presented him with a ring, which is now in the possession of a descendant—Sir Henry Shiffner.

During the seventeenth century the town suffered severely from the raids of the sea, and in Defoe's time, could only boast of six decent streets. The women employed themselves in weaving nets ; the boatmen were glad to obtain employment from the Yarmouth merchants in the herring-fishery. In 1703 and 1706 it was further desolated by violent storms. In the latter year no less than 130 houses were swept away, and £40,000 worth of property destroyed by the inundations which accompanied the tempest. In a few years all traces of ancient Brighton were lost under an accumulation of shingle. In 1818, during some excavations between Middle and Ship Streets, the walls of one of the streets of the lower town, called South Street, were discovered under a layer of beach, 15 feet in depth.

Brighton, like Ventnor, owes its present prosperity, in the first place, to a physician, Dr. Russell, who removed here from Malling, in 1750, and resided in a house on the Steyne,—*i. e.*, stane, a rock—where the Albion now stands. His portrait, by Zoffany, is preserved in the Old Ship Hotel. He published a treatise on the advantages of sea-bathing, and drew several patients from London to test the soundness of his theory. The Duke of

Cumberland, the victor of Culloden, was one of Brighton's earliest patrons, and lived in a house north of the Pavilion. The Duke and Duchess of Marlborough also sought the Brighton physician, and resided at Elm Grove. Dr. Johnson accompanied hither Mr. and Mrs. Thrale and Fanny Burney, in 1770, and declared the country " so desolate, that if one had a mind to hang one's self for desperation at being obliged to live there, it would be difficult to find a tree on which to fasten a rope." Miss Fanny visited the " King's Head Inn" (originally the George), in West Street, and gazed with loyal satisfaction on its sign — a head of his " black-wigged Majesty" Charles II., who slept there the night before his escape from Shoreham. The Thrales and their friends resided at No. 75 in the same street. George IV., then Prince of Wales, paid his first visit to Brighton in 1782, and built a house here in 1784 — an epoch in the fortunes of the town duly remembered by all loyal Brightonians. It was not completed until 1817, when it was taken to pieces, remodelled, repaired, gilded, decorated, and moulded into the present bizarre architectural model — the PAVILION. The THEATRE was opened in 1807. BEDFORD SQUARE was commenced in 1810. The CHAIN PIER was begun in 1822 and completed in 1823. KEMP TOWN, on the estate of Mr. Thomas Kemp, rose into existence between 1821 and 1830. The MARINE WALL, 23 feet thick at the base and 60 feet in height, was built in 1827-8 at a cost of £100,000. In 1841 the BRIGHTON RAILWAY was opened throughout, having cost £2,569,359, and occupied two years and a half in its construction. Among the attractions of Brighton can scarcely be included its public buildings, and yet there are two or three points of interest to which the tourist must be formally introduced.

The CHAIN PIER, " where for the sum of 2d. you can go out to sea, and pace the vast deep without need of a steward with a basin," is only equalled as a marine promenade by its modern rival the West Pier. From this point the entire " sea-face " of Brighton is seen in a striking manner. It was commenced in 1822, and completed in the following year, under the direction of Captain Sir S. Brown, R.N., and at a cost of £30,000. It is 1136 feet in length and 15 feet in width, is supported by four piers which stand upon piles of oak driven 10 feet into the solid chalk, and by four cast-iron towers, 25 feet high, over which are carried the wrought-iron suspending chains, four deep and two

BRIGHTON.

inches in diameter. Each of these four divisions or bridges is 258 feet in length, and has 117 links of one foot each. A fearful storm in November 1836 overthrew this fragile structure, snapping the suspending rods and breaking the central bridges, and necessitating repairs which cost £2000. Some injuries were done by a gale during the night of October 15, 1838, but, since that event, it has withstood in security the heaviest tempests which have visited our shores.

The PAVILION cannot be visited by the tourist without recalling to his mind the luxurious days when George, Prince Regent, was eulogized as " the finest gentleman in Europe," and Mrs. Fitzherbert, " fat, fair, and forty," was the cynosure of admiring eyes. Among his companions were Lord Barrymore and his two brothers—a trio, known by the expressive nick-names of " Hellgate," " Cripplegate," and " Newgate ;" Sir John Ladd, of four-in-hand memory; and Colonel Hanger, renowned as " the Knight of the Black Diamond." Well might Lord Thurlow reply to the Prince's query, " Thurlow, how is it you have not called on me ? You must find a day for dining with me."—" I cannot, your Royal Highness, until you keep better company." On another occasion, when Thurlow had consented to dine with the Prince, he was informed that Sir John Ladd would also be a guest. The Prince apologized to the surly Lord Chancellor, but with little effect. " I do not object," said Thurlow, " to Sir John Ladd in his proper place, but that I take to be your Royal Highness's coach-box, and not your table."

The Pavilion occupies with its gardens about eleven acres and a half, and is a curious combination of domes, minarets, and cupolas, looking, according to Sidney Smith, " as if the dome of St. Paul's had come to Brighton and pupped." Cobbett suggests that " a good idea of the building may be formed by placing the pointed half of a large turnip upon the middle of a board, with four smaller ones at the corner." Nor is this description exaggerated in its ridicule, and he who gazes upon the monstrous pile can well understand " the intensity," of Sir Walter Scott's feelings when he wrote to his friend Morritt, then residing at Brighton (A.D. 1826) :—" Set fire to the Chinese stables, and if it embrace the whole of the Pavilion, it will rid me of a great eyesore."

The original Pavilion was commenced for the Prince Regent by the architect Holland in 1784, but was entirely reconstructed

by Nash in 1818 under the immediate direction of the Prince.
The royal stables, now converted into an assembly room, cost
£70,000. The diameter of the great dome is 250 feet. The
Chinese gallery measures 162 feet by 17 ; the banqueting-hall,
60 by 42 ; the music-room, 62 by 41 ; and the rotunda is 55 feet
in diameter. These, and several other apartments, elaborately
decorated after the Chinese manner, are open to inspection at 6d.
admission. In the same suite of buildings is the Corn Exchange
(formerly the riding-school) on the west, whilst on the east is
the Free Library, the Museum, and the Picture Gallery.

William IV. sometimes resided here, and Queen Victoria
occasionally visited it before she purchased Osborne. Her refined
taste, however, was disgusted at its semi-Chinese monstrosities,
and she intimated her intention of abandoning it as a royal residence. It was then (1849) purchased by the town for £53,000
—not a fourth of the sum originally lavished upon it—and has
since been adapted for concerts, public meetings, balls, and general entertainments, remaining a building of no ordinary interest,
though of more than ordinary architectural deformity.

In the QUEEN'S PARK, a pleasant plantation north of the
town, is situated the ROYAL GERMAN SPA, where chemical imita-
tions of the different German mineral waters are manufactured—
to the great benefit of those who are unable to patronize the
springs of Marienbad, Pyrmont, Seidschütz, and Seltzer.

The only relic of ancient Brighton is ST. NICHOLAS' CHURCH,
situated on the hill north-west of the town. It is mainly Perpendicular in style, was built in the reign of Henry VII., and
restored, in 1853, in memory of the Duke of Wellington, who
often worshipped within its walls, and was for some time a pupil
of the vicar. The memorial then erected is a richly decorated
Cross, by Carpenter, 18 feet high, in the south chancel. A
scroll, entwined about the shaft, bears the magic words, " Assaye,
Torres Vedras, Vittoria, and Waterloo." A figure of St. George
is inserted in the canopied niche at the top. The east window
represents, in rich colours, the miraculous draught of fishes. The
perpendicular screen, of painted oak, has been painted and gilded.
The Norman circular font, brought, it is said, from Normandy,
has its sides adorned with sculptures representing the Lord's
Supper, and its base disfigured with the names of the churchwardens who officiated in the church in 1743.

In the churchyard are placed the memorial-stones of Captain

Nicholas Tattersall, " through whose prudence, valour, and loyalty, Charles II. was faithfully preserved and conveyed to France, 1651 ;"—*Phœbe Hessell,* panegyrized by George IV., from whom she received a yearly pension of £18, as " a jolly old fellow," and who, according to her epitaph, " served for many years as a private soldier in the 5th Regiment of Foot in different parts of Europe, and in the year 1745 fought, under the command of the Duke of Cumberland, at the battle of Fontenoy, where she received a bayonet wound in the arm. Her long life, which commenced in the reign of Queen Anne, extended to George IV., by whose munificence she received comfort and support in her latter years. She died in Brighton, where she had long resided, December 12, 1821, aged 108 years." There is also a memorial to Mrs. *Crouch,* the actress ; and the base of the old churchyard cross is still extant.

The Bishop of Chichester has the right of presentation to the vicarage of St. Nicholas. The vicar himself nominates to eight incumbencies—1. ST. PETER'S (perpetual curacy), at the end of the Steyne, built in the Late Perpendicular style, by the late Sir Charles Barry, at a cost of £20,000 ; 2. ST. PAUL'S, in West Street, built by Carpenter in 1847 ; 3. ALL-SOULS ; 4. CHRIST CHURCH (perpetual curacy, valued at £420), built in 1838 ; 5. ST. JOHN THE EVANGELIST; 6. ALL SAINTS' CHURCH (perpetual curacy, £200) ; 7. CHAPEL ROYAL, in Prince's Place, built by Saunders in 1793 ; and 8. ST. STEPHEN'S. There are, besides ST. JAMES'S CHAPEL, ST. MARY'S CHAPEL, ST. GEORGE'S, TRINITY, and ST. MARGARET'S CHAPELS, and ST. MARK'S CHURCH.

In the way of public buildings Brighton can boast of the School of Science and Art at the foot of Carlton Hill, an elegant building in the modern Romanesque style, the SUSSEX COUNTY HOSPITAL, founded in 1828, and built by the late Sir Charles Barry at a cost of £10,000,—the Victoria wing was added in 1839, and the Adelaide wing in 1841. It is " open to the sick and lame poor of every country and nation." The BRIGHTON COLLEGE, a proprietary school established in 1847, occupies a handsome Tudor building. ST. MARY'S HALL, in Kemp Town, is an institution for educating the daughters of poor clergymen, and preparing them for governesses. The TOWN HALL, a large and imposing structure, 144 feet long and 113 feet deep, was erected at a cost of no less than £50,000. Here the magistrates meet ; the market is held ; offenders are imprisoned ; and

the borough elections (Brighton returns two members to Parliament) are conducted.

Resuming our rambles, and cursorily glancing at those points
of interest which have hitherto escaped our notice, we start from
the western suburb of Hove. Here there is an interesting old
church, chiefly Norman in its structure. Passing eastward by
Brunswick Square we descend upon the beach. Here we may
gaze upon a scene as full of life as the greatest London thoroughfare,—and fuller, perhaps, of contrast,—for fishermen hauling
up the dingy boats—bathing machines dipping their grotesque
hoods into the brine—coils of old cable—fragments of spars,
and a net or two—are combined with invalids in Bath-chairs,
with pedestrians eager to indulge their locomotive propen-
sities, and amateur artists outlining sundry picturesque and
uncouth objects upon their tablets. A short stroll takes us
to the West Pier, which extends 1115 feet out to sea. It ac-
commodates 2000 people, and affords a pleasant lounge, with a
view of the shore and town. Proceeding eastwards along King's
Road, Grand Junction Road, and passing the Aquarium, the
Chain Pier is reached. The King's Road, which forms the
westernmost portion of the Promenade, or Esplanade, is terminated by the open space called the Steyne, over the trees of
whose enclosure the minarets and domes of the Pavilion rise
against the sky. From this spot the Marine Parade commences,
and the ground rises until the roadway is full 60 feet above the
level of the beach.

We pass Brill's Bath, leaving the Town Hall to our left, and
continue our road to Kemp Town. On the beach here we may
notice the GROYNES or jetties,—rows of piles running down into
the water, and planked on one side—intended to prevent the loose
shingle from being tide-driven out to the east.

The AQUARIUM, between the Steyne and the Chain Pier, now
one of the principal attractions of Brighton, was erected by a
joint-stock company at a cost of £50,000, and opened in
August 1872. With its elegantly ornamented corridors, conservatory, saloons, etc., it forms a most agreeable lounge and
promenade, and is provided with newspapers, periodicals, and
the latest telegrams, for the use of visitors. The fish are placed in
tanks—forty-one in number, and some of them very large—which
are ranged in two of the corridors. These are respectively 220
and 160 feet long, and the length of the whole buildings exceeds 700

feet. The sea-water is pumped by steam into reservoirs capable of holding 500,000 gallons. Another attraction in the department of natural history is the Museum of British Birds in the Dyke Road, one of the best collections in England, admission 1s.

Returning from the east end of the town, we may notice Sussex Square and Lewes Crescent, where a tunnel leads underneath the road to an esplanade formed upon the beach.

Arrived at the Steyne we may visit the Pavilion—and the Steyne Gardens, where Mrs. Honeyman resided (*See* "The Newcomes"). In the North Steyne, which is reserved for subscribers, there is a statue of George IV. by Chantrey. The South Steyne is open to the public, and contains the Victoria fountain. The Western Road is a thoroughfare deserving notice, and the Hospital and St. Nicholas Church may next be visited.

[HINTS FOR RAMBLES.—1. By rail to Lewes; visit the Castle and Priory, and Mount Harry. Return by road, *viâ* Falmer. 2. Across the Downs to Rottingdean, and thence to Newhaven. Keep along the bank of the Ouse to Lewes, and return by rail. 3. To the Devil's Dyke, and thence descend into the plains at Kingston. Visit Shoreham, and return by rail. 4. To Worthing, thence to Sompting, and descend into Lancing. Return by rail. 5. Keep northward to Patching. Cross the hills to Stanmer, and thence to Falmer. Walk over the Downs to Ovingdean, and return to Brighton by way of the race-course.]

BRANCH ROUTE—BRIGHTON TO NEWHAVEN.

The walk to Newhaven, along the crest of the glorious South Downs, is one not easily to be forgotten, but rather to be remembered as "a joy for ever." Their crisp green sward, their swelling lines of beauty, their shadowy *coombes* and *denes*, whether seen in the gray light of early morning, or reddening with the retiring glory of the sunset, have an inexpressible attraction—a charm and a character of their own. And from these lofty heights the eye surveys a wonderful expanse of country; quiet leafy villages with a gray old church-tower or so; a picturesque many-gabled house, dating from the stormy days of Tudor and Stuart; broad reaches of verdurous pasture; ample stretches of yellow cornfields; a whirling, sweeping mill, on the brink of a bubbling rivulet; a noble mansion, crowning a gentle knoll which rises above a mass of vigorous foliage. Then, too, far away to the south glimmers the broad mirror of the Channel;—its rolling waves seem fixed in repose from the elevation at which we stand, and only a dim, faint echo of its music falls upon the

attentive ear. If we descend to the shore by one of those gaps in
the cliffs, always to be met with near a Coastguard station, we
shall find a scarcely less interesting scene. Above us towers a
wall of glittering chalk, 300 feet in height,—spotted with layers
of flint which incline southward to the sea. Observe the broad
masses of calcareous strata, 50 feet thick, in which are frequently
found the bones and teeth of the fossil elephant,—brought hither,
it may be, from a far off land by floating icebergs during some
great natural convulsion in the pre-historic period. On the shore
are occasionally discovered fossil sponges of rare beauty, huge ammonites, and those lumps of black bitumen mixed with salt and
sulphur, which are known as *stromballen*, or stream-balls,—the
name given to them by the Early Flemish fishermen.

The epicure's delicacy, the *wheat-ear*, is an inhabitant of the
Downs. The shepherds entrap him in this wise: they incise the
turf in the shape of the letter T, cover over the hollow, and place
at the mouth a horse-hair springe, into which the wheat-ear flut-
ters at the slightest cry or movement, and is consequently caught.
" Wheat-ears," says Fuller, " is a bird peculiar to this country—
hardly found out of it. It is so called because fattest when the
wheat is ripe, being no better than a lark, which it equalled in
the fineness of the flesh, and far exceeded in the fatness thereof. The
worst is, that being only seasonable in the heat of summer, and
naturally larded with lumps of fat, it is soon subject to corrupt,
so that (though abounding within 40 miles) London poulterers
have no mind to meddle with them, which no care in carriage
can keep from putrefaction. That palate-man shall pass in silence,
who being seriously demanded his judgment concerning the abili-
ties of a great lord, concluded him a man of very weak parts,
' because he saw him at a great feast feed on chickens when there
were wheat-ears on the table.' "

The numerous *fairy-rings* and *hay-tracks* upon the green slopes
of the Downs will not fail to attract the tourist's attention. It is
now generally admitted that they originate in the growth of
various species of *fungi*, but the Sussex shepherds believe them
to be formed by the feet of dancing fairies, or, as they are locally
called, *Pharisees*, who,

> " In their courses make that round
> In meadows and in marshes found,
> Of them so call'd the fairy ground,
> Of which they have the keeping"—(*Drayton*).

OVINGDEAN has a picturesque little CHURCH, partly Norman in style, and partly Early English. For a description of the scenery of the neighbourhood see Ainsworth's novel of " Ovingdean Grange."

ROTTINGDEAN (*Hotel:* White House) is a quiet village with a pebbly beach on the south coast, and lies in a sheltered hollow which opens pleasantly upon the sea. Its neat cottages are embowered in trim gardens. Its Early English CHURCH, dedicated to St. Margaret, is maintained in decorous neatness. Here, at a school kept by Dr. Hooker, the author of " The Caxtons" received his early education. Here, too, a band of marauders was bravely repulsed, in September 1377, by Prior John de Cariloco, of Lewes, and his retainers, though the priest militant was unfortunately taken prisoner.

The Earl of Abergavenny has the patronage of the vicarage, which is valued at £332 per annum.

☞ BALSDEAN, another hamlet sequestered in a hollow of the downs, lies about two miles inland. An ancient Decorated CHAPEL is now used as a barn. Remark its thatched roof.

The tourist, at 7 miles from Brighton, descends the hills to NEWHAVEN (population, 2549), lying in a deep valley, at the junction of the Ouse with the Channel. A swing-bridge is thrown across the river. The railway station is on the opposite bank, and communicates with a pier, whence the steamers for Dieppe start daily in connection with certain London trains. The harbour is held in considerable estimation from its position on the exposed coast of the Channel, and is defended by a battery on the hill above. The depth at the mouth in spring-tides varies from 18 to 20 feet ; in neap tides, from 13 to 15 feet. Two wooden piers protect the entrance, which is 106 feet in width.

Since the establishment of the Dieppe packet-service, Newhaven has risen into a place of some importance. The entries of coasting ships, *inwards*, average 280 vessels of 30,000 tons — *outwards*, 65 vessels, of 7000 tons ; of foreign vessels, *inwards*, 135 vessels of 20,000 tons, and *outwards*, 120 of 18,000 tons.

On a hill above the town—which consists of one long street, crossed by two smaller ones—stands the CHURCH, dedicated to St. Michael, a Norman building, with a nave, north aisle, central tower ornamented by a single spire and aspidal chancel. The nave and aisle are of recent erection. An obelisk over the grave-yard commemorates the loss of the war-brig Brazen, stranded off the port on the 2d of January 1800, with the loss of her commander and 104 men. Only one life was saved.

The rectory, valued at £550, is in the patronage of the Lord Chancellor.

It was at Newhaven Louis Philippe and his queen landed, as Mr. and Mrs. Smith, in 1840, after crossing from Triport in a small fishing-smack. Among those who welcomed him on his arrival was a Mr. Smith ; much to the astonishment of the de-posed sovereign, who naïvely remarked, in ignorance of the myriads of Smiths existing in England—that " he thought he had heard the name before ! "

The passage from Newhaven to Dieppe is effected in about five hours. The steam-packets start according to the changes of the tide.

In the neighbourhood are some Celtic earthworks ; the nearest is an oval encampment on the summit of Castle Hill.

[Between Newhaven and Lewes are the Norman churches of SOUTHEASE (population, 102), and PIDDINGHOE (population, 258), which have a strong family-likeness, as Mr. Lower has pointed out, to the churches in Normandy. Piddinghoe, according to a local saying, is the place where "they shoe magpies." On the opposite bank of the Ouse are the villages of EAST TARRING (population 79), or Tarring-Neville; HEIGHTON (population, 84), and DENTON (population, 195), commemorated by the jesters of the Downs as " Heighton, Denton, and Tarring all begin with an A." BISHOPSTONE (population, 328), which may be easily reached from Newhaven, has a remarkable CHURCH. The tower rises in four stages, each gradually diminishing in diameter. In the first and second stories is a single round-headed window; in the third, a circular moulded window; in the fourth, a double window with balusters. The tower-arch is low, but there are traces of an earlier and loftier one. A small spire surmounts the tower. The chancel is in two divi-sions, with Norman and English arches. The present windows are all English. Observe the curious porch, and the stone dial and crown over the door, lettered with the name of some Saxon king, Eadric, who was probably its builder. A stone slab, inscribed with a cross, bearing in circular compartments the Agnus Dei, and the symbol of two doves drinking, should be carefully examined. It appears to be the work of some Norman sculptor, who, however, was not ignorant of the spirit and influences of Italian Art.

A monument in the chancel commemorates the Rev. *John Hurdis*, Oxford Pro-fessor of Poetry, and an agreeable didactic rhymester, d. 1801. The epitaph is by Hayley.]

BRANCH ROUTE FROM BRIGHTON TO THREE BRIDGES.

[By the London, Brighton, and South Coast Railway.]

Allowing ourselves to be borne, with all the speed of a Brighton express train, through the magnificent landscape which spreads away to the eastward, and through PATCHAM TUNNEL, we pass the village of PATCHAM (pop. 490), which lies to our right. Here there is an old church of the Transition-Norman period, with chancel, nave, and tower, in which were lately discovered some frescoes, formerly overlaid with white wash. We then run through a deep cutting and enter the CLAYTON TUNNEL (cost £90,000, and 1¼ mile in length), piercing the chalk mass of the Downs, and opening out upon the meadows of KEYMER (pop. 2397), whose Saxon and Norman Church lies about 1 mile east of HASSOCK's GATE STATION (*hassock*, a small wood or coppice). The curacy of CLAYTON (pop. 1111) is attached to the rectory of KEYMER, in the patronage of Brasenose Coll, Oxon. The church, which is lofty but plain, has a Saxon chancel arch somewhat unique in form.

Beyond Keymer is situated, on the slope of the hills, DITCH-LING (pop. 1069), whose cruciform CHURCH is an interesting and handsome structure (restored). The nave and aisle are Transition-Norman; with tower, chancel, and transepts Early English. The pillars are built of sandstone, while the arches and window tracery (beautifully carved) are of chalk.

Passing through the village, we climb the steep and lofty Downs to their highest elevation, DITCHLING BEACON, about 858 feet above the sea level. What a landscape spreads beneath and around! The rich and leafy plains of the Weald, the vales and groves of southern Sussex, and the bright waters of the boundless sea, lie before us in a light as magical as that which floats over a picture by Turner. The remains of a Roman encampment crown the summit, and recall to the memory the grand old times when yonder rich and fertile Weald was an impenetrable forest, when tidal waters seethed and fretted in the broad valley of the Ouse, when Lucullus built his villa on the grassy slopes, and Aglaia wandered in love-musing upon the pebbly shore. The Roman road up the ascent, trod 1500 years ago by the stalwart legionaries of imperial Rome, may still in many places be distinctly followed.

West of Hassock's Gate, nearly three miles from the station, and belted round with oak, beech, and ash, lies HURST-PIER-POINT (population, 2827),—the wood (*hurst*) of the Pier-points, —its Early Norman lords. The CHURCH was carefully restored and rebuilt, in the Decorated style, by the late Sir Charles Barry, and its interior is one of unusual interest. The defaced effigy of a templar, *temp.* Henry III., in the S. transept, and another of a nameless knight, *temp.* Edward III., in the N. aisle, are worthy of notice. The view from the churchyard extends to the Surrey hills on the north, Ashdown forest on the north-east, the South Downs on the south, and the forest ridge on the east.

DANNY PARK, an old seat of the Dacres, into whose hands it passed from the Pierripoint family, lies under the hills, south of the village,—a pleasant breadth of green sward and venerable oaks, and an Elizabethan brick mansion, dating from 1595. WOLSTANBURY HILL, in the rear of the house, is crowned with a Celtic encampment of a circular form.

To the left of the road, between the village and the station, stand the headquarters of a society called St. John's College, founded in 1848 to supply education to those in different ranks of life, and now possessing four schools in Sussex, with an aggregate of about 1000 pupils. These are—(1), *Lancing*, for the sons of gentlemen. (2), *Hurst-pier-point*, for the sons of farmers, tradesmen, professional men, etc. (3), *Ardingly*, for the sons of small tradesmen and farmers, mechanics, etc. (4), *Bognor*, for the daughters of gentlemen, with separate schools under the same roof for the daughters of tradesmen and farmers, and for poor children to be trained as household servants.

St. John's College is itself only a branch of a larger institution, which possesses also a college in Staffordshire with two schools, now open, corresponding to those at Hurst-pier-point and Bognor.

Resuming our railway journey, we speedily pass the Burgess Hill Station, 41½ miles, and there the point of divergence of the Lewes line. To the right may be descried the village of WIVELSFIELD (population, 1616), with its Early English CHURCH, its masses of trees, and smiling meadows. The County Lunatic Asylum at Hayward's Heath contains accommodation for about 700 inmates.

Crossing Hayward's Heath, and the main road from Cuckfield to Maresfield, we reach the HAYWARD'S HEATH STATION, 37½ miles from London, and 13 miles from Brighton. Here there is a new district church of some pretension. About 2 miles to our left lies

☞ CUCKFIELD (pop. 1700 ; *Hotel :* The Talbot), an agreeable little town, with good hotel accommodation, though not so busy as before the railway passed it by. It is situated in a charming country, all pasture and grove. Its goodly Early English CHURCH (with a tower and steeple), contains some interesting memorials, and monuments by Flaxman and Westmacott. The vicarage, valued at £613, is in the Bishop of Chichester's patronage. There is a district church, dedicated to St. Mark, at Staplefield Common.

CUCKFIELD PLACE (W. Sergison, Esq.) is situated west of the town, and is not only interesting as a fine Elizabethan mansion, but as having suggested to Ainsworth the "Rookwood Hall" of his striking romance. "The supernatural occurrence," he says, "forming the groundwork of one of the ballads which I have made the harbinger of doom to the house of Rookwood, is ascribed, by popular superstition, to a family resident in Sussex, upon whose estate the fatal tree (a gigantic lime, with mighty arms and huge girth of trunk) is still carefully preserved. Cuckfield Place, to which this singular piece of timber is attached, is, I may state, for the benefit of the curious, the real Rookwood Hall ; for I have not drawn upon imagination, but upon memory, in describing the seat and domains of that fated family. The general features of the venerable structure, several of its chambers, the old garden, and, in particular, the noble park, with its spreading prospects, its picturesque bits of the hall, 'like bits of Mrs. Radcliffe' (as the poet Shelley once observed of the same scene), its deep glades, through which the deer come lightly tripping down, its uplands, slopes, brooks, brakes, coverts, and groves are carefully delineated." In the avenue that winds towards the house the Doom-Tree still stands :—

" And whether gale or calm prevail, or threatening cloud hath fled,
By hand of Fate, predestinate, a limb that tree will shed ;
A verdant bough, untouched, I trow, by axe or tempest's breath,
To Rookwood's head, an omen dread of fast approaching death."

In this neighbourhood are OCKENDON HOUSE, TYE, SLOUGH, and BOARD HILL, all seats of some importance and considerable antiquity ; and LEIGH POND (50 acres in extent), a fen haunt of the wild-fowl during the winter months.

[On the Croydon road, about 1¼ m. north-east of the station, is situated LIND-FIELD (population, 1814). HORSTED-KEYNES is 3½ m. north-east ; FLETCHING, 6½ m. east ; BOLNEY, 4¼ m. south-west.]

We resume our journey through a country side of exquisite luxuriance, and in a few minutes cross the valley of the Ouse by means of the OUSE VIADUCT, a magnificent specimen of engineering skill, 1437 feet long, and supported by 37 arches, each 30 feet in span, and about 60 feet high. It was constructed at a cost of £58,000, and is one of the finest in the world. Noble prospects of the surrounding landscapes are here commanded.

At 4½ miles from Hayward's Heath, 16¾ miles from Brighton, and 33¾ miles from London, we arrive at BALCOMBE (population, 961), with its Early English CHURCH, and quiet village lying at the foot of the clay hills, on the southern skirts of the great Tilgate Forest. This district was formerly the delta of a mighty river, and offers to the persevering geologists the remains of enormous reptiles, palms and tree-ferns of an oriental character. Dr. Mantell here discovered the first bones of the huge Iguanodon, and the earliest traces of the mighty Hylæo-saurus. · Tilgate Forest covers about 1500 acres, and presents some pleasant woodland pictures at various points. WAKEHURST PLACE (Sir Alexander Cockburn) is situated 2 miles east. SLAUGHAM (population, 1418), with SLAUGHAM PLACE, 3 miles west. The latter is a Tudor house of some interest, the ancient seat of the Coverts, whose landed supremacy, in the days of Elizabeth and her successor, extended "from Southwark to the sea." SLAUG-HAM CHURCH is Early English, and contains some richly-coloured glass, and brasses for *John Covert*, d. 1503 ; and *Richard Covert*, d. 1547, and his three wives ; *Jane Covert* d. 1586.

The rectory, valued at £300, is in the gift of W. Sergison, Esq.

After leaving the Balcombe Station we quietly enter the BALCOMBE TUNNEL, 6 furlongs and 3 chains in length. The line then skirts the eastern boundary of Tilgate Forest, and crossing an open country, reaches the THREE BRIDGES Junction Station, so named from the intersection of the main roads by the river Mole. These branch lines diverge to EAST GRINSTEAD, 7 miles east, and CRAWLEY, 1½ mile. HORSHAM, 8½ miles west.

☞ The village of WORTH (population, 3209) lies about 1¼ mile east of the station, and should be visited for the sake of its curious CHURCH, the only perfect ground-plan of a Saxon church extant in England. It is seated on a knoll, and embowered in trees, and approached by an ancient lich-gate which opens into a quiet and picturesque yard. The plan of the building is cruciform, —the chancel and nave intersected by north and south transepts. The chancel is apsidal. The walls are of roughly-hewn stones and rubble. Round the building, carefully restored in 1871, and half-way between the ground and the roof, is carried a string-course of stone, and bands of stone at various places diversify the surface. On a double course of stone rise pilasters of irregular long and short work, which support the string-course. The outer buttresses are recent, and the west and south sides are Decorated insertions. In the window over the west door are the De Warrenne arms. The transept arches are unornamented; the chancel-arch has a rude moulding. A small Saxon window remains in the east wall of the north transept. The font is ancient, and consists of two basins, one placed above the other.*

This interesting church may have been built (as a writer in the Sussex Archæological Collections suggests) by a Saxon " earl" who had settled down in the wild forest of Worth—some traces of which still linger in the high ground—for the sake of hunting the deer. It afterwards belonged to the barony of Lewes, and passed from the De Warrennes in 1347 to the Fitzalans.

The rectory, valued at £930, is in the patronage of Mr. G. Banks.

At Worth, and in Tilgate Forest, flourishes the *scyphophorus microphyllus,* a lichen of great rarity; *rhynchospora alba, heliocharis acicularis, carex curta,* and *epilobium angustifolium.* The sandstone dug here, " of a white, pale fawn, or yellow colour," often affords the leaves and stems of ferns and other plants.

After leaving the Three Bridges' Station, a ride of about 2 miles carries us over the county-border into Surrey. We cross the Mole, and at 25¼ miles from London reach the Horley Station. But this portion of the line will be found described in Black's " Guide to Surrey."

* At the restoration of the church two Saxon windows and balustors were found in the north wall of the nave, and one in the south wall.

G

BRANCH ROUTE—BRIGHTON TO HORSHAM.

[Coach from Brighton to Horsham (5¼ miles), Monday, Wednesday, and Friday.]

The road at first skirts the base of the South Downs, and passes the sequestered village of PRESTON (population, 2470)—*i.e.*, Priest's town, because it formed a part of the possessions of the see of Chichester—where the little Early English CHURCH, dedicated to St. Peter, and consisting of nave, chancel, and tower, is worthy of a patient examination. On the walls of the nave are some rude frescoes, in red and yellow, of the murder of Thomas à Becket, shewing the four knights, and the monk Grim protecting the Archbishop with his arm. St. Michael, with his scales, is figured on the other side. In the nave lies the tomb-stone of *Francis Cheynel*, D.D., d. 1665, the bitter antagonist of Chillingworth, whose grave he profaned with his unseemly violence. Douglas, the erudite author of the " Nenia Britannica," and the father of Sussex archæology, lies interred in the churchyard.

The vicarage, valued at £250, is in the patronage of the Bishop of Chichester. Hove, and its two churches, St. Mark's and St. John the Baptist's, are within this parish. Anne of Cleves resided here for a short period.

From this point HOLLINGSBURY CASTLE (2 miles north), a square camp, five acres in extent ; WHITE HAWK HILL, a triple entrenchment, near the Brighton race-course, three quarters of a mile in circumference, and the camps on Ditchling Beacon may be visited, as the three points of a triangle which commanded the sea-coast, and overlooked the passes of the Weald.

- The tourist should now leave the high road and ascend the downs to the DEVIL'S DYKE (5¼ miles from Brighton), a remarkable natural fosse, steep, abrupt, and of unusual depth (300 feet), which looks as if the Titans had excavated it as a defence for some enormous stronghold. The legend attached to it is curious : —the Devil, or, as the Sussex hinds more sympathizingly call him, the Poor Man, wroth at the number of churches which sprang up yearly in this neighbourhood, resolved to dig a trench from this point down to the sea, and so to inundate the whole country side. But as he was toiling by night with assiduous energy, he was descried by an old woman from the cottage window, who held up a candle that she might the better comprehend his

THE DEVIL'S DYKE, NEAR BRIGHTON.

design, and frightening the devil into the belief that it was the sunrise, he immediately disappeared. When he found out his error, he was too ashamed of his folly to return, and the Dyke to this day remains—a witness to an old woman's curiosity and the devil's discomfiture !

On the brow of the hill beyond this immense verdurous fosse, the Romans formed, or rather adopted what the British formed, an oval encampment, defended by a wide ditch and huge vallum, about one mile in circumference. By such means a natural position of defence was rendered more secure from sudden attacks.

A pleasant " hostelry," where reasonable " creature-comforts" may be obtained, stands on the brink of the down—a point from which the tourist will enjoy the most magnificent prospect in this part of Sussex. " If Nature had endeavoured to create a surprise for man, she could not have done it more effectually than by leading him over the gradual ascent of a vast down, and then suddenly sinking the earth 600 or 700 feet in a bold escarpment, until it formed a plain almost limitless to the eye, and rich in summer foliage and yellow corn. For miles on each side the Downs descend into this plain in an almost perpendicular manner. If you throw yourself down on the edge of this fearful descent on a fine summer's afternoon, and strain your eyes over the wonderful plain beneath, you gain a sensation of space that scarce another landscape in England can afford. The valley before you stretches north-east to south-west a space of no less than 120 miles, commencing at Maidstone, and only terminating at the Hampshire Downs, near Portsmouth. To the north and north-west the eye reaches, it is affirmed, but we confess to some misgivings, as far as Croydon and Norwood ; no fewer than six counties being rolled out, in this gigantic map, at the spectator's feet, and these, for the most part, garden or park-like in culture and appearance. Those who are curious about the matter may, it is said, count upwards of sixty churches dotted over the wide landscape. Turning to the southward, the spectator traces distinctly the extensive bay sweeping between Beachy Head and Selsey Bill, with Brighton in the centre. Looking over the ocean to the west, the Culver Cliffs of the Isle of Wight are, on a clear day, seen distinctly by the naked eye, although upwards of forty miles distant ; and a vast expanse of ocean stretches before you"—(Thorne).

Descending into the high road, beneath the Downs, we arrive
at POYNINGS (population, 261), where the Perpendicular
CHURCH, dedicated to the Holy Trinity, with its central tower,
transepts, aisle, and nave, will remind us of that of ALFRESTON
(see p. 42), and induce us to accept Mr. Hussey's conclusion, that
both were built by the same architect. The font is octagonal,
and there are three sedilia in the chancel. The rectory, valued
at £375, is in the gift of the Lord Chancellor.

NEWTIMBER (population, 161) lies about one mile east of
the main road. The CHURCH, dedicated to St. John, has some
good painted glass in the east window, and two grave-slabs despoiled of their brasses. NEWTIMBER PLACE (Lady Gordon) is a
moated mansion of venerable age. To the north is situated
DANNY PARK (W. T. Campion, Esq.), already described (see
p. 94.)

Beyond the 48th milestone (from London) we pass the parliamentary boundary of West Sussex, and one and a half mile
further reach WOODMANCOTE (population, 326), in a well-
wooded but thinly-populated district. The tree-embowered
CHURCH is Early English, with nave, chancel, and turret. The
rectory is in the Lord Chancellor's gift.

[About two miles north lies ALBOURNE (population, 377), on a *bourne*, or
branch of the Adur—it was formerly in the hands of the Juxon family, and
ALBOURNE PLACE (Miss Long) is reputed to have been built by the good prelate
who soothed the last hours of Charles the First.—The rectory, worth £225, is in the
gift of John Goring, Esq.]

At ten miles from Brighton we gain the hill whereon the
village of HENFIELD (population, 1850) clusters, some of its
cottages quaint enough in aspect to merit a place in the sketcher's
note book. The CHURCH, dedicated to St. Peter, is chiefly Perpendicular. The nave and south aisle are separated by elongated
arches. There is a brass, on an altar tomb, for *Thomas Bisshopp*,
d. 1552, and an epitaph upon *Meneleb Raynsford*, d. 1627, aged
nine, of so ludicrous a character in its combination of the Pagan
and Christian as to merit quotation :

" Great Jove hath lost his Ganymede, I know,
    Which made him seek another here below ;

And finding none, not one like unto this,
Hath ta'en him hence unto eternal bliss.
Cease, then, for thy dear Meneleb to weep;
God's darling was too good for thee to keep;
But rather joy in this great favour given,
A child on earth is made a saint in heaven."

The Bishop of Chichester has the presentation to the vicarage, which is valued at £412 per annum.

At Chestlem's Bridge we cross a tributary of the Adur, and passing through a fertile country reach SHERMANBURY (population, 458), upon another branch of the same river. SHERMANBURY PARK (S. Copestake, Esq.), was erected, about sixty years ago on the site of an Elizabethan mansion. The CHURCH, dedicated to St. Giles, is a small Early English building, close to the house. It contains a Perpendicular font, and some good modern painted glass.

A little to the west of the Place stand the venerable remains of the old moated mansion of EWHURST, the ancient seat of the Peverels. The arched gateway, with its pointed roof, dates from the reign of Edward I.

An open country lies before us, meadows and corn-fields spreading on either hand, and in due time we arrive at COW-FOLD (population, 975), whose very name savours of abundant and fertile pastures. The CHURCH stands on the left side of the road. The chancel is Edwardian, the nave and south aisle Tudor, and the tower at the west end Late Perpendicular. It contains a very fine brass for *Thomas Nelond*, prior of Lewes, d. 1433, with figures of the Virgin and Child, St. Pancras trampling on a sword-brandishing knight, and St. Thomas à Becket with mitre and crosier.

A monastery for Carthusian monks has quite recently been erected here.

Our road now enters the woodlands, and passes " under the shade of melancholy boughs." We turn aside from the highway to visit the leafy hamlet of NUTHURST (population, 727), and as we penetrate the shady groves of Highhurst—a portion of the once extensive forest of St. Leonard's—from the hills we look back upon the fair landscapes of southern Sussex, bounded afar off

by the glowing waters of the Channel. Near NUTHURST LODGE
(J. Nelthorpe, Esq.) are the ivy-shrouded remains of an old moated
mansion, and a spring lined with large blocks of stone, and called
the Wren's Well. The CHURCH, dedicated to St. Andrew, is a
Decorated building, with panelled ceiling, and remains of ancient
painted glass. The Bishop of London is the patron of the rectory.

We regain the high road at Monk's Gate, and 3 miles further,
reach the ancient town of HORSHAM (population, 6804. *Inns:*
King's Head, Anchor), so named from *hors-ham*, the horses' meadow, and not, as some speculative antiquarians would pretend,
from Horsa, the Saxon chieftain, whom they slay at this place.
The town stands on the Arun, in the heart of much agreeable
and well-wooded scenery, and consists of two main streets intersecting each other at right angles—a green to the north where
bull-baiting used to be practised, and an open area to the south
wherein the court-house is situated. Its markets for corn, cattle,
and poultry are held high in repute. It returns one member
to Parliament.

The lordship of the borough has descended from William de
Braose to the Duke of Norfolk. To one of the wealthy and
powerful members of the De Braose family may be ascribed the
foundation of the CHURCH, which is a large and venerable Early
English building, dedicated to St. Mary, and consists of a nave,
chancel, two aisles, and lofty tower surmounted by a spire. The
east window is Perpendicular, and has five lights. There is a
note-worthy memorial to *Thomas, Lord Braose*, d. 1396, representing him in the armour of the period. Unfortunately it is
much mutilated. An altar-tomb of Sussex marble belongs, it is
said, to *Thomas, Lord Hoo*, Chancellor of France to Henry VI.,
d. 1455. A finely sculptured effigy and tomb of pure white
marble, commemorate *Elizabeth Delves*, d. 1654. Two brasses
remain,—one of a priest in his cope, the other of a man in a
furred gown and a woman in appropriate dress,—but their inscriptions have disappeared.

The vicarage, valued at £751, is in the patronage of the
Archbishop of Canterbury. The vicar himself presents to the
curacy of ST. MARK'S, and the perpetual curacy of SOUTHWATER,
(1½ mile south), two churches of recent erection.

The GRAMMAR SCHOOL, adjoining the churchyard, was founded

in 1532, by Richard Collier, for the support of a master and usher, and the instruction of sixty scholars. The *worthies* of Horsham are, Nicholas Hortresham, or Horsham, a physician of eminence in the reign of Henry VI.; and Barnaby Lintot, born in 1675, the publisher of Pope's "Iliad," and Gay's "Trivia," and prose and verse by other "eminent hands."

South of the town lies DENNE PARK (C. G. Eversfield, Esq.) The ivy-decorated mansion stands on an elevated site, and over-looks a considerable portion of Sussex and Surrey. It is ap-proached from the London road by a fine avenue of beech-trees. One mile east is COOLHURST (C. S. Dickens, Esq.), a picturesque Elizabethan house, with gabled roof and mullioned windows, partly rebuilt about thirty years ago. There are some remains of the ancient edifice at CHESWORTH, half a mile south-east, the resi-dence of the De Braoses, lords of Bramber.

From Horsham we may conveniently penetrate into ST. LEONARD'S FOREST, a tract of about 9000 acres, which takes its name from a chapel, dedicated to St. Leonard, formerly situated in the north-eastern recesses. A great portion of the forest is included in the northern division of the parish of Beeding. It was formerly held by the De Braose family, but is now divided amongst various proprietors. The principal avenue contains nearly 16,000 trees, not one, however, of more than eighty years' growth, their predecessors having been uprooted in a violent storm,—is 1½ mile in length, and, from an unhappy athlete who ran the distance for a wager, and fell dead at the moment of victory, is called MIKE MILL'S RACE. The pleasant vistas in the wide wood-land, through columned aisles of pine, and larch, and oak, and beech, are numerous, and there are many delightful little dells, and a running stream or so lends life, and light, and music to the scene. Nightingales occasionally fill the shadowy arcades with their "most musical, most melancholy" song, and disprove Andrew Borde's assertion that "they will never singe within the precincts of the forests, as divers keepers and other credible parsons did show me."

"The violet of a legend" blows, as one might easily conclude, in these obscure and dreamy glades. The daring horseman who penetrates their mirky depths at night must prepare to ride with a headless phantom, which will not quit him until the forest sha-dows are past. St. Leonard engaged here in a fearful contest with a "mighty worm," struggling with him in many places

before he conquered him, and clumps of lilies sprang up wherever
the saint's pure blood was spilled—a sort of allegory, we fancy,
if read aright, and a dim reflection evidently of the old "St.
Michael and the Dragon" story. As late as 1614, a dragon, we
are told, haunted the forest glens; and "a discourse" concerning
this "strange monstrous serpent" was printed and published in
London by one John Trundle. "There is always left in his track
or path," says the writer, "a glutinous and shine matter (as by a
small similitude we may perceive in a snail's), which is very corrupt and offensive to the senses; the serpent is reputed to be 9
feete, or rather more, in length, and shaped almost in the forme
of an axeltree of a cart, a quantitie of thicknesse in the middest,
and somewhat smaller at both ends. The former part, which he
shootes forth as a necke, is supposed to be an elle long, with a
white ring, as it were, of scales about it. There are likewise on
either side of him discovered two greate bunches so big as a large
foote-ball, and, as some think, will in time grow to wings; but
God, I hope, will so defend the poor people in the neighbourhood
that he shall be destroyed before he grow so fledge."

Within a compass of three or four miles, near the south boundary of the forest, the Arun, Adur, and Ouse have their source;
and not far from Coolhurst are two of "the hammer posts" formerly the indispensable adjuncts of the Sussex iron works.

☞ At FAYGATE, 3 miles north-east of Horsham, there is a
station on the Horsham branch of the London and South Coast
Railway. It adjoins the large estate of Lord St. Leonards, who
derives his title from his property in this neighbourhood.

About 3 miles further, and the railway traveller will see on
his left the village of IFIELD (population, 1112), seated on a
broad and pleasant green, and surrounded by a vigorous growth
of oaks. It was once the seat of a considerable iron trade, of
which the disused "hammer posts" are now the sole remains.
Its CHURCH, dedicated to St. Margaret, is partly Early English
and partly Decorated. There are two tombs under the nave
arches, bearing respectively the effigies of a cross-legged knight,
and a lady in Edwardian costume, which are reputed to be those
of Sir *John de Ifield*, and his wife, d. 1317. The vicarage (£180)
is in the gift of Mr. Lewin.

[RUSPER (population, 539) lies about 3 miles to the west of Ifield. The road
across the hills is a pleasant one, and commands some good views of the Weald of

Surrey, Leith Hill, and the country about Dorking. Gervaise, Archbishop of Canterbury, founded here a Benedictine nunnery, *temp.* Richard I., of which there are no remains. The farm of NORMANS has been held by a family named Multon, ever since the Norman Conquest. "The present proprietor has the chest brought over the water, as he terms it, by his ancestor, the Norman, who first settled at Rusper" —(*Horsfield*).

The Early English CHURCH, dedicated to St. Mary, a small and antique building, contains a brass for *John de Kyngesfold*, and *Agnes*, his wife ; and another for *Thomas Challoner*, d. 1532, and *Margaret*, his wife. Mrs. Greene is the patron of the rectory, valued at £202 yearly.]

We now arrive at the CRAWLEY STATION, adjoining the old posting-town of CRAWLEY (population 500), not yet shorn of all its glories. The Brighton four-in-hand still rattles through its streets, but besides the blithe horn of "the guard," a shrill railway whistle awakens its echoes. The neighbourhood is very pleasant, and Tilgate Forest lies within a moderate distance. On the high road stands a venerable elm, a well-known object, which arrests the eye of the stranger at once by its tall and straight stem, which ascends to the height of 70 feet, and by the fantastic ruggedness of its widely-spreading roots. The trunk is perforated to the very top, measuring 61 feet in circumference at the ground, and 35 feet round the inside at 2 feet from the base." An old and time-worn oak in the centre of the village is a remarkable object.

CRAWLEY CHURCH is chiefly Decorated in style, and has recently undergone a careful restoration. One of the tie beams of the roof is lettered—

"Man yr wele bewar; for warldly good maketh man blynde.
Bewar for whate comyth behinde."

Situate north of the railway, between West Brighton and Hove, is the newly erected Nunnery of the Sacred Heart, with a chapel handsomely furnished with carved oak stalls.

After leaving Crawley a few minutes' ride brings us to the junction-station at THREE BRIDGES.

MAIN ROUTE RESUMED—BRIGHTON TO SHOREHAM.

The road from Brighton to Shoreham lies along the coast, in sight and hearing of the glorious sea. We cross a level of great fertility, the downs rising up to the northward like a formidable bulwark, and descend a slight incline into the valley of the

Adur. To our right we pass, in succession, the hamlet of HANGLETON, 1 mile west, with an Early English CHURCH, and a Tudor manor-house, and the neat little church of Aldrington, which, after being in ruins for 150 years, was rebuilt in 1877, and arrive at the three Portslades.

PORTSLADE—the station is between the two villages of PORTSLADE-BY-SEA, to the south, on the banks of the Ship Canal—a modern uninteresting place, and PORTSLADE (the old village), 1 mile north of the line, hidden away in a hollow. This is the prettiest village in the immediate vicinity of Brighton. The Early English church of St. Nicholas has a fine "ivy-mantled tower."

After Portslade is seen the small village of FISHERGATE, and on the south bank of the canal, almost on the sea-beach, are the works of one of the large Brighton gas companies.

SOUTHWICK (population, 2400), 5 m. from Brighton, with a handsome church dedicated to St. Michael. Charles II. is said, whilst waiting for a ship to convey him to the continent, to have hidden himself in an old house (still shown), and in gratitude for his escape to have given the piece of land called the Green. A little farther stands KINGSTON-BY-SEA, where goods are forwarded for the Shoreham shipping. The CHURCH is uninteresting, and is but a portion of the original edifice. The railway is carried across the Shoreham flat by a viaduct—the Adur Viaduct—550 yards in length. OLD SHOREHAM lies to the right, just beyond the Portsmouth road ; NEW SHOREHAM occupies the banks of the Adur, in one long, squalid, and winding street, irregularly crossed by other streets.

NEW SHOREHAM (pop. 3505. *Hotels:* Dolphin, Surrey Arms, Buckingham Arms, and Swiss Cottage) rose into importance as Old Shoreham, owing to the gradual silting-up of its harbour, fell into decay. The ancient haven, formed by the estuary of the Adur, was early regarded as of some maritime importance, from its position with respect to the coast of Normandy, and to defend this important pass a Norman stronghold was raised at BRAMBER, up the river, just as Lewes commanded the Ouse, and Arundel the Arun. King John landed here in 1199, immediately after the decease of Richard Cœur-de-Lion. He also embarked from hence in the following June on his way to France. In 1346, when Edward III. fitted out two large fleets of 706 ships, Old

Shoreham contributed 26, whilst London furnished but 25, Southampton 21, and Hull only 16. But early in the fifteenth century the sea made rapid encroachments upon its insecure marshes—the port was destroyed—and the town had fallen into so sad a decline, that in 1432 it could but number 36 inhabitants.

It was long before brighter fortunes dawned upon the natives of Shoreham, but, by degrees, a new town sprang up along the banks of the Adur, and in 1724, the population had increased to 640 souls, chiefly employed in " the building and fitting up of ships." The attention of the Government was at length directed to the condition of the harbour, and considerable improvements were effected. The entrance, however, continued to the eastward, at the rate of a mile in forty years, until the present substantial piers were erected by Clegram, in 1819, and a species of canal fenced in. The mouth is now 218 feet wide, and at spring tides has about twenty feet depth of water, fourteen feet at neap, and only four feet at low. A light-house has been erected for the convenience of mariners. The principal imports are corn, deals, firewood, and potatoes ; the export, coke, etc. About 670 vessels, of 75,000 tons, enter the harbour yearly.

The handsome SUSPENSION BRIDGE, built in 1833 at the expense of the Duke of Norfolk, by Clarke, the architect of the Hammersmith Bridge, is not only an ornament but an advantage to the town. It shortens the distance between Brighton and Worthing by 2 miles.

The CUSTOM HOUSE was built in 1830, and designed by Smirke. Two Hospitals, and a Priory of Carmelite Friars, are said to have existed here. During the summer months the Swiss Gardens are a great attraction. The timber bridge over the Adur (dwr, water), at Old Shoreham, 500 feet long and 12 feet wide, was erected in 1781.

The principal historical association of Shoreham is the escape of Charles II. after the defeat at Worcester, and his preservation at Boscobel. Crossing the country, attended by Lord Wilmot, he reached Brighton on the evening of October 14, 1651, and passed the night at the George (now the King's Head) Inn, in West Street. Early on the following morning they set out for Shoreham, where Captain Nicholas Tattersall had moored his bark, and when the tide served, effected their embarkation undetected. On the same day (October 15th) the Earl of Derby, one of Charles's stoutest adherents, was executed at Bolton.

The Churches, both at Old and New Shoreham, possess an unusual interest for the archæologist.

OLD SHOREHAM CHURCH ($\frac{3}{4}$ mile west) is an Early Norman church, cruciform in plan, and " remarkable for the small number of windows, and the consequent darkness of the nave ; as also for possessing on the tie-beams of the chancel the tooth-moulding which is very rarely found carved in wood." The central tower is supported by four enriched circular arches of conspicuous beauty. An oblong window in the south transept has a zigzag moulding. Mr. Ferrey has " restored " this interesting edifice with commendable care—The vicarage, valued at £458, is in the gift of Magdalene College, Oxford.

NEW SHOREHAM CHURCH was probably erected about 1100. It contains some Norman portions, and additions in Transition-Norman and Early English. " When entire it was a stately and capacious edifice of a cruciform shape, having a tower 83 feet high, rising from the centre of the cross. The nave has been long destroyed, and what remains consists of a choir, with side aisles, transept, and tower. The walls of the choir, now used as the parish church, rise considerably higher than those of the transept ; two massive flying buttresses support the upper part "—(*Horsfield*). The windows in the aisles are semicircular ; in the south side they are of a later date. The choir is divided into five bays by Early English arches, springing from columns whose richly foliated capitals should receive a careful examination. The exterior mouldings of the arches are similarly enriched. The east end has a triple lancet window, surmounting three semicircular Norman windows. The transept and the tower are Norman and Transition-Norman. There is a brass of the time of Edward IV.

The vicarage, valued at £127, is in the patronage of Magdalene College, Oxford.

BRANCH ROUTE FROM SHOREHAM TO HORSHAM.

[The branch line of the Brighton Railway to Horsham embraces much the same tract of country as is hereinunder described. The stations are Bramber, 4 m. ; Steyning, 4½ m. ; Henfield, 8 m. ; Partridge Green, 10 m. ; West Grinstead, 12½ m. ; Southwater, 15½ m. ; Horsham, 20 m.]

As we ascend the Downs from Old Shoreham to Bramber, two quiet, secluded, but picturesque villages may be discerned in the valley beneath, and on the west bank of the Adur—COOMBES and ST. BOTOLPH'S.

COOMBES (population, 72), whose situation is indicated by its name, lies in a hollow, from which, on every side, rise the verdurous hills. A thick environment of trees is about it. Its CHURCH is Early English, and would, perhaps, accommodate, in an emergency, 150 persons. The Wyndham family hold the patronage of the rectory, which is valued at £201 per annum.

ST. BOTOLPH'S (population, 55) lies upon a ridge of chalk, which slopes somewhat abruptly into the valley of the Adur. The church is small, consisting of a nave, chancel, and low tower. The vicarage has long been annexed to the rectory of Bramber.

And it is at BRAMBER (population, 130), 5 miles from Shoreham, that, crossing the river, we next arrive. Bramber, the Saxon fortress (*Brynamburh*), the Norman stronghold, the considerable market-town, the corrupt parliamentary borough, the quiet old-world village—for such are the mutations it has undergone. Here, on the hill, against whose base the tidal waters of the Adur fretted, the Saxon kings, probably on the site of a Roman encampment, erected a castle, which commanded the narrow pass. After the conquest, castle and barony were bestowed upon William de Braose, the builder of the massive fortress whose scanty ruins still excite the tourist's admiration. It occupied an area of three acres (560 feet by 280), on the brink of a steep abrupt spur of chalk which jutted out into the morasses of the Adur. On the west, south, and north, the castle was defended by a stout vallum and deep fosse, on the east the river-marshes were sufficient protection. Only a fragment of the barbican tower, and some crumbling stones, remain as the solemn "Hic jacet" of the once powerful race of De Braose.

Beneath the castle ruins stands the old Norman Church, dedicated to St. Nicholas, the patron saint of the Anglo-Normans. It consists of a nave and chancel, divided by a Norman arch, but has evidently been of larger proportions. Magdalene College, Oxon, has the patronage of the rectory, which is valued at £160.

STEYNING (population, 1664. *Inn:* the White Horse)—from *stean*, a stone—a Roman *via*, or Stane Street, having formerly connected Arundel with Dorking, lies about half a mile beyond Bramber. An omnibus runs between it and Shoreham thrice a-week.

The tide anciently rose as high as Steyning, whose harbour was the well-known PORTUS CATHMANNI. It stands at the foot of a hill—one wide street running north-west, from which another diverges in a north-easterly direction to the Church. The chief traffic is in cattle, a market being held once a fortnight.

The ancient CHURCH (dedicated to St. Andrew) was founded by St. Cuthman, a saint whose life was one long series of miracles. When, as a youth, appointed to the care of his father's sheep, he defied all hostile influences, and saved himself " a world of trouble" by drawing around them a mysterious circle, into which none could break. He travelled with his widowed mother into "the far east," wheeling her in a sort of barrow, whose cords snapping asunder he made use of some elder twigs. At the expedient some haymakers sillily laughed, and lo ! the rain ever afterwards descended upon their fields when the hay was ready for the garner. At Steyning the elder twigs broke, and there he consequently resolved to locate himself. Having built a hut, he erected a wooden church, where he regularly worshipped, and where he was interred. To his grave in due time flocked the wayfaring devout, and around the little timbered sanctuary a town speedily arose, and St. Cuthman became a word of love and reverence for all the country side. The Saxon Ethelwulf, king Alfred's father, was afterwards buried here (?), and Edward the Confessor bestowed the church on the Benedictine Abbey of Fécamp (in Normandy), whose monks established a small cell.

The present CHURCH probably occupies the site of Cuthman's building, and is purely Norman, with additions in the Early English style. It appears to have been designed as a cruciform structure, and never completed. The nave is exquisitely beautiful. It has five bays, whose arches, as well as the capitals of the piers, are elaborately enriched. Each column is 3 feet 8 inches in diameter. The chancel was restored by the late Duke of Norfolk ; the chancel-arch is 38 feet in height. There is a large square Norman font. Most of the building and the ornamentation date from 1150.

Some old wainscoting is preserved in the panelling of the vicarage dining-room, and two ancient crossed stones will be observed in the garden. In Church Street stands an ancient house, called Brotherhood Hall, bestowed by Alderman Holland of Chichester upon the Grammar School in 1614.

In this neighbourhood the ornithologist will meet with the

wood-warbler, purple heron, reed-warbler, and little bittern ; and
the botanist with salicornia radicans, vicia lutea, spiridia ful-
mentosa, and polysiphonia fibrillosa.

One mile and a half east of Steyning lies WISTON (population,
256), a neighbourhood of the highest interest, from the picturesque
character of its scenery, and the romantic nature of its associations. Just beyond the Church the Downs rise up to a noble
elevation, inferior only to Ditchling and Firle, and the fir-crowned
height of CHANCTONBURY RING, at 814 feet above the sea-level,
becomes "a thing of wonder" to all West Sussex. The views
from this glorious eminence are worthy of the Downs, and
embrace all that vast variety of scenery—of dale and hill, and
glen and grove ; of gabled farmhouse and ivied tower—which
is peculiar to the landscapes of England.

The circular encampment called "the Ring" is British, but
Roman coins have been discovered here, and the Roman *via*
passes at the foot of the hill.

WISTON HOUSE (Rev. John Goring), with "its ancient and
well-wooded park," lies below the Downs, and overlooks a valley
of unusual beauty. The grounds are well arranged,—its "undulating surface" and "stately forest-trees" lending them all the
charm of varying light and shade. The house is a goodly Tudor
pile, erected by Sir Thomas Shirley about 1576, and much "improved upon" by his successors. The hall, 40 feet in length,
breadth, and height, has a noble groined roof ; the dining-room
retains the original oaken wainscot.

The manor passed, by marriage, from the family of De Braose
to that of Shirley. Of the latter race came several Sussex worthies. Sir Hugh Shirley was one of the knights who, disguised
as the King, fought with the Douglas on the field of Shrewsbury,
1403,—"the spirits of *Shirley*, Stafford, Blunt," alike unequal to
cope with the valour of the Scot. Another Shirley fought at
Agincourt. Sir Thomas, who built the Wiston manor-house,
begat three extraordinary adventurers,—"The Three Brothers, Sir
Thomas, Sir Anthony, and Mr. Robert"—whose romantic career
was made the subject of a play, "written by a trinity of poets, John
Day, William Rowley, and George Wilkins," in 1607.

Thomas, the eldest, fitted out three vessels, manned them with
500 choice spirits, cruised in the Greek Archipelago, was captured
and imprisoned at Negropont, ransomed himself for 40,000

sequins, and died in the Isle of Wight. *Anthony* fought at Zutphen with Sir Philip Sidney, and against the Portuguese in Africa; departed to Persia in 1598, on a mission of political importance; drank at Aleppo of coffee—"a drink made of seed that will soon intoxicate the brain;" was created a Mirza by the Shah; despatched to Europe with the powers of an ambassador; quarrelled with the Persian Court; became Admiral of the Venetian fleet in the Levant, and died in 1631. *Robert Shirley* accompanied his brother to Persia; obtained a distinguished military command; was sent as ambassador to Europe to form a confederacy against the Turks; married a Circassian lady, named Teresià; was received in Germany, Rome, and England with great distinction; deceived, and finally disavowed by the crafty Persian; and died of chagrin and disappointment, at Kazveen, in 1628. His adventures have been graphically narrated by Stowe.

WISTON CHURCH, dedicated to St. Mary, is a Decorated building. The manorial chapel, at the east end, contains a beautiful brass, inlaid with the words "Jesu Mercy," for Sir *John de Braose*, d. 1426, who is figured in full armour, a helmet on his head, and a gorget round his neck. The inscription runs—"Es testis Xte, quod non jacet lapis iste corpus ut ornetur, sed spiritus ut memoretur. Hinc tu qui transis, medius, magnus, puer an sis. Pro me funde preces, quia . . . spes." On the north side, under an arch, lies the effigy of a child. Sir *William Shirley* is commemorated by a monument which represents him standing on a rock, in an attitude of prayer, and lifting his hands towards a dove— the symbol of the Holy Spirit. Against the wall are the effigies of Sir *Thomas Shirley*, the builder of Wiston, and his wife *Anne*, daughter of Sir Thomas Kempe of Ollantighe, in Kent.

As we continue our journey northward we pass, 3 miles from Steyning, through the village of ASHURST (population, 441)—the Ash-wood—whose Early English CHURCH stands at some slight distance from the road, and consists of a nave, chancel, south aisle, and low shingled spire. The patronage of the rectory, valued at £352, belongs to Magdalene College, Oxon.

Three miles further, we arrive at WEST GRINSTEAD (population, 1252), the centre of a great corn-growing district. The CHURCH, dedicated to St. George, stands on the right side of the road, at a small distance from the river Adur. Its architecture

exhibits specimens of the Norman, Decorated, and Perpendicular
styles. The projecting wooden porch has a niche above the
entrance, wherein a figure of the Virgin formerly stood. The
Burrell Chapel contains two large and fine brasses: one for a
female, reported to be *Philippa*, wife of John Halsham, and one
of the co-heiresses of David de Strabolge, Earl of Athol, d. 1385;
the other for *Hugo Halsham*, d. 1441, and his wife *Joan*, d.
1421. A monument, with two figures in *Roman* costume, by
Rysbrach, commemorates *William Powlett*, d. 1746, and his wife
Elizabeth. Flaxman is said to have admired it—an extraordinary proof of the great sculptor's good nature! The sarcophagus and urn for *William Burrell*, d. 1796, the collector of
the Burrell MSS. (British Museum) on points connected with
Sussex history, were executed by Flaxman. The Wyndham
family hold the patronage of the rectory, which is valued at
£791.

WEST GRINSTEAD PARK (Sir W. Burrell, Bart.) skirts the
Horsham road, which divides it from Knepp Park for some distance. It was erected by Walter Burrell, Esq. in 1806, and if
not designed in the purest form of Gothic architecture, is certainly an imposing and stately pile. Indeed its position would
redeem from mediocrity a far inferior building. It stands near
the site of an old mansion, which was long the residence of the
Caryls, one of whom was the host and friend of Pope, and suggested to him the "Rape of the Lock:"—

> " What dire offence from amorous causes springs;
> What mighty contests rise from trivial things,
> I sing.—This verse to Caryl, muse! is due:
> This even Belinda may vouchsafe to view:
> Slight is the subject, but not so the praise,
> If she inspire, and he approve my lays."

" Pope's Oak" is still pointed out in the park, which is luxuriantly wooded and charmingly diversified.

KNEPP PARK (Sir W. W. Burrell, Bart.) lies upon our left.
Its stately castellated mansion, built by the late proprietor,
stands on an ascent overlooking some attractive scenery and
a magnificent piece of water, whose banks are fringed with some
noble trees. There is here a good collection of portraits :—
Anne of Cleves, by *Holbein;* Cromwell, Earl of Essex, *Holbein;* Stafford, Duke of Buckingham, *Holbein* (engraved by Hol-

H

!ar) ; Sir Henry Guldeford, Comptroller of the Household to
Henry VIII., *Holbein* (engraved by Hollar) ; Lady Guldeford
(engraved by Hollar) ; Sir Richard Rich, Chancellor to Edward
VI., *Holbein ;* Algidus, a learned person employed by Francis I.
to visit the East on a commercial mission, *Holbein ;* a Woman of
rank, name unknown, *Holbein ;* Sir Robert Cotton, founder of
the Cottonian Library, *Vansomer,* engraved by Vertue ; William
Herbert, Earl of Pembroke, *Vansomer,* engraved by Papæus in
1617 ; Loyens, Chancellor of Brabant, *Philip de Champagne ;*
Cornelius Van Tromp, *Frank Hals ;* Henrietta Maria, a whole
length, *Vandyke ;* Charles II., *Sir Peter Lely ;* Lord Lumley,
Vansomer ; A Head, *Quintin Matsys ;* Sir Merrik Burrell, *Opie ;*
Sir William Burrell, who mainly formed this interesting collection, *Reinagle ;* Lady Burrell, *Leslie ;* and Sir C. M. Burrell,
Reinagle. Observe, also, the sea-views by *Vandervelde,* a battle-
piece by *Bourguinon,* and two specimens of *Albert Durer.*

The ruin of KNEPP CASTLE—a part of a Norman inner tower
or keep—stands on a knoll about half a mile west of the present
mansion. It was erected as a " hunting-box" by one of the De
Braoses, who here maintained a numerous establishment and a
large kennel, and often "roused the hart" in the neighbouring
woodlands. KNEPP is derived from the Saxon *cnæp,* a hillock,
indicative of its position. It is situated in the parish of SHIP-
LEY (population, 1160)—*i.e.,* the sheep meadow—whose Norman CHURCH, dedicated to St. Mary, stands to the left of a lane
which joins the Horsham road near Southwater. The tower is
two stories in height, and surmounted by a low shingled spire.
The flat oaken ceiling has been enriched with colours. A curious
reliquary of wood is preserved in the church chest. It is 7 inches
long and 6 inches high, enamelled, and gilt on the sides and ends
with the subject of the Crucifixion and angelic figures. The letters X P S, in Greek characters, surmount the Cross. It was
possibly brought from Byzantium by the Knight Templars, to
whom the church formerly belonged. Remark the altar-tomb
and effigies, in vari-coloured marble, and restored about thirty
years ago by Carew, for Sir *Thomas Caryll,* d. 1616, and his
Margaret. The epitaph is very quaint :—

> " Aske not who lyes entombed, that crime
> Argues you lived not in his time ;

His virtues answer, and to fate,
Outliving him, express their hate,
For stealing away the life of one
Who (but for fashion) needs no stone
To seek his praise. His worst did dye,
But best part outlives memorie.
Then view, reade, trace his tombe, praise deeds
Which teares, joy, love-strains causeth, breeds."

☞ From Shipley to Horsham is about 7 miles. The road lies through a pleasant agricultural district, but passes no object of particular interest. At 3 miles from Horsham we pass through SOUTHWATER, a pretty well-wooded hamlet, with a new district church, and afterwards skirt the grounds of DENNE PARK (see p. 103), turning to the right out of the main road, and entering Horsham at a point near the Church.

ITCHINGFIED (population, 371) lies to the west, in the heart of numerous leafy *shaws*, and surrounded by many fine old oaks. At almost every point the sketcher will find a charming woodland landscape. The rude Decorated CHURCH, dedicated to St. Nicholas, consists of a nave, chancel, low oaken spire and tower. An old font of Sussex marble was dug up in the churchyard some years ago. It is said that a skull and cross bones used to be adhibited to one of the rafters of the church.

BRANCH ROUTE—SHOREHAM TO PETWORTH.

The Petworth road, as far as Steyning and Wiston, has been already described. After leaving Wiston Place it skirts the base of the chalk downs until at Storrington it makes a sudden curve, and strikes inland towards the hills of Pulborough.

Our first halting-place is at WASHINGTON (population, 884), whose small CHURCH is mainly Early English. It consists of a nave, chancel, north aisle, and low embattled tower, and contains a monument to *Johannes Byne*, with two figures in the costume of the sixteenth century. The vicarage, valued at £63, is in the patronage of Magdalene College, Oxon.

A grave-slab in the churchyard bears the following curious epitaph upon one *Carolus Goring*, d. 1821 :—

> " Ab orienti redux incorruptus,
> Optimatibus improbusque invisus,
> Divitiarum honorumque spretus,
> Populi salutis et potentiæ vindex."

SULLINGTON (population, 243), a settlement of the Saxon Syllingas (so Angmering of the Angmeringas, Poling of the Polingas, Beeding of the Bedingas ;—see Kemble's "Saxons in England"), lies about 1 mile south of the turnpike road. The Downs, which are spotted with numerous Saxon tumuli, form the southern boundary—a glorious swarded rampart, which seems to reach the very skies! Ascend them, and before you stretches the valley of the Adur—the third of the great passes or defiles in the huge chalk range which runs across Sussex in a line parallel with the coast—and beyond it the glittering expanse of the Channel, while far away to the south-east rises the gleaming cliffs of the Isle of Wight. The view to the north embraces a considerable portion of the verdurous and leafy Weald, watered by the Adur, the Arun, and their numerous tributaries :—

> "A land of streams! some, like a downward smoke,
> Slow-dropping veils of thinnest lawn, did go ;
> And some through wavering lights and shadows broke,
> Rolling a slumbrous sheet of foam below."

Sullington has an Early English church, dedicated to St. Mary, which contains the mutilated effigy of a knight, *temp.* Henry III., said to be that of Sir William de Covert, but with that exception there is nothing special to interest the visitor.

Not above 1½ mile beyond Sullington we pass through the village of STORRINGTON (population, 1038). The common (on the right) is a favourite resort of the rabbit tribe. The village consists of two long streets, intersecting each other at right angles.

The CHURCH has a nave, chancel, north aisle, and low square western tower. The chancel alone is ancient ; the rest of the building was rebuilt in 1731. It contains two sculptures by Westmacott ; a sarcophagus, with military emblems, for Sir *Henry Bradford*, d. 1816 ; and a female figure for Major *Falconer*, d. 1827, and his daughter. There is an inlaid slab commemorative of *Henricus Wilshe*, a priest, d. 1591.

There is a comfortable inn, the White Horse, in the village of Storrington.

The road now bends to the north, and brings us to the PARK and VILLAGE of PARHAM (population, 55), the latter a mere cluster of cottages situate on the outskirts of Lord Zouche's noble domain.

PARHAM HOUSE, a *picquant* Elizabethan structure, nestles in the shadow of the Downs, and looks out upon a luxuriantly wooded breadth of hill and dale, and glen and lawn. Under the leafy branches of the vigorous trees repose a fine herd of deer. Rare plants and glorious blossoms brighten and enrich the well-ordered parterres.

The house was built by Sir Thomas Palmer about 1540, and, in 1597, passed into the hands of the Bisshopp family, afterwards Lords de la Zouch. The present representative is the Baroness de la Zouch, who married, in 1802, the Hon. Robert Curzon, the well-known traveller, and author of an interesting work on the " Levantine Monasteries." Mr. Curzon has formed here a most valuable library, rich in MSS. and early printed books, as well as a collection of works of art of the most *recherché* character. Permission is readily given to the tourist to inspect the greater portion of these costly treasures, and we shall briefly indicate the objects of the highest interest.

In the HALL, remark the escocheon of Queen Elizabeth pointing out the spot where the great lady sat at dinner, in 1592, when she visited Parham on her way to Cowdlay. Remark, too, the interesting collection of armour, principally of the fifteenth century, brought from the church of St. Irene at Constantinople by Mr. Curzon, and carefully arranged in veritable *armoires*. These helms, and gorgets, and hauberks encased the stout frames of the gallant Christian knights who, in 1652, defended Constantinople against Mahomet II. Here, too, are the sword of a German *Heidenmauer*, or headsman, beneath whose sharp edge many a chivalrous life has gasped out ; a thumb-screw, and an old iron lock from a house which formerly stood in Chichester High Street ; two ancient helmets (one Etruscan), recovered from a tomb at Bari in Calabria ; a shield which was borne by the handsome and ill-fated Courtenay, Earl of Devon, whose misfortune it was to attract the favour both of Mary and Elizabeth ; some pieces of armour engraved by Hans Burgmais for Maximilian of Austria ; the garniture of the Mameluke horse : an English helmet of the twelfth, and some Venetian helmets of the fifteenth centuries; a model of a Greek casque, discovered at Delphi, and probably "the *salve* (or offering) of some ingenious Greek who had vowed a helmet to Apollo," and cheated the god in this subtle fashion; some richly ornamented oriental armour; and a copper-gilt chamfron and gauntlet, which appear, from the purport of their Arabic inscriptions, to have belonged to the chivalrous Saladin

Remark, in the SMALL DRAWING-ROOM, two Interiors by *Ostade ;* four pictures of the Seasons, finely enamelled on copper, by *Pierre Courtois* of Limoges ; and a Holy Family, *Pontormo*, purchased in Italy by Mr. Curzon.

In the DINING-ROOM, a portrait of Lady Wilmot Horton, with Lord Byron's verses, in his own handwriting,—" She walks in beauty, like the night of cloudless climes and starry skies ;" and a portrait, by *Gainsborough*, of Lady Frederick Campbell, widow of the Earl Ferrers, who was hanged at Tyburn with a silken cord for the murder of his steward.

The DRAWING-ROOM contains—Sir Philip Sidney, Lady Sidney, and Robert, Earl of Leicester, by *Zucchero ;* Mary Curzon, gouvernante of Charles the First's children, *Vandyke ;* the great Constable Bourbon, *Titian ;* St. John the Evangelist, a sketch, *Raffaelle ;* two landscapes on copper, *Ricci ;* the Holy Family, *Jacobello Flores ;* a Holy Family, *Carlo Maratti ;* and numerous portraits by unknown masters, including those of Sir Francis Walsingham, Lord Crewe, bishop of Durham, and the Prince of Orange, father of William the Third.

The GALLERY, 150 feet long, is a noble room, full of valuable relics and interesting portraits. Observe the Egyptian ark, of sycamore, brought from Thebes by Mr. Curzon, and adorned with hieroglyphics, indicating its construction during the reign of Amunoph, 1550 B.C. Its dimensions, compared with those of the ark of the covenant (see Exodus, chap. 25), which is generally dated from 1500 B.C., are as follow :—

	Length.	Width.	Height.
Parham Ark,	2 ft. 9 in.	1 ft. 1 in.	1 ft. 4 in.
Ark of the Covenant,	4 ft. 6 in.	2 ft. 3 in.	2 ft. 3 in.

When discovered, numerous figures of the Egyptian gods were in its interior.

Observe the collections of rare china, and literary antiquities, equally unique in their way. The pen-case of Henry VI. is among the latter.

Among the portraits are Charles Paget, brother to the Lord Paget, implicated in Babington's conspiracy; Sir Henry Wotton, by *Jansen;* and Queen Elizabeth at the age of 25. A Roman pig of lead, excavated at Pulborough, lies upon the floor.

The CHAPEL, at the end of the Gallery, contains figures of St. John and two monks, by *Andrea della Robbia;* some good stained glass, a curious Elizabethan font, and much admirable wood-carving.

The picturesqueness of the Park will enchant the artist. Clumps of venerable trees chequer with floating shadows the crisp green sward, while the soft swell of the Downs is seen through a frame-work of the richest foliage. A famous heronry is located in the depth of the pine wood. Its history is curious: From Coity Castle, in Wales, the birds were removed, *temp.* James I., by Lord Leicester's steward, to Penshurst. Two hundred years later they emigrated to Michel Grove, near Arundel, whence, twenty years ago, disturbed by some meditated improvements of the Duke of Norfolk's, they transported themselves to Parham. They assemble early in February, repair their nests, lay early in March, and watch over the young fledglings through the summer. "The trees are never entirely deserted during the winter months, a few birds, probably some of the more backward of the preceding season, roosting among their boughs every night." There are now fifty-eight nests.

PARHAM CHURCH, repaired and modernized in 1800, adjoins the house. The leaden font bears the armorial distinctions of Andrew Purcell, 1351, and the inscription, in Lombardic letters, Ih'C NAZAR (*Jesus Nazarenus*). There is nothing noteworthy in the church besides this, and visitors will find more objects of interest in the house and park.

After leaving Parham, the road crosses Wiggonholt Common, and leaves WIGGONHOLT (population, 39), or rather its church, for half-a-dozen houses can scarcely be termed a village, on the left. Just beyond is GREATHAM (population, 76). Both churches are Early English, and both parishes—chiefly arable and meadow-land, comprising 1770 acres — are very scantily populated. The two rectories are held by one incumbent valued at £205, and in the gift of the Hon. R. Curzon.

On the bank of the Arun, and at the foot of a considerable range of hills, stands PULBOROUGH (population, 1825—*Inn:* The Swan)—*i. e., pwl,* water, and *byrig,* an encampment—two words which aptly indicate its position. The church is situated very near the point of intersection of the Horsham and Retworth, and Arundel and Dorking roads. The great Roman via, from Regnum (Chichester) to Londinium, passed through this neighbourhood ; and possibly the Latin epicures appreciated, as highly as the gastronomes of a later day, the eels, pike, and trout which here disport themselves in the Arun.

At OLD PLACE there are some remains of a house built in the reign of Henry VI., and of a barn whose general style of architecture seems Edwardian. The manor formerly belonged to the Apsleys.

Numerous Roman relics have been found, as might be expected, in this parish, and in the vicinity of the great Regnum highway. Four pipes of lead—one of which is at Parham—were discovered here in 1824. They were lettered—

" TCLTRPVTBREXAVG,"

which has been interpreted, with much ingenuity, as an abbreviation of Ti. Cl. Tr. Pvt. B. Rex. Avg., *i. e.,* " Tiberius Claudius, Tribunitiæ Potestatis, Britanniæ Rex, Augustus."—(*Gentleman's Magazine*). At Mare-hill, in 1817, the remains of a Roman mausoleum were excavated. On a circular mound, to the right of the village, remains a Roman arch, a portion of a Roman castellum commanding the Arun and the Rother. Extensive traces of a Roman villa—the foundations 150 feet by 190 feet—may still be examined on the hill, at *Borough,* north-east of Pulborough street.

The CHURCH, dedicated to St. Mary, is partly Early English, and occupies a conspicuous position on a hill of sandstone. The clerestory windows are worth examination. The single-pillared font is Norman. There are brasses for *Thomas Harling,* d. 1423, a canon of Chichester ; *Edmund Mille,* d. 1652, and *Matilda* his wife, and *Edmund Mille,* his son. The Mille sepultuary-chapel, from which these were removed, is no longer in existence. It formerly stood in the churchyard.

☞ From this point the tourist may proceed to Billinghurst and into Surrey, or *by rail* to Horsham, or even through Chiltington to West Grinstead ; or descend, by way of Amberley, into Arundel.

The Arun valley will now be left behind, and at one and a quarter miles we shall cross the Rother. Here, at the foot of a tolerably steep ascent, we come upon the pretty village of STOP-HAM (population, 161), and its quaint church, a building partly Norman and partly Decorated, and containing a series of brasses to members of the Bartelott family, hereditary stewards to the Earls of Arundel. The stained glass in the chancel window was the work of one Roelandt, a Flemish glass-stainer, and removed from the hall of the old manor-house. This church is worthy of a passing visit.

One mile beyond, but on the left of the road, stands the church of FITTLEWORTH (population, 696), 8 miles from Arundel, 3 miles from Pulborough, and 3 miles from Petworth. It is partly Early English and partly Decorated, with a chancel, nave, and north aisle, but is void of interest. The vicarage, valued at £391, is in the patronage of the Bishop of Chichester.

In a quiet valley, half a mile distant, lies EGDEAN (population, 76), with an antique manor-house, formerly the seat of the Dykes, and a small church, which need not delay the tourist. Both Egdean and Petworth are reached from the Petworth station of the Pulborough and Midhurst line.

We now ascend the hill to PETWORTH (population, 3439— *Inns:* The Half-moon, the Swan), which looks down, from its breezy elevation, on a small stream of the Rother, winding its silver trail through pleasant meadows. A modest and commodious market and court-house of stone, built by the Earl of Egremont, occupies a convenient position in the centre of the town. The market is generally well attended, and the fairs, for corn and cattle, draw hither a bustling throng of Sussex farmers. The Wyndham family are the principal landed proprietors.

PETWORTH CHURCH, a Perpendicular building, restored at an expense of £15,000 by the late Earl of Egremont—a liberal and judicious benefactor of the town and its neighbourhood—boasts a lofty spire, 180 feet in height, the work of the late Sir Charles Parry. The chapel of St. Thomas contains several memorials of the Percies, the early lords of Petworth—a monument erected by the late Earl, in 1857, when he was eighty-six years old, representing religion leaning on a cross, at whose

base a Bible lies open. The touching inscription is, " Mortuis
Moriturus." Carew was the sculptor.

Among the notabilities interred at Petworth, are Dr. Price,
a former rector, who, as chaplain to Monk, exercised considerable influence upon the transactions of the Restoration ; Henry,
ninth Earl of Northumberland, who was implicated in the Gunpowder Plot, fined £20,000, and imprisoned for sixteen years
in the Tower, d. 1632 ; Algernon, the tenth Earl, a parliamentary leader, d. 1668 ; and Josceline, the last Earl, d. 1670.
Josceline de Louvaine, who received the manor of Petworth
from Queen Adeliza, and Lucy Percy, Countess of Carlisle, the
beautiful intriguante of Charles the First's court, whom Bishop
Warburton called " the Erynnys of her time," and whose charms
were celebrated by Voiture and Suckling, are also buried here.
A fine sculpture by Baily commemorates the late Earl of Egremont.

The Wyndham family are the patrons of the living—a rectory
valued at £856.

PETWORTH PARK (Lord Leconfield) is the great art-treasury of
Sussex, and must on no account be neglected by the tourist.
The glorious scenery of the grounds, and the unequalled interest
of its picture-gallery, render it a shrine worthy of any pilgrim's
devotion.   The manor was granted by Adeliza, the dowager-queen
of Henry I., to Josceline de Louvaine, her brother, who married
Agnes, heiress of the Northumberland Percys.   It remained with
the Lords Percy and the Earls of Northumberland until the
death of the last Earl in 1670, when his daughter, Lady Elizabeth Percy, brought it as her dower to her third husband, Charles
Duke of Somerset (her second husband was Thynne of Longleat,
murdered in 1682, by Count Königsmarck).   By the marriage
of their daughter Catherine with Sir William Wyndham, it passed
into the hands of the present representative of the Wyndhams and
Percys.

The ancient castellated edifice occupied the same site as the
present mansion.   It was " most famous for a stately stable, the
best of any subject's in Christendom, as it afforded standing
in state for threescore horses, with all necessary accommodation."   Charles, Duke of Somerset, almost entirely rebuilt it,
and the late Earl of Egremont effected considerable alterations.
The frontage forms one unbroken range, 332 feet long, and
62 feet high, which is imposing from its size, but possesses no

architectural recommendations. In the rear rises the spire
of Petworth Church, with an effect which is not at all to be
admired.

The PARK, which is about 14 miles in circumference, and
open to all comers, is very beautiful. From the Prospect Tower
on the higher ground a noble view may be enjoyed. The ancient
stag park (between 700 and 800 acres), enclosed and cultivated
by the late Earl of Egremont, spreads out its fertile expanse
beneath. All around stretch exquisite turfy lawns, and shadowy
dells, and bold abrupt knolls, crowned by magnificent oaks, and
clumps of beech, and ash, and elm rear their dark green crests at
every "place of vantage." A fine sheet of water dimples and
sparkles in the hollow before the house, and herds of deer toss
up their branching antlers in the cool and leafy coverts. In the
distance rises the swelling line of the South Downs, light and
shadow chasing each other across their verdurous slopes ; and
Chanctonbury Ring, with its diadem of trees, towering sublime
above the exalted range. Far away to the north-east, the dark
leaf-masses and burnished plains of the Weald present a striking
contrast, and when reddened in the rare splendours of the sunset,
offer a landscape eloquent in beauty.

Let us now enter the HOUSE, which is thrown open to visitors
with the utmost liberality, and glance at the precious works of
art for which it is so deservedly famous. They are too numerous
to be specified with much detail. We can but select the most
noteworthy, and recommend the reader to the temperate criticism
of Dr. Waagen in his "Art-Treasures of England," for fuller information.

[1. The GRAND STAIRCASE was painted by *Laguerre* (twin spirit with " sprawl-
ing Verrio "), for Charles "the proud" Duke of Somerset. Here Pandora and Pro-
metheus figure in the most marvellous of attitudes, and the Duchess of Somerset
rides in a car of triumph, attended by her daughters, while an allegory does justice
to her singular fortunes. Her father, Earl Joscelin, died at Turin at the early age of
twenty-six, leaving his daughter Elizabeth "heiress of all the immense estates of
her family, and sole inheritrix of the hereditary glory of the Percys." It became her
lot to be three times a wife, and twice a widow before she was sixteen. In her
thirteenth year she married Harry Cavendish, Earl of Ogle, who survived the cere-
mony a few months only. In 1681, she married Thomas Thynne, of Longleat,
separating from him at the altar, and pursuant to a previous arrangement, travelling
on the Continent for a twelvemonth. Thynne, Monmouth's "wealthy western
friend," and the "Issacher" of Dryden's satire, was assassinated by Count Königsmarck, February 12, 1682. The adventurer, however, did not obtain the wealthy
prize he aimed at. In less than two months after the murder the heiress of the

Percys was married to Charles Seymour, known as the proud Duke of Somerset, from his extraordinary arrogance. "He seemed little less in his conduct than if vested with regal honours. His servants obeyed by signs. The country roads were cleared that he might pass without obstruction or observation."—(*Burke's Romance of the Aristocracy*). The Duchess died in 1722, aged fifty-five; the Duke in 1748, aged eighty-seven.

2. The SQUARE DINING-ROOM contains—By *Titian* :—Portrait of a Noble ; Catherine Cornaro, Queen of Cyprus ; his daughter Lavinia fondling a kitten. By *Vandyck* :—Earl of Strafford ; Henry Percy, 9th Earl of Northumberland (a master-piece in colouring and expression) ; Prince William of Orange, father of the "Great Deliverer ;" Algernon, 10th Earl of Northumberland, his wife and child ; Lady Rich ; Anna Cavendish ; Sir Charles Percy ; Mrs. Porter, Henriette Maria's lady of the bedchamber ; Lord Percy of Alnwick ; Lord Goring and his Son. By Sir *Joshua Reynolds* : Woodward the Actor ; Virgin and Child.

Holy Family attended by Angels, *Andrea da Sarto* : Allegory of Events in the Early part of Charles the First's reign, *Teniers* : Jacob and Laban, with landscape, morning—one of the most important works of the master—*Claude Lorraine* : Portrait of himself, *Tintoretto* : Philip II. of Spain, Sir *Antonio More* : Philip le Bel, father of the Emperor Charles V., a pupil of *Van Eyck's* ; A portrait, *Geovanni Bellini* ; Queen Catherine Parr, *Holbein* ; Oliver Cromwell, *Walker* ; The Young Singer before the aged Connoisseur, *Hogarth* ; Joscelin, eleventh and last Earl of Northumberland, Sir *Peter Lely*.

3. DUKE OF SOMERSET'S ROOM :—Edward VI., when 10 years old (1547), *Holbein* ; Archduke Leopold, *Teniers*, and a priest, *Teniers* ; Thomson, author of "The Seasons," *Hudson* ; Henry ninth Earl of Northumberland, *Vansomer* ; Breughel the Painter, *Vandyck* ; Prince Regent, *Varelst*.

CARD PLAYERS, Matsys the younger ; A sea-shore landscape, *Claude* ; Two land-scapes, *Hobbima* ; Landscape with a Man Angling, *Gaspar Poussin* ; Landscape, *Van Goyen*.

4. The NORTH GALLERY.—By *Turner* ; Echo and Narcissus ; Jessica ("Mer-chant of Venice") ; An East Indiaman and a Man-of-War ; Cattle at a Pool, and Men Peeling Osiers ; Evening Landscape, with Willows Dipping into a Pond ; The Lake and Tower at Tabley, Cheshire ; The Thames near Windsor, at Evening ; The Thames from Eton College ; The Thames near Weybridge ; and the Thames and Windsor Castle. *Northcote* :—Richard III. receiving the Sons of Edward IV. in the Tower ; Murder of the Two Young Princes ; and Bridget Plantagenet, daughter of Edward IV., at the Nunnery of Dartford. *Gainsborough* : — Landscape, with Cattle ; landscape with Shepherd and Shepherdess. *Romney* : — Mrs. Charlotte Smith, the Novelist, as Melancholy, and Lady Emma Hamilton as Mirth ; Shak-speare watched by Tragedy and Comedy (the latter a portrait of Lady Hamilton). Sir *Joshua Reynolds* :—The Witch-scene in "Macbeth ;" and Death of Cardinal Beanfort, from Henry VI. ; Admiral Lord Viscount Rodney ; Mrs. Masters ; General Gardiner ; Lady Craven and her Son ; the Earl of Thanet's Children, with a dog. *Allston*, the American artist :—A figure of Contemplation ; and Jacob's Dream.

Children of Charles I., Sir *Peter Lely* ; Venus asleep, and Cupid attending her, *Hoppner* ; A sea-scape, with storm, Sir *Augustus Callcott* ; Still water, with rock and Castle, *Wilson* ; the Cognoscenti, *Patch* ; Windsor Park, *Howard*, R.A. ; Musi-dora, *Opie* ; A copy of the Punch-drinkers, of *Hogarth* ; Rydal Water, *Copley Field-ing* ; Invention of Music, *Barry* ; Rape of Europa, *Hilton* ; Alexander Pope, *Richardson* ; Sancho and the Duchess, *C. R. Leslie* ; Herodias, with John the Bap-tist's Head, *Fusch* ; Adam and Eve, expelled from Paradise, are abandoned by St.

Michael, *Phillips;* A Storm in the Alps, *Loutherbourg;* and Edwin, Beattie's Minstrel—" And yet poor Edwin was no vulgar boy, "—*Westall.*

SCULPTURE :—A Shepherd Boy ; and the Archangel Michael piercing Satan with his spear (from " Paradise Lost "), by *Flaxman.* A Bas-relief by Sir *Richard Westmacott,* in illustration of the Horatian passage—

Non sine dies animosus infans.

5. RED ROOM.—By *Vandyck :*—Sir Robert Shirley, and his Circassian bride Teresia (see p. 112); Frances Howard, Duchess of Richmond ; and Anne Bull, wife of Lionel Cranfield, Earl of Middlesex, " the citizen who came to be Lord Treasurer, and was very near coming to be hanged " (*Walpole*). By *Vansomer :*—Ludovic Stuart, Earl of Richmond ; Ralph, Lord Hopeton. Sir *Joshua Reynolds :*—Prince Boothby : a Lady in a turban ; a Lady with letter. *Van der Meulen :*—Attack by Banditti upon a travelling-party ; Louis XIV. and the Dauphin at Lisle. Adoration of the Kings, *Albert Durer* (ascribed by Waagen, but, perhaps, on insufficient grounds, to *Hieronymus Bosch*); Scene near Nimeguen, with figures, *Albert Cuyp;* Battle of the Boyne, *Maas;* Storm at sea, *Vlieger;* Two Prelates kneeling, *Rubens;* A Lady, costumed in black, *Rembrandt ;* Charles II. passing Whitehall in his carriage, *Theodore Stoop;* Countess of Egremont, *Gainsborough ;* and Admiral Van Tromp, *Van der Helst.*

6. ANTE-ROOM.—Vandyck, *Dobson;* Sir Isaac Newton, *Kneller;* Colonel Wyndham (Lord Leconfield), his wife and sons, *Grant;* Marquis of Granby, *Reynolds;* Sir Edward Coke, *Jansen;* A nobleman at prayers, *Van Eyck;* Study for " the preaching of Knox" in Sir Robert Peel's Collection, *Wilkie.*

7. CARVED DINING-ROOM.—Remark here the exquisite carvings in wood of dead game, wreaths of blossoms, and foliage by *Grinling Gibbons.* They enrich the walls and cornices of this noble chamber (60 feet long, 24 feet wide, and 20 feet high), with almost priceless ornamentation. " Appendant to one is a vase with a bas-relief of the purest taste, and worthy the Grecian age of Cameos. Selden, one of his disciples and assistants—for what one hand could execute such plenty of laborious productions—lost his life in saving this carving when the house was on fire "—(*Horace Walpole*). The decorations were completed by Jonathan Ritson, a Cumberland artist, who was employed for the purpose by the late Earl of Egremont and the present Lord Leconfield.

The pictures are inserted in deep, red-coloured panels, which seem to require some relief. Observe the following—By *Turner :*—Petworth Park, a sunset landscape of extraordinary beauty ; The Lake in the Park ; a sea-view of Brighton ; Chichester Canal, at sunset. By *Clint :*—Portraits of Ritson, and Grinling Gibbons. *Kneller :*—The proud Duke of Somerset, and thrice-married heiress of the Percys. By *Jansen :*—Lord and Lady Seymour of Trowbridge. By *Holbein :*—Henry VIII. (painted about 1541).

8. The LIBRARY.—Newmarket Heath, in 1724, introducing the Duke of Somerset, who is addressing the Duke of Cumberland, *Wootton;* Visit of the Allied Sovereigns to Petworth in 1814, *Phillips;* Charles III. Emperor of Germany, who visited the house in 1703, and Ferdinand d'Adda, Papal Nuncio to James II., both by *Kneller;* Giving Bread to the Hungry, a sketch, *David Teniers;* The Primitive Christians engaged in teaching, *Pasqualino;* and Virgin, Infant Jesus, and Joseph, *Correggio.*

9. The WHITE and GOLD ROOM.—By *Vandyck :*—Lady Dorothy Sidney, Countess of Sunderland, Wallis's " Saccharissa ;" Lady Lucy Percy, Countess of Carlisle, " undoubtedly the most enchanting woman at the Court of Charles I."—(*Jesse*)—" flattered in French by Voiture, and in her native tongue by almost all the

contemporary wits and poets, and more especially by Waller in verse, and in prose
by that singular and mysterious person Sir Toby Matthew"—(*Miss Aikin*); Lady
Dorothy Percy, Countess of Leicester, sister of the aforesaid beauty, and mother of
Algernon Sidney.; Lady Elizabeth Cecil, Countess of Devonshire ; and Lady Anne
Carr, Countess of Bedford, daughter of Carr, Earl of Somerset, James the First's in-
famous minion.   By *C. R. Leslie:*—Lady Lucy Percy, Countess of Carlisle, brings
his pardon to her father, the 9th Earl of Northumberland, imprisoned in the Tower
for his share in the Gunpowder Plot.   Raleigh, and those famous mathematicians,
Harriot, Hughes, and Warner, " the Earl of Northumberland's Three Magi," are also
introduced.

10. The BEAUTY ROOM contains the following panelled portraits :—By *Dahl :*—
The Countess of Portland ; Duchess of Ormond ; Duchess of Devonshire ; Countess
of Carlisle ; Lady Howe ; Countess of Pembroke ; Lady Longueville.   The portraits
of Louis XIV. in this chamber are by *Van der Meulen.*

11. The MARBLE HALL :—Portraits of unknown personages, *Holbein ;* Peg
Woffington, *Hogarth ;* Macpherson (" Ossian), Lord North, and Lady Thomond,
Reynolds ; The Ferry-boat, with sailors, and figures on the shore, *Cuyp ;* A Youth,
Bronzino : Leo X., *Titian ;* His own portrait, *Vandyck ;* Cervantes, *Velasquez ;*
Marshal Turenne, *Frank Hals ;* Guidobaldi, Duke d'Urbino, *Rafaelle ;* and Rem-
brandt and his wife, *Rembrandt.*]

Among the royal visitors to Petworth have been Edward
VL in 1551, the emperor Charles VI. in 1703, Prince George
of Denmark ; and the Prince Regent, Alexander of Russia, the
King of Prussia, the Prince of Wirtemburg, and the Grand
Duchess of Oldenburg, in 1814.

The CHAPEL attached to the ancient mansion is in excellent
preservation.   Both walls and windows are radiant with the emblazoned escutcheons of the lords of Petworth.

The Petworth marble, dark-coloured and interlaced with
purple veins, resembles that which is found in the quarries of
Bethersden in Kent.

* The late Lord Egmont was a munificent patron of Leslie's, and Leslie spent
many of his happiest hours and painted some of his best pictures at Petworth.
Those broad Venetian mirrors, tapestried chairs, China jars and monsters, brocade
and damask hangings, and recherché vases which he has introduced upon his
canvas with an accuracy so minute, he saw at Petworth.   You may see there the
screen and chairs which he has painted in the " Rape of the Lock ;" the old globe
introduced in the " Lady Carlisle ;" the carved mirror and jewelled casket of the
Duchess's toilet-table ; Sophia Western's china jars and console ; the window, with
its look-out on the swelling slopes of the park, where sweet Lady Jane Grey sits
absorbed in *Plato,* while the hounds and horns are making merry music in the sunshine without.   Poor Haydon was another of the Petworth artists, and warmly
appreciated the munificence of the noble owner.   " The very flies," he writes, " seem
to know there is room for their existence—that the windows are theirs.   Dogs,
horses, cows, deer, and pigs ; peasantry and servants, guests and family, children
and parents, all share alike his bounty, and opulence, and luxuries."   For interesting details relative to Petworth and Lord Egmont, see the " Autobiographical
Recollections of Leslie," edited by Mr. Tom Taylor.

☞ North of Petworth, and about one mile west of the Guildford road, lies LURGASHALL (population, 744), with an uninteresting church dating from about 1730. " On the south side of the nave is a kind of cloister, of timber frame, furnished with benches for the accommodation of the parishioners at *Sunday dinner.*" Lord Leconfield is the patron of the rectory, which is valued at £235 per annum.

NORTH CHAPEL (population, 864), is situated on the Guildford road, 5 miles north of Petworth. The CHURCH is dedicated to St. Michael, and the rectory, valued at £363, is in Lord Leconfield's patronage.

Two miles north of this quiet hamlet we cross the boundaries of Surrey.

WORTHING.

The rail, after passing through Shoreham, crosses the Adur, and, following pretty nearly the coast line, soon reaches LANCING (population, 1069), which derives its name from Wlencing, son of King Ælla, and skirts an ample stretch of pleasant turf, terminating in a shingle-bank, some few feet above the sea-level. The *Inn* here is The Farmers'. The lodgings of the place are moderately dear, the air is wholesome, the bathing is good, and society is anything but—lively. Philanthropic monarchists will remember that here Queen Caroline embarked in 1822 ; the lover of poetry, that Coleridge favoured its seclusion and marine scenery. On the hill above the village, and conspicuous from the railway station, stands ST. NICHOLAS' COLLEGE. It was established on the principles of the Church of England, and is in connection with the commercial school at Hurstpierpoint. At both schools there is accommodation provided in the head masters' houses, for which higher fees are exacted. About 900 boys are educated annually in the two schools.

Lancing Church is partly Norman and partly Decorated. Two and a half miles farther and we arrive at

WORTHING, a popular watering-place (population, 10,976— *Hotels :* Marine, Royal Sea-House, Westworthing, Steyne), 52 miles south of London. From a poor fishing village it rose into

sudden importance when George IV.'s patronage of Brighton
attracted the attention of the fashionable world to the pleasures
of sea-bathing and the beauties of the south coast. For their
convenience an agreeable sea-walk or esplanade has been constructed three quarters of a mile in length, and a pier on the
" non-resistance " principle. The sands extend their firm and
pleasant surface for quite ten miles. The temperature is well
adapted to invalids, the sea-views are beautiful, and the town is,
in all respects, identical with other popular sea-side resorts.
There are two rinks, and one excellent swimming-bath.   There
are a CHAPEL OF EASE, built in 1812, and CHRIST CHURCH,
in 1843, besides two other churches more recently erected.
Queen Adelaide resided here in 1850.   The Downs raise their
green crests in the rear of the town, at a distance from the sea
of upwards of a mile.

EXCURSIONS FROM WORTHING.

[Chantonbury Ring, with fine view; Bramber, 5 m.; Broadwater, ½ m.; Cissa-
bury Hill, 2½ m.; Clapham, 5 m.; Findon, 4¼ m.; Highdown Hill, 4 m.; Michelgrove, 6 m.; Muntham, 7 m.; Offington, 2 m.; Salvington, 1¼ m.; Sompting, 2¼
m.; Steyning, 6 m.; Warminghurst, 8 m.; West Tarring, 1 m.]

DESCRIPTIVE NOTES.—BROADWATER (population, 10,000, including Worthing), is situated in a country of " thick hedgerows and hedgerow elms." The
parish, formerly included in the possessions of the knightly family of Camoys, could
number but 300 inhabitants in 1724. In 1801 it boasted of 1018, in 1831 of 4576.
The CHURCH, Transitional Norman, should certainly be visited. It is cruciform in
plan, with a low square central tower. Remark the groined roof of the chancel,
and the rich four-lighted east window. The cross (in flutes), on the north wall.
The palm leaves on the capitals of the columns indicate that the founder was a
crusader. Early English arches separate the nave from the aisles. The tower arch
is enriched with a zig-zag moulding. Observe the canopied monument, in Caen
stone, to *Thomas Lord Delawarr*, d. 1526; a rich memorial, in the same style, for
Thomas, 3d *Lord Delawarr*, d. 1554; and a brass to *John Mapleton*, rector, chancellor to Catharine, wife of Henry V., died 1432. The Rev. E. K. Elliot is patron
of the rectory, which is valued at £600 per annum.

CISSBURY HILL (i. e., Cissa's byrig—from Cissa, one of the sons of Ælla, king of
the South Saxons) rears its stately head above the plains at about 2½ miles north
of Worthing, from which point it is easily reached. A single FOSSE, from 8 to 12
feet in depth, and a broad and lofty VALLUM, enclose an oval camp, about 60 acres
in extent. Roman coins and pottery have been discovered here, and traces of the
foundation of a prætorium; so that it is probable the Roman legionaries kept
" watch and ward " upon this solitary height long before Ælla and his sea rovers
hunted the Britons out of their woodland villages. Some circular pits on the west
side appear to be of British origin, and resemble those at Rowborough in the Isle of
Wight. Celt, Roman, and Saxon, may therefore in turn have had their stronghold
here. Southey, in February 1837, ascended this noble hill, and was delighted with

the landscape which it commands—a landscape embracing the whole coast from Beachy Head to the Selsea Bill. " Worthing," he says, " appeared like a ruined city, such as Baalbec or Palmyra, in the distance, on the edge of what we knew to be sea, but what as well might have been a desert, for it was so variegated with streaks of sunshine and of shade, that no one ignorant of the place could have determined whether it was sea or sky that lay before us."

CLAPHAM (population, 252), is very picturesquely situated in the heart of green sloping downs and richly wooded dells. The village, one long irregular street, winds up a gentle ascent, at about 6 miles from Worthing. The CHURCH consists of a chancel, nave, north and south aisles, and low tower surmounted by a shingled spire. It is principally Transition Norman. Among the memorials observe—a monument of Caen stone, with effigies, for Sir *William Shelley*, Justice of the Common Pleas, and his wife *Alice*; a brass for *John Shelley, temp.* fifteenth century; and figures of an armed knight and his wife, Sir *John Shelley*, d. 1550, and his wife *Alice*.

FINDON (population, 559), as its name indicates, is situated on the chalk-hills, on the road from Worthing to Horsham. The beautiful seat of MUNTHAM (Marchioness of Bath), with its wooded slopes, is but a short distance north of the church; and FINDON PLACE (M. W. Richardson, Esq.), is close at hand. The Early English CHURCH is dedicated to St. John the Baptist, and consists of a chancel, nave, north aisle, and manorial chapel. A shingled spire surmounts its low, square, western tower. The patronage of the vicarage is vested in Magdalene College, Oxon. Its yearly value is computed at £500.

HIGHDOWN HILL rises like a tower out of the green Clapham woods, and looks out upon pleasant Clapham Common. "On crossing the hill," says Pennant, "we saw a curious monument, protected by rails, with a funereal yew at each corner, and a shrubbery adjacent, built by a miller still living, for his place of interment; the monument is strewed with many a pious text out of the burial-service, and some poetical inscriptions—the effusions of his own muse. He is said to have his coffin ready; it runs on castors, and is wheeled every night under his bed. I was told that he is a stout, active, cheerful man; and, besides his proper trade, carries on a very considerable one in smuggled goods." This eccentric miller was named John Olliver, and died in 1793. His coffin, at his funeral, was borne round the meadow by persons dressed in white, and was preceded and followed by some young women attired in white muslin. A funeral sermon was read over his grave by one of these white-stoled virgins. The tomb, a flat stone slab supported by some brick work, stands almost in the centre of an irregular earthwork, which encloses an area of 360 feet by 180. The view from this point is good, but not extensive.

The hill is situated in the maritime parish of FERRING (population, 332),—i. e., the horse-pastures. The manor-house contains some remains of an ancient building where St. Richard of Chichester fed 3000 persons with bread only sufficient for 90— not so difficult a miracle as his monkish biographers would have us believe !

MICHELGROVE (Duke of Norfolk) was the seat of an ancient family of the same name, and afterwards of the Shelleys. The house was pulled down by the Duke of Norfolk about thirty years ago, but this spot is still to be visited for the sake of its exquisite bits of paint-like scenery. Hill and vale here succeed each other in agreeable alternation.

OFFINGTON—i. e., a settlement of the Offingas—is a manor included in the parish of Broadwater. The ancient seat of the Delawarrs is now the residence of Thos.

I

Gaisford, Esq. It lies about half a mile west of Broadwater, in a small park which
has long been colonised by "a family" of rooks.

SOMPTING (population, 682)—i.e., a settlement of the Somptingas—has an interesting church, picturesquely situated on the slope of a hill, embosomed amid
venerable elms. A portion of the manor formerly belonged to the Norman Peverels,
and another to the Abbey of Fécamp; hence the names, retained to the present day,
of Sompting Peverel and Sompting Abbots. The church is cruciform in plan, with
a nave, chancel, and transept, and a western tower terminating in a pointed gable,
out of which rises a shingled spire. The tower and east end of the chancel are said
to be Saxon; the remainder of the edifice seems Transition Norman, unless we
ascribe a pure Norman origin to the chancel. Perpendicular windows have replaced
the original circular-headed lights. Early English arches, springing from circular
pillars, divide the north transept into two aisles. Both north and south transepts
open into the nave with lofty circular arches. Remark the triangular piscina on
the south side of the chancel,—a Perpendicular altar-tomb without name or date,—
and the double aumbry over the altar. A rude sculpture (Early English) of a bishop
in the act of benediction is placed in the south transept, and in the north, a similar
figure of the Saviour with an open book, surrounded by the Evangelist symbols.
The lower outer wall of the tower is evidently Saxon. Remark its courses and
bands of stone. The upper portion has Norman enrichments. The church may
therefore be regarded as a Norman enlargement of a small building erected towards
the close of Edward the Confessor's reign.
Sompting village lies about 2 miles to the north-east of Worthing, and Warminghurst about 9 miles north-west.

WARMINGHURST (population, 116), nestles among the trees, 1 mile north of
Ashington, and 1½ mile west of the Worthing and Horsham road. A long but pleasant day's excursion may be made from Worthing to this pretty village, by way of
Sompting, Findon, and Washington : returning through Sullington, across the downs
to Clapham, and home by way of DURRINGTON (where some remains of an ancient
chapel may be noticed), Salvington, and West Tarring.
The view from the hill on which Warminghurst is perched embraces a considerable portion of the east of Sussex. From the site of the ancient manor-house the
prospect eastward extends to the windmill at Cross-in-hand, and the monument to
the memory of "the hero of Gibraltar," at Heathfield.
The church is Early English, with a large pointed east window, temp. Edward III.
A brass, with figures of a man and woman, their seven sons and three daughters,
commemorates Edward Shelley, d. 1554, Master of the Household to Henry VIII.,
Edward VI., and Queen Mary, and his wife Joan, d. 1558.
The Duke of Norfolk is lord of the manor, and patron of the perpetual curacy.]

We resume our westward route. On our right lies WEST
TARRING (population, 573)—a settlement of the Terringas—at
about 1½ mile north-west of Worthing. The tourist will not fail
to notice the abundant fig-orchards for which this parish is remarkable. It was planted in 1745 from some old stocks in the
parent garden, which are traditionally reputed to have been
brought from Italy by Thomas à Becket. The compiler of the
Acta Sanctorum, however, ascribes them to the horticultural tastes

of St. Richard of Chichester (Bishop Richard de la Wych). There are now about 120 trees, which annually produce upwards of 2000 dozen.*

Tarring was given by King Athelstane to the see of Canterbury, and the Archbishops long had a palace here, of which some portions are embodied in the National School-House. The south part is Early English, but has undergone considerable modification. The tracery of the windows is Perpendicular, and was inserted long after the windows were completed. The hall, on the west side of the building, is Edwardian.

"A range of buildings adjoining the premises of the rector, and still called the Parsonage Row, affords good specimens of domestic architecture in the reign of Henry VI." The vicarage is inhabited by the vicar and rector, the Rev. J. W. Warter, B.D., son-in-law of the poet Southey, who visited Tarring in 1837.

The Early English CHURCH, dedicated to St. Andrew, has a lofty shingled spire, a chancel with a fine five-light window, a nave with clerestory windows, and north and south aisles. The tower-window was placed by Mrs. Warter, the eldest daughter of Southey, as a memorial of the poet. The vicarage, valued at £562, is in the patronage of the Archbishop of Canterbury.

Crossing the churchyard, and following the meadow-path for about half a mile, the tourist will reach SALVINGTON, a small hamlet in the manor of Tarring. A small house called LACIES, at the entrance to the village, was the birth-place of John Selden, the illustrious author of "De Jure Maritima," "History of Tythes," and "Titles of Honour" (born December 16, 1584, died November 30, 1654). His father was, it is said, an itinerant musician, and Selden received his early education at the Free School of Chichester. When only ten years old he carved on the lintel of the cottage-door a Latin distich, singularly illustrative of his character,—

"Gratus, honeste, mihi, non claudar, inito, sedebis,
Fur abeas, non sum facta soluta tibi."

From Tarring we may easily regain the high road at GORING (population, 569), a distance of 1¼ mile. There is here a station on the Brighton and Portsmouth Railway, and we may therefore

* Admission may be gained to the Fig Gardens, 2d. each person. The rare and beautiful golden oriole bird is known to breed here.

abandon pedestrianism. and once more call to our aid the locomotive.

To the north rises CASTLE GORING (Sir G. T. Petchell Bart.),
out of an environment of trees. The mansion is imposing in appearance, but in its combination of Gothic and Grecian is somewhat *bizarre*.

GORING CHURCH, dedicated to St. Mary, is partly Norman,
partly Early English. The chancel, however, dates from the
fourteenth century. An inlaid brass commemorates *John Cooke*,
"and Emma Lys, his wife." The vicarage, valued at £320, is in
the patronage of David Lyon, Esq.

We next arrive (2½ miles) at ANGMERING (population,
1012), whence we may proceed north to ANGMERING PARK (Duke
of Norfolk), a richly wooded demesne of great beauty. A colony
of herons migrated here from Penshurst, when some venerable
trees were felled in that extensive chase, and, on some trees being
again cut down at Angmering, again departed, and settled themselves at Parham, where they still abide.

New Place was the seat of the Palmers, of whom Sir Edward
Palmer married Alice Clement, of the Moat, at Ightham, and by
her had three sons, born on three Sundays successively,—Whit-
sunday, Trinity, and the first Sunday after Trinity,—who were
all three knighted for their valour by Henry VIII.

There were churches both at East and West Angmering, but
of the former there are no remains. The latter, dedicated to St.
Peter, dates from the fifteenth century. The escocheon of the
nunnery of Sion is carved over the entrance-door, with the date
—*Anno Dom. Milesimo Quingesimo Septimo*—from which it would
appear that the tower was built in that year, and at the expense
of the nuns of Sion. Angmering station, on the South Coast
line, is about ¾ of a mile from the village.

PATCHING (population, 271) is situated on the left of a
lane which diverges from the Arundel road, about 2 miles from
the Angmering station. PATCHING PLACE (Col. Payne) is, indeed,
visible from the line. The land here is divided between corn-
fields and cattle-pastures ; and Patching butter has more than a
local reputation. The angler may try his skill with, possibly,
satisfactory results in PATCHING POND, a large piece of water,
stored with trout, eels, pike, tench, and carp ; the architectural

student may occupy himself in studying the details of the Early English CHURCH.

In the beech-woods here, truffles are very abundant.

At 2½ from Angmering, and 18 miles from Brighton, we reach Ford Junction, the station for ARUNDEL and LITTLE-HAMPTON—the former lying about 2 miles north, the latter on the coast, 3 miles south. But we must first take note of Poling and Leominster, both of which lie to the right of the line, between Goring and Arundel. POLING has a large decoy for wild fowl, supplied by a tributary of the Arun ; a modern dwelling-house transformed out of the chapel, formerly attached to a Commandery of the Knights Hospitallers ; and a fifteenth century CHURCH, containing some fragments of stained glass, and a brass for *Walter Davys*, vicar.

LEOMINSTER contains a picturesque Church, partly Transition-Norman in its style, and partly Early English, dedicated to St. Mary Magdalene. The font, standing on five pillars, is Norman.

ARUNDEL.

[*Hotels :* The Norfolk Arms. 59 m. from London by rail; 61 m. by road ; 10 m. by road, and 11 m. by rail, from Chichester ; 19 m. from Brighton, by road ; 8 m. from Bognor; 11 m. from Petworth. Population, 2748.]

Descending a steep hill, says Pennant, we crossed a narrow tract of rich meadows ; opposite to us was a range of lofty banks clothed with wood, diversified every now and then with a contrast of chalk which bursts out in the face of the cliffs. Arundel Castle filled one space, and impended nobly over the river Arun and the subjacent meads. We crossed the bridge, and immediately entered the town of Arundel, which consists chiefly of one handsome broad street running straight up the steep slope of the hill, with the castle on the summit on one side, and the church on the other. A brief but graphic description of the position of the most picturesque town in southern England, but since Pennant's time an uninteresting suburb has sprung up on the left bank of the river.

Crossing the neat stone bridge of three arches which here spans the Arun, we breast a steep and abrupt hill, crowned by the towers of Arundel Castle, winding through a street which, happily, still rejoices in many an old gable-fronted, half-timber house. Here, at the NORFOLK ARMS, we may obtain excellent accommodation while we glance at the annals of the ancient town. The origin of the name has not been settled, and it is a question whether it arose from *arundo*, a reed (the neighbouring marshes abounding in reedy growth) from the river Arun, from *hirondells*, a swallow, the device of the corporation seal, or from *Hirondelle*, the famous horse of the notable giant Bevis, the mythic warder. of the Castle, whose bones, with those of his steed's, were interred in the hollow of Pughdean. The reader may choose for himself.

Arundel, as an old prescriptive borough, returned members to Parliament from the reign of Edward the First, but it has been wholly disfranchised by the Reform Acts of 1832 and 1868. It was incorporated by Queen Elizabeth, and is duly governed by a mayor and six aldermen. Its port has been held in some estimation from a period anterior to the Conquest, but its trade now, in timber, coal, and corn, is quite inconsiderable. During the Civil Wars it suffered severely from the outrages of Waller's soldiers, when the Roundhead leader besieged the castle (December 1643), and his artillery terribly shattered the beautiful Church. A canal from the river affords a water communication with the inland agricultural districts, and extends to the Wey, thus bringing Guildford, Weybridge, and the Thames into correspondence. To many the most agreeable association of Arundel will be with the famous *Arundel mullets* which are found in the river, and prove welcome to the epicure.

ARUNDEL CASTLE (" Castrum de Hirundel "), the principal seat of the Duke of Norfolk (who inherits from it his second title of Earl of Arundel), is interesting alike in a historical and architectural point of view. It occupies a commanding position on a richly wooded height, overlooking the town of Arundel and the vale of the Arun. Being precipitous on one side, and protected by a deep fosse on the other, the castle was impregnable in olden times. The area of the walls extends to about 950 by 250 feet, or nearly five and a half acres. The walls are 30 feet high in the oldest part, and from 6 to 12 feet thick. The most interesting, as well as the most ancient part of the castle is the NORMAN KEEP, crowning a mound upwards of 100 feet in height. This is the original and oldest part of the building, which was besieged by King Stephen (1139). As an "ivy-mantled tower," says Dr. Beattie in his *Castles and Abbeys of England*, " this keep is without a rival in all we can recollect of foreign or domestic

ARUNDEL CASTLE, SEAT OF THE HOWARDS—DUKE OF NORFOLK.

castles." It is approached by a gateway, flanked by two square towers of four storeys, in the lowest of which lie the dungeons. In the north wall of the archway is the old sallyport, which opens into the ditch. A portion of the well-tower still remains, and the well itself (always an object of great concern to a garrison) is said to have been 300 feet deep. Near this are the remains of an ancient ORATORY, from the ruined window of which there is a romantic view. The keep is now abandoned to the owls and bats, and of the former Arundel was long famous for its peculiar horned breed.

The modern castle is a reconstruction on a grand scale of the ancient pile, made at the end of the last century by Duke Thomas. The work was continued by his successor for a period of thirty years, during which time he is said to have expended a sum of £600,000 on the execution of his plan, which was still left incomplete at the time of his death in 1805. The noble proprietor, who was an amateur in architecture, as well as a great patron of art, superintended the designs himself, and exercised a careful concern for every relic of antiquity found among the ruins.

The grand entrance is formed by a lofty arched gateway flanked by two hexagonal towers. This gives admission to the court-yard, on entering which the eye is first attracted by a large bas-relief representing Alfred the Great instituting the trial by jury. On the right stands a modern chapel of Florid Gothic. Adjoining the chapel is the BARON'S HALL, a banquet-room much admired. This room is the most interesting in the castle, and was designed to commemorate the triumph of the barons over King John in the signing of the Magna Charta, the story of which is effectively illustrated in its numerous splendid painted glass windows. Its architecture, like that of the chapel, is in the style of the 14th century. The hall is 115 feet in length, by 35 in breadth, and lofty in proportion. The roof is of Spanish chestnut, elaborately carved. The south part of the quadrangle is an entire renewal of this part of the ancient building, and exhibits the insignia of the Howards in union with those of their predecessors. It has a grand entrance in the Norman style, elaborately carved, surmounted by colossal emblematical statues of Hospitality and Liberty. The north-east wing contains the LIBRARY (commenced in 1801), an apartment of great magnificence, measuring 120 feet in length, by 24 in width. The

GREAT DRAWING-ROOM is a fine apartment, commanding an extensive prospect of the vale of the Arun, and containing the family portraits. The DINING-ROOM embraces what was anciently the family chapel, and is spacious and lofty. Its central large window of stained glass represents the meeting of Solomon with the Queen of Sheba.

In point of antiquity the property of Arundel goes back to a very early date. It is mentioned in the will of Alfred the Great, and in *Domesday Book*. It was bestowed on Roger de Montgomery, commander of the Breton soldiers at Hastings, and held by him and his two sons till 1118, when it was granted to William de Albini, Earl of Sussex and Arundel, who married Queen Adeliza, widow of Henry I.

In mentioning the great families which have succeeded each other in the possession of Arundel, it is needless to say that the personal history of the Fitz-Alans and Howards is an integral portion of the history of England.

William Rufus occupied the castle in 1097 on his return from Normandy. It was besieged by Henry I. in 1102, and surrendered to him; and again by King Stephen in 1139, because the Empress Matilda had been granted refuge there by Queen Adeliza. Edward I. came here as a guest, and dated a Patent from the castle September 9, 1302. In 1397 a confederacy against Richard II. was formed within its walls.

In 1247 the castle and earldom passed to John Fitz-Alan, who married Isabel, sister and co-heiress of Hugh, the last earl. It remained in the family of the Fitz-Alans till 1580, when Henry, the last earl of that line, left an only daughter, Mary, and this lady, by marrying Thomas Howard, fourth Duke of Norfolk, brought Arundel and its honours to the great family which now holds them.

When Philip Howard, Earl of Arundel, was attainted in 1585, commissioners were appointed to make a return of the castle and its furniture to the Exchequer; and the inventory of the furniture of twenty-one rooms in it is preserved among the Burleigh MSS. in the British Museum. It is a very curious document, as showing the state and manner of living of a great nobleman in the time of Queen Elizabeth.

Few, if any families, have more greatly distinguished themselves in the service of their country than this; and few have suffered more severely, whether by confiscation of property or loss

of life. Of the latter class were Henry, the last earl of the
Fitz-Alan line, who espoused the cause of Queen Mary of England in opposition to that of Lady Jane Grey, and was imprisoned in the Tower by order of Queen Elizabeth. The keep
of the castle, the dairy, and park are thrown open to the public
on Mondays and Fridays. The cicerone to the keep will tell
the visitor that the subterranean passage in the centre of the
building once led to Amberley Castle, 5 miles distant. The new
and handsome ROMAN CATHOLIC CATHEDRAL (not yet completed)
was built by the present Duke at a cost of £100,000, and was
opened for worship in 1873.

Next in interest to the castle is ST. NICHOLAS' CHURCH, a
Perpendicular building, partly of flint and stone, which is still
beautiful, despite of Roundhead iconoclasts and eighteenth
century churchwardens. Waller's soldiers were quartered here
in 1643, and found ample scope for the exercise of their religious
zeal. In 1782 the carved roof was taken down and destroyed.

Roger de Montgomery established here in 1094 a Benedictine
Priory, which he bestowed upon the Abbey of Seez, in Normandy.
In 1380, this Priory was converted, by Richard Fitz-Alan, Earl of
Arundel, into a College, dedicated to the Holy Trinity, for a
master and twelve secular canons. He then began building the
present CHURCH, with the view of connecting it with his new
foundation. The College Chapel (82 feet by 28 feet) still
exists, at the east end, beyond the chancel. It is large and lofty,
and contains five of the Arundel tombs. The Church is cruciform, with nave, and aisles, transept, and low square tower, surmounted by a leaden spire. The nave measures 82½ feet by 50½
feet, and is ceiled with Irish oak; two frescoes on the north
wall represent the Seven Deadly Sins and Seven Works of Mercy.
The clerestory windows enclose quatrefoils. The vicarial pew
seems to have been the ancient stone pillar. In the south aisle
stands the original high altar, the only one in England said to
have escaped destruction at the Reformation. The College
Chapel opens through three Pointed arches into the Lady Chapel,
54 by 20 feet, containing brasses of a knight and spouse, 1418;
and "Sir" *Ewan Ertham*, first master of the College, d. 1432.

The Arundel tombs are as follow :—

1. *Thomas, 15th Earl of Arundel*, Lord Treasurer, and his wife *Beatrice*,
daughter of John, King of Portugal. The former, "a beardless figure in
white marble, recumbent, in robes and coronet, with a horse at his feet;"

the latter, "dressed in her robes, lies on an altar-tomb, surrounded by
twenty monkish figures, under a rich canopy of Gothic work." Died, 1215.

2. *John*, 16th Earl, who defended Southampton against the French,
and d. 1422; and *Eleanor*, daughter of Sir John Berkeley. The brasses
have been despoiled. This tomb is in the centre of the Lady Chapel.

3. *John*, 17th Earl (died 1434), in plate armour, with a close surcoat
and collar of SS. "Beneath, in the hollow of the tomb, he again appears
in his shroud, emaciated by death, well cut in white marble."—(*Pennant*).

4. *William*, 18th Earl, d. 1488, and his Countess *Joan*. Recumbent
effigies upon the altar-tombs of *Thomas*, 20th Earl, d. 1524, and *William*,
21st Earl, d. 1544. Their own tomb, without figures, stands under a
exquisitely light canopy, supported by four richly carved pillars. The lady
Joan with the peculiar oblong head-dress, was the sister of Richard Neville,
the king-making Earl of Warwick.

5. *Thomas*, 20th Earl, d. 1524. On the north side of the altar, and
bearing by a curious misappropriation, the effigy of Earl William. He was
the patron of Caxton the printer. In the same tomb lies the dust of
William, 21st Earl, d. 1544.

6. *Henry*, 22d Earl, d. 1579, last of the Fitz-Alans, commemorated by
a tablet over the tomb last described. He was imprisoned in the Tower
by Elizabeth for his share in his brother-in-law—the Duke of Norfolk's—
conspiracy in favour of Queen Mary of England. He introduced the use of
coaches into England.

There are no monuments to the Howards, though many of them are
here interred, and among them *Thomas*, 24th Earl of Arundel, d. 1646,
the collector of the Arundelian marbles and the friend of John Evelyn.

Some remains of the collegiate buildings, especially the
entrance gateway, adjoin the churchyard. The master's house
occupied the south-east angle; the refectory stood on the east;
the cells of the brethren ranged along the south and west sides of
the quadrangle. This college possessed the privilege of sanctuary.

A Hospice, dedicated to the Holy Trinity, and named the
Maison Dieu, was founded, about 1380, by Earl Robert. It provided for 20 poor men. It formed a small quadrangle, with
chapel and refectory, and was destroyed by Waller's soldiers in
1643. The present bridge was built out of the ruins in 1742.

The TOWN HALL, an ambitious castellated building, was
erected by Bernard, Duke of Norfolk, about 1832, at a cost of
£10,000. The principal room is 50 feet by 30, and 23 high.

LITTLEHAMPTON, 5 miles south of Arundel, forms one long
street on the Arun. It is reached in a few minutes by a short
branch line from Ford Junction on the L. B. and S.-C. Railway.
The mouth of the river forms a harbour from which there is
steam communication with France. Here the Empress Matilda
landed in 1139. The piers are of modern construction, a canal,

formed 1820-3, extends between Littlehampton, Arundel, and Portsmouth, and costs £160,000. A floating-bridge, as at Portsmouth, extends from shore to shore (370 feet). The CHURCH, 100 feet by 50, was erected in 1826 at a cost of £3000. It embodies some remains of the ancient building.

On the coast, about 1 mile east of Littlehampton, stands RUSTINGTON with a CHURCH partly Transition-Norman. The chancel and aisle are of later date. Preston is a small village, half-a-mile from the shore, where a CHURCH (at some distance) dates from the fifteenth century. The north door is Norman. CLIMPING is situated on the western bank of the Arun in a sequestered position. The CHURCH is an Early English cruciform building of singular design, and supposed to have been founded by John de Clymping, bishop of Chichester, in 1253.

ARUNDEL TO RUDGWICK.

This road conducts through the glades of Arundel Park, studded with majestic trees, shady avenues, and dells, dotted with herds of deer. To the east of the park, and beyond the Arun, lies Burpham, where there is a church of some antiquity. Near the churchyard there is a considerable entrenchment of uncertain origin. The soil here is chiefly chalk, and layers are frequently found composed of an aggregate of "detached ossiculæ of star-fishes." By following the course of the river we come to South Stoke, with our Early Norman church, and one mile farther to North Stoke—both of them seated in a neighbourhood which abounds with Celtic relics. At North Stoke, in 1834, a British canoe was dug up on the river-bank.

About 1 mile from the north boundary of the park the road passes to the left of Houghton. Chapel containing a brass, inserted in a slab of Petworth marble, for *Thomas Cheyne*, d. 1486.

About 5¼ m. from Arundel lies the picturesque old village of Amberley, containing an ancient CHURCH, half Norman, half Early Eng., with traces of mediæval frescoes. Its red consecration crosses, pulpit hour-glass, and brass for *John Wanlett*, d. 1424, are of interest. There are still some remains of the palace of the Bishops of Chichester, and the CASTLE, built by Bishop Rede, *temp.* Richard II. (1369-79). They occupy a low rock of sandstone, over-

looking the Wild Brook, and its fringe of cranberry bushes. The
original plan was nearly that of a parallelogram. At each corner
a square tower rises above the walls, which were 40 feet high;
the massive and imposing gateway was flanked by two round
towers (compare that of Lewes Castle) ; and the south side was
defended by a fosse. The present dwelling-house in the Green
Court was built by Bishop Sherbourne, in 1508.

The best view is obtained from the bridge which spans 'the
fosse. Over these ruins, the handiwork of Waller's Roundhead
troopers in 1643, the eternal ivy has thrown its rank luxuriance
and unwholesome beauty.

The patron of the vicarage of Amberley is the Bishop of
Chichester.

Beyond the sixth milestone, our road diverges to the right,
and passes through COLDWALTHAM (population, 120), i. e., the
village in the bleak woodland—and HARDHAM (population,
98), to PULBOROUGH. At HARDHAM there is a small Early
English church, and the river Arun flows through a tunnel, 400
yards long, bored in the hill of sandstone on which the village is
situated.

We cross the downs at PULBOROUGH (see p. 120), and proceed
over North Heath, and through a wild romantic countryside, to
BILLINGHURST (population, 1458), one of the settlements of
the Saxon tribe of the Belingas, situated on the main road in a
richly-wooded and well-watered district. It is 14 miles N.E. by
N. of Arundel. The Roman STANE STREET, from Regnum (Chichester) to London, crossed this parish, and terminated at
BILLINGSGATE. The CHURCH, dedicated to St. Mary, has a spire
which rises to the height of 120 feet, a landmark for the peasants
in the depths of the surrounding Weald. It contains a brass for
Thomas Bartlett, d. 1489, and *Elizabeth* his wife. Sir C. Goring
is the patron of the vicarage.

Five miles further, and our road joins the highway which
connects the Dorking and Guildford roads. Turning to the right,
we may reach Rusper, Ifield, and Crawley ; turning to the left, we
shall arrive at RUDGWICK (population, 1031). The village is
seated on a hill, commanding some fair prospects of Sussex and
Surrey. The CHURCH, dedicated to the Holy Trinity, consists of

a chancel, nave, north aisle, and western tower. There are three stone sedilia, under an arched canopy, in the chancel. Patron of the vicarage, Bishop of Chichester.

Having conducted the tourist to the borders of Surrey, we again return to our Chichester route.

MAIN ROUTE RESUMED—ARUNDEL TO CHICHESTER.

The FORD STATION (2¼ miles) affords the advantages of railway communication to the villages of FORD (population, 106),—a ferry across the Arun, and TORTINGTON (population, 104), where a house of Black Canons was founded by Hawse de Corbet, *temp.* Richard I. The CHURCH was probably built about the same time. Its font is enriched with Lombardic ornaments, and the chancel-arch with a moulding of grotesque heads of birds and beasts.

YAPTON (population, 609) is situated on the turnpike-road. Its CHURCH, except the chancel, is Early English. The font is very curious, and either Saxon or Early Norman. It is composed of black granite ; is large, circular, and rests on a square base. A cross patie fitchy is sculptured in each of the six semicircular niches which enrich the sides.

Yapton vicarage is attached to that of Walberton, valued at £218, and in the patronage of the Bishop of Chichester. WAL-BERTON (population, 578) lies one mile north of the Yapton station. WALBERTON HOUSE (R. Prime, Esq.) is a stately mansion set at the head of an ample lawn. It was built in 1817, from the designs of Smirke. The CHURCH, dedicated to St. Mary, is partly Early English.

We run through a country of little interest, catching pleasant glimpses of the sea on the one hand, and of the undulating crest of the Downs on the other, until, at 5 miles from Arundel, we reach BARNHAM JUNCTION and there take the branch line to BOGNOR (3½ miles south). There are several trains daily to and from Brighton.

BOGNOR (population, 3289. *Inns:* York, Norfolk)—*i.e.,* the rocky coast — is Worthing's twin-sister, a quiet, healthy watering-place, seated on a level, in face of the ever restless channel. A reef of rocks, about 2 miles in length, juts out from the shore, and forms a natural but insufficient breakwater. The geologist will find here septaria, turritella, rostellaricæ, and nautili.[*]

About 1785, Sir Richard Hotham, a wealthy Southwark hatter, determined upon acquiring the glory of a sea-side Romulus, and set to work to erect a town of first class villas in this pleasant spot, with a view of creating a truly *recherché* watering-place, to be known to posterity as "Hotham town." He spent £60,000, erected and furnished some commodious villas, but did not succeed in giving his name to his own creation, and died broken hearted in 1799. Fashion, however, after some slight delay, patronized the new English bath, and Bognor grew by degrees into its present prosperity.

The best streets are the Crescent, Hotham Place, and the Steyne. The CHURCH, dedicated to St. John, was built in 1793.

The PARISH CHURCH is at SOUTH BERSTED (population, 781), dedicated to St. Mary Magdalene, and built in 1405. The Archbishop of Canterbury is patron of the vicarage, which is valued at £381.

One mile east of Bognor, at a short distance from the shore, and, perhaps, in a situation which is even pleasanter than that of Sir Richard Hotham's "salubrious" but not very "lively" watering-place, is FELPHAM (population, 596). Here, in a delightful villa—standing almost in the centre of the hamlet—lived and died *William Hayley*, the author of the "Triumphs of Temper," but certainly better known to the readers of to-day as the friend and biographer of the poet Cowper. His death took place on the 12th of November 1820. Only forty years ago, and yet who reads a line of the poems of the man whom Mrs. Opie panegyrized, whom Cowper and Romney esteemed, whom his contemporaries regarded as "a gifted minstrel?"

FELPHAM CHURCH, dedicated to St. Mary, is mainly Perpendicular. The font is large and ancient. Remark the monument to Hayley, with an epitaph, long and verbose, by Mrs. Opie.

In the churchyard lies interred Dr. *Cyril Jackson*, d. 1819,

[*] "The sandstone rocks of Bognor are the ruins of a deposit once very extensive; the lowermost part is a dark grey limestone, the upper part is silicious. The Barn rocks, between Selsea and Bognor, the Houndgate and Sheet rocks on the west, and Mixen rocks on the south of Selsea, are portions of the same bed"—(*Dr. Mantell*).

Dean of Christ Church, Oxon, and tutor to George IV. He
spent the last years of his life at Felpham, and was visited here
on his deathbed by his royal pupil.

The following lines, on the tombstone of one William Steele,
a blacksmith, were written by Hayley :—

" My sledge and hammer lie reclin'd ;
My bellows, too, have lost their wind ;—
My fire's extinct,—my forge decay'd,
And in the dust my vice is laid ;—
My coal is spent,—my iron gone,—
The nails are driven,—my work is done."

Felpham Churchyard had the wall that surrounded it swept
away in a storm, the gravestones broken, and some of the bodies
washed into the sea.

[A pleasant excursion may be made either from Bognor, the Barnham, or Dray-
ton Stations to PAGHAM (population, 1022), a fishing village situated upon an inlet
of the sea, named Pagham Harbour, which dates from the fourteenth century. It is a
tidal harbour, with two islands before its narrow mouth. In a place called the
PARK,* outside the entrance, anchorage may be obtained in 4½ fathoms of water.
The "curiosity" of Pagham is its HUSHING WELL. The air is forced by the sea
from some submarine gully or cavern in the Pagham Bank, through the shingle, so
as to fret and disturb the whole surface of the water in an area of 130 feet by 30
feet, and produces a peculiar hissing noise which may be heard at a considerable
distance. The "edible" of Pagham is the Selsey cockle, found off this part of the
coast in great quantities, and to be classed by Fuller with the Amberley trout, the
Arundel mullet, and the wheat-ear of the Downs, among the "good things" of Sussex. There is excellent sport in this vicinity for the disciples of Bishop and Joe
Manton. In every little creek, on every solitary spur of sand, the wild fowl congre-
gate like a cloud of wings,—osprey, and tern, and the shrieking gull,—dusky sand-
pipers, whirling ring-dotterels, choughs, puffins, and guillemots.

The Early English CHURCH of Pagham, spite of repairs, is interesting. It is
dedicated to Thomas à Becket, and was therefore built after his canonization. The
manor belonged to the see of Canterbury, and the Archbishop had a palace here, of
which there are no remains. Observe the three-lighted east window, the paintings
of the sixteenth century were brought from a church in Rouen.

From Pagham the pedestrian may keep along the sands, when the tide is out, for
some miles, and visit Selsea (Seal's Island), and the bold promontory of SELSEA BILL.
The whole peninsula was at one time green, with an extensive forest,—the Forest of
Manwood, whose name may be traced in that of the Hundred (Manhood) wherein
the peninsula is now included. It is now a low flat plain, of London clay, with
occasional deep marshes, and is given up without remorse to the grazier. Nothing
of the romantic, nothing of the beautiful relieves its dreary uniformity. The sea itself seems to have surrendered its ancient grandeur, and instead of rolling in thunder
against a precipitous wall of chalk, steals craftily and silently over the muddy shore.

---

* The PARK, as late as the reign of Henry VIII., was a chase for deer. Bishop
Rede excommunicated certain unfortunates who had presumed to "rouse the hart"
in this episcopal preserve.

Its power as a Destroyer, however, has been asserted here for centuries, and the coast-line yearly recedes before its insidious advance. Selsea Isle is famous in Ecclesiastical History. Here Wilfred of York was wrecked about 680, and hospitably received by Edilwalch, King of the South Saxons, who with his Queen had previously been converted to Christianity, but reigned over a Pagan people. "Bishop Wilfred," says Bede, "by preaching to them, not only rescued them from the torment of eternal perdition, but also from the sufferings of temporal death, for no rain had fallen in that country side for three weary years, and a terrible famine had arisen, and cruelly struck down the people. Indeed, it is said, that groups of 40 or 50 men, worn out with want, would rush together to some steep rock, or down to the sea-shore, and perish by the headlong fall, or be devoured by the waters. But on the very day whereon the people accepted the baptism of faith, there fell from Heaven a soft and plenteous rain : once more the earth grew glad, the verdure again sprang up in the meadows, and a pleasant and abundant harvest followed"—(*Eccl. History*, v. iv. c. 13). The good bishop, however, was wise enough not to trust himself wholly to miraculous interposition. "He taught the people to get their food by fishing, for their seas and rivers abounded in fish, but they had no skill to catch any fish but eels. So the bishop's men, having borrowed eel-nets everywhere cast them into the waters, and by God's blessing they caught 300 fish of various kinds; and dividing these into three portions, bestowed a hundred upon the poor, a hundred upon those from whom they had hired the nets, and a hundred they reserved for their own use." A practical reading of the monkish homily, "Laborare est orare"—Work is Prayer—which we commend to the reader's admiration.

Here Wilfred founded a monastery, and he placed in it those of his disciples who had been banished from Northumbria. Its site, it is said, was about 1 mile east of Selsea Church, but the waters long ago overwhelmed its foundations, and neither of the old Saxon abbey, nor of the cathedral of the Episcopate of Selsey, can a stone be found by the most industrious archæologist.

SELSEY CHURCH was built, it is supposed, by Bishop Rede of Chichester, about 1369-1385. It stands about 2 miles inland. The roof is of recent date. The tower has never been completed. Here are several grave-stones of Sussex marble, inscribed with a cross, memorials probably of the old Saxon priests, removed from the ruins of the ancient cathedral. Effigies of a man and woman, with figures of St. George and St. Agatha, their patron-saints, commemorate *John Lews*, and *Agatha* his wife, d. 1537. A grave-stone in the churchyard, to the memory of two young men drowned while rendering assistance to a wrecked vessel, bears an epitaph by Hayley.

The fosse and vallum of the British encampment adjoin the churchyard.

☞ There is little to interest the tourist in the numerous villages which stud the Selsey peninsula. For his convenience, however, we append a few notes in a tabular form :—

BIRDHAM (population, 531), 4 miles from Chichester. CHURCH dedicated to St. Leonard. Rectory valued at £396, is in the patronage of the Dean and Chapter of Chichester.

EARNLEY (population, 137), 6½ miles from Chichester. Rectory valued at £450, in the patronage of the Bishop of Chichester, and, every third presentation, the Duke of Norfolk.

ITCHENOR, WEST (population, 254), 6½ miles south-west of Chichester. Small Early English CHURCH, dedicated to St. Nicholas. Rectory, valued at £174, in the patronage of the Lord Chancellor.

SIDLESHAM (population, 941), retains the name of its Saxon proprietor, whose "ham" or "home" is now situated at the head of a deep creek of the channel, and on the road from Chichester (6½ miles) to Pagham Harbour. There is an extensive tide-mill on the bank of the estuary already spoken of, "occasioned several centuries ago by a sudden irruption of the sea at Pagham, by which 2700 acres were devastated." The CHURCH, an Early English building, dedicated to St. Mary, is worth a visit. It contains an Edwardian font (*Dallaway*). Its embattled tower is probably Perpendicular. There is here an oaken chest, finely carved, and near the chancel is placed a mural monument, with effigies for *Rebecca Taylor*, d. 1631. The vicarage, valued at £182, is in the patronage of the Bishop of Chichester.

EAST WITTERING (population, 233), 1 mile from the sea, and 7 miles south-west of Chichester. "From the mouth of Chichester Harbour to the extremity of Chichester Hill, a distance of about 8 miles, the sea has encroached so as to have absorbed a considerable portion of the prebendal manor of Bracklesham"—(*Horsfield*). The bay thus formed has excellent sands, affording at low water a capital promenade, and its occasional "patches of soft clay" are full of fossil shells. The most interesting spot is immediately in the neighbourhood of Bracklesham Barn, " especially at about a furlong to the east, where there is a small break or chine in the low clay cliff. Here there is a stratum of light green marly sand, abounding in venericardii planicosta" (*Bowerbank*), myliobates, turritella, lucina serrata, cerithium giganteum, and other fossils.

EAST WITTERING CHURCH is partly Early Norman. The Bishop of London is the patron of the rectory, which is valued at £200.

Between East and West Wittering lies the hamlet of CAKEHAM. The Bishops of Chichester had a marine residence here, and Bishop Sherbourne, inspired by the noble sea-view which this position commands, erected a lofty prospect-tower of brick, hexagonal in construction, which is still in existence. We take our hats off, as we pass it, in honour of a prelate of such excellent taste.

WITTERING, WEST (population, 609), is 7½ miles south-west of Chichester. The district is low and level, but nevertheless it affords "marine views" of uncommon extent, variety, and magnificence. The CHURCH dates from the thirteenth century. Three oaken stalls are preserved in the chancel, and a canopied tomb of Caen stone, sculptured with bas-reliefs of the Annunciation and Resurrection, commemorates *William Ernley*, d. 1545. The vicarage, valued at £300, is in the patronage of the Bishop of Chichester.]

During this long digression we must fain suppose that "the gentle reader" has sped through a rich but level country, past the BARNHAM STATION [OVING (population, 1404,—*i.e.*, the sheepfold—lies to the right], and arrived at the cathedral city of

CHICHESTER.

[Population, 8114. *Hotels*: Dolphin, Anchor, Globe. 60 m. from London, by road; 79 m. by rail; 28 m. from Brighton, by rail; 13 m. from Petworth; 10 m. from Arundel; 16 m. from Portsmouth; 3½ m. from Boxgrove; 6 m. from Bognor; and 10 m. from Midhurst.

☞ Omnibuses run between the city and the station. Coaches run daily to and from Godalming, three times a week to Petworth, and daily to Midhurst.

CHICHESTER, the ancient REGNUM, presents, in its main streets, running in straight lines east and west, and north and south, and its lesser streets diverging at right angles from them—an exact reproduction of the old Roman plan. Its walls, 1½ mile in circuit, stand on the fcundations of the ancient walls, and are fashioned out of their materials. A portion of the old wall, on the west side of the city, now forms a pleasant public walk. Coins, urns, bits of tesselated pavement, and other relics, remind us, at almost every step, of its Roman masters—of the city where Cogidubnus, King of the Regni, and the viceroy of the Emperor Claudius, held his royal state. It stood at the point where the Stane Street, which connected Regnum with Londinium, crossed the great via to Portus Magnus (Porchester) ; at the head of the east branch of the creek now known as Chichester Harbour, and in the shelter and shadow of the lofty Southern Downs. When Ella landed on the Sussex coast, his forces pushed forward from their point of disembarkation (at CYMEN'S ORA, now Keynor, 7 miles south, so named from one of Ella's sons) across the level marshes into Regnum, which they devastated with fire and sword, and out of its ruins built up a Saxon settlement, called, in honour of their chief leader, CISSA'S CEASTER. We hear but little of it during the Anglo-Saxon supremacy. After the Conquest it was absorbed among the possessions of Robert de Montgomery, who built a small castle in its north-east quarter, destroyed in the first year of Henry the First. Three mints were established here, temp. King John. Its walls, strengthened by 16 semicircular towers, were frequently repaired, but could not resist the assault of Sir William Waller's troops, who surprised here Lord Hopton and the royalists in 1643. The siege was of the briefest. "They within the town were easily reduced to straights they could not contend with ; for besides the enemy without, against which the walls and the weather seemed of equal power, and the small stock of provisions, which in so short a time they were able to draw hither, they had cause to apprehend their friends would be weary before their enemies, and that the citizens would not prove a trusty part of the garrison ; and their number of common men was so small that the constant duty was performed by the officers and gentlemen of quality, who were absolutely tired out ; so that, after a week or ten days' siege, they were compelled, upon no better articles than quarter, to deliver the city "—(Clarendon).

The victorious Roundheads immediately began their icono-

CHICHESTER CATHEDRAL.

clastic labours. They demolished the cathedral organ, " crying
in scoff, ' Hark ! how the organs goe !'" defaced its ornaments,
destroyed its tombs, and despoiled them of their brasses ; battered
down the churches of St. Pancras and St. Bartholomew ; and
pillaged the houses of all who were suspected of being " malig-
nants." Sir William Waller fixed his head-quarters at the Grey
Friary House, and " billeted " his soldiers in the Cathedral.

It may be added that Algernon Sidney was governor of
Chichester in 1645.

The poet Collins was born in this quiet cathedral city on
Christmas day, 1720, and died here, in a house in the cloister,
in 1756. Another of its worthies was Bishop Juxon, born August
24, 1591. Hayley was also a Chichester celebrity — " a star of
the sixth magnitude," which hid " its diminished head" after the
uprising of greater minds. During the greater part of his life
he resided on his estate of Gartham, Sussex. His own poetry
is now almost never read, but he will be remembered as the
friend and biographer of Cowper. Mention may also be made
of the art-labours of George Smith and John Smith, "whose
genius in the art of landscape-painting obtained for them a
merited distinction in their native city."

The first object in Chichester to which the tourist's attention
will naturally be directed, is its CATHEDRAL, established here
temp. William I., on the removal of the episcopate from Selsey
to the ancient Regnum. It was erected on the site of a Saxon
monastery, dedicated to St. Peter, and had but a brief existence.
It was destroyed by fire in 1114. Bishop Ralph immediately
commenced another building, and so energetically pushed forward
its works, that it was nearly completed in 1123. Of this venerable structure much remains. The additions it has received will
best be understood from the following chronological state-
ment :—

STYLE.	ADDITIONS.	DATE.
Norman.	The Nave, North and South Aisles, and Tri-forium, are Bishop Ralph's	1091-23
Early English.	The higher stones of the South-west Tower, and the Clerestory of the Nave, the West and South Porches, were added by Bishop Seffrid, who lengthened the Choir and vaulted the Roof	1188-99

148 CHICHESTER.

STYLE.	ADDITIONS.	DATE.
Early English.	The Marble Shafts, chiefly of Petworth marble, were erected by Bishop Fitzrobert	1204-10
„	The Spire and Chapter House, by Bishop Neville	1222-45
„	The two Exterior Aisles, North and South, Bishop de la Wych . .	1245-53
,,	The Lady Chapel (now the Library), Bishop de St. Lespard	1288-1304
Decorated.	The Presbytery, Sacristy, South Transept, and Bell Tower, by Bishop John de Langton,	1305-38
„	The Reredos and Carved Stalls and Decorations of the South Transept, by Bishop Sherbourne	1508-36
Perpendicular.	The Oratory, now the Organ Screen, by Bishop Arundel	1458-78
„	The Organ, built by Harris, 1678, improved by Gray and Davidson, 1844, and Hill	1851
„	The Throne, by Bishop Mawson . .	1740-54

Entering the Cathedral by its WESTERN PORCH (Early English, and built by Bishop Seffrid II.), we first remark the five divisions of the NAVE—a characteristic which distinguishes it from all other English Cathedrals, but which is not altogether to be admired. Much picturesqueness of effect, however, is produced by their constantly shifting lights and shadows. The clerestory, and the Purbeck marble of the piers are to be ascribed to Bishop Seffrid. Bishop Richard de la Wych (1245-1253), was the builder of the additional aisles, designed for chantries or side chapels. The piscinas and aumbries in the walls indicate the positions of the different altars. Observe that the sideshafts are triple, the bearing shafts " clustered in threes," with three triple vaulting-ribs above, symbolic of the Holy Trinity, to whom Bishop Seffrid dedicated this part of the Cathedral.

The stained glass in the two western windows is by Wailes. The larger one is a memorial to the late Dean Chandler, erected by the parishioners of All Souls, St. Marylebone, where he was rector for many years. The memorial window, in the north aisle, to Sir Thomas Reynell, is by O'Connor, that to F. E. Freeland, by Willement.

The ARUNDEL CHANTRY is in the north aisle. It contains the tomb of Caen stone—restored in 1843 by Richardson,—for

Richard Fitzalan, Earl of Arundel, beheaded for high treason in
1397. This tomb was opened by order of Richard II. shortly
after the earl's interment, because the common people believed
that a miracle had been wrought, and that his head had grown
to his body again.

A CHANTRY, dedicated to ST. JOHN THE BAPTIST, occupies
the end of the aisle. Here there is a stately Decorated tomb,
with effigy, of a nameless lady, supposed by some authorities to
be Maud, countess of Arundel, and pronounced by Flaxman the
finest in England.

☞ MEMORIALS IN THE NAVE.—The Hon. *William Huskis-
son,* d. 1830, the statue by Carew ; *Collins,* the poet, d. 1756,
the medallion by Flaxman. The poet is pictured as studying
the Scriptures. " I have but one book," he said to Dr. Johnson
shortly before his death, " and that is the best." At his feet lies
a volume of " The Passions." Two female figures, Love and
Religion, are placed upon the pediment, and underneath is lettered an epitaph by Hayley and Sargent,—

" Ye who the merits of the dead revere,
Who hold misfortune's sacred genius dear,
Regard this tomb ; where Collins' hapless name
Solicits kindness with a double claim.
Strangers to him, enamour'd of his lays,
This fond memorial to his talents raise.
For this the ashes of the bard require,
Who touch'd the tenderest notes of Pity's Lyre."

The monuments (in the south aisle) of *Jane Smith* and *Agnes
Cromwell,* are also Flaxman's handiwork. The memorial window,
representing the martyrdom of St. Stephen, is by Wailes.

The CHOIR, and the east aisles behind it, were built by
Bishop Seffrid. The latter are Transition Norman in style, and
exhibit the gradual change from the circular to the pointed arch.
Observe the grotesque bones in which the vaulting ribs terminate.
It is difficult to imagine what object the sculptor could have had
in view when he carved those monstrous human faces. Was it
satirical ? Did any of his contemporaries trace a likeness to certain
living notabilities in those exaggerated lineaments ? Behind the
altar-screen stand the monuments of Bishop *Storey,* d. 1503 ;
Bishop *Henry King* (1641-69), poet and prelate ; Bishop *Grove,*
d. 1596 ; and Bishop *Carlton,* d. 1685. A purbeck slab, in
the pavement, is figured with two hands holding up a heart

and inscribed "Ici git le cœur de Maud." The rest. is illegible. The tomb of Bishop *Day*, d. 1556, is on the right.

The SCREEN which separates choir and nave was erected by Bishop *Arundel* (1458-78), and is known as his "Oratory." A nicked arcade surmounts these arches, which are enriched with quatrefoils in their spandrils. The stalls in the choir, the altar-screen, and the decorations of the south transept, were the gift of Bishop Sherbourne, and justify old Fuller's quaint eulogy :— " Now though Seffride bestowed the cloth and making on the church, Bishop Sherbourne gave the trimming and best lace thereto."

The NORTH TRANSEPT forms the parish church of St. Peter the Great, more commonly called the Sub-Deanery. The SOUTH TRANSEPT was lengthened, and its beautiful window inserted, by Bishop Langton (1305-38), but the Roundhead troopers destroyed the stained glass. The Bishop's .tomb, considerably defaced, stands beneath it, and close at hand, the memorial of *John Smith*, Esq. of Dale Park. The tomb near the choir is considered to be that of Bishop *Richard de la Wych*, d. 1253, the last Englishman who received " the honour " of canonization. In the ACTA SANCTORUM may be read, in considerable detail, the miracles wrought by St. Richard of Chichester. The tomb was restored by Richardson in 1847, and the small figures in the arches are entirely his handiwork. Hither the devout pilgrims of Kent, Sussex, and Hampshire were wont to repair, and lay their offerings, and branches plucked on the road, on the shrine of the Sussex saint.

The figures of the Bishops of Selsey and Chichester which enrich the walls were Bishop Sherbourne's donation to his Cathedral. From the "family-likeness" between them, one would imagine that they respresent a succession of great grand-fathers, fathers, and sons, all of the same remarkable race. The English sovereigns are presented on the opposite wall, and above them a picture, in two panels, represents Cadwalla bestowing Selsey upon St. Wilfrid, and Henry VIII. confirming the grant to Bishop Sherbourne. Cadwalla is a portrait of Henry VII, and all the kings, nobles, and ecclesiastics introduced are costumed in the Tudor style. A Flemish artist, Theodore Bernardi, and his sons were the artists employed by Bishop Sherbourne.

The railed-off portion of the transept is now made use of as an ecclesiastical court. The old consistory (Perpendicular in style) was a room over the porch, to which access was obtained by a spiral staircase in the nave. It opened upon the Lollards' Prison through a sliding panel.

A very curious oaken chest, 8 feet long, preserved in the SACRISTY; and two carved slabs (discovered in 1829) which represent the Raising of Lazarus, and Martha and Mary meeting the Saviour, are supposed to have been removed from Selsey. Near these sculptures stands the tomb of Bishop *Sherbourne*, d. 1536, restored at the expense of New College, Oxon, to which foundation the prelate had intrusted its custody.

At the extreme east end of the Cathedral is the LADY CHAPEL, built by Bishop de St. Lespard (1288-1305), at an expense of 1250 marks. It is now little better than a mortuary chapel for the Duke of Richmond's family. A slab is inscribed "DOMUS ULTIMA, 1750,"—an inscription which suggested to Dr. Clarke, one of the residentiaries, the following bitter epigram :—

" Did he who thus inscribed this wall,
Not read, or not believe, St. Paul,
Who says there is, where'er it stands,
Another house, not built with hands ?
Or may we gather from these words
That house is not a house—for Lords ?"

Under two arches in the passage which leads to the Lady Chapel, is placed the black marble slab inscribed to Bishop *Ralph*, d. 1123,

The large canopied tomb in the north aisle is that of Bishop *Moleynes*, a faithful adherent of the Lancasterian party, murdered at Portsmouth in 1459.

The CHAPTER LIBRARY, with its rare MSS., printed books, and relics, is preserved in the Lady Chapel. Among the relics are a silver chalice and paten, an agate thumb-ring (or Basilidian gem) inscribed with a Gnostic talisman, two other rings, and a leaden cross, discovered in 1829 in the stone coffins of two prelates, who are supposed to have been *Godfrey*, the second bishop of Chichester, d. 1088, and Bishop *Seffrid II.*, d. 1205.

From the south aisle we pass into the quiet CLOISTERS (Perpendicular), which afford some fine views of the general characteristics of the Cathedral. The space they enclose is called " Paradise." The SPIRE* (which is a copy of the original) is 270

* The original spire fell in 1861 during a gale of wind; the new one, under the direction of Sir G. G. Scott, was erected in 1866.

feet high, and so resembles that of Salisbury that the local saying
ran,—" The master-mason built Salisbury, and his man built
Chichester." Mr. Truman, in an able paper on the architecture
of the Cathedral, to which the tourist may with advantage refer
(*Sus. Arch. Coll.*, vol. i.), points out that in these Cathedrals alone
there is " a visible centre and axis to the whole building, viz., the
summit of the spire, and a line let fall from it to the ground.
Salisbury was so constructed at first. Chichester was made exactly
central, to an inch, by the additions of the Lady Chapel and west
porch. Michael Angelo's most perfect outline, the pyramidal, is
thus gained. The eye is carried upward to the spire point from
the chapels clustering at the base, along the roof of pinnacles."
Detached from the building, on the north side, rises the campanile
or bell-tower, 120 feet high. It has four turrets at its summit,
exactly similar to those at the base of the spire, whence it has
been conjectured that it was built (at the same period) to receive
the bells from the old tower. The stone made use of was quar-
ried near Ventnor, in the Isle of Wight.

DIMENSIONS OF THE CATHEDRAL.

	Length in feet.	Breadth in feet.	Height in feet.
Nave	156	91·9	62·3
Choir	105	59	60
Presbytery	52·2	...	...
Lady Chapel	62·9	20·7	22
Spire	...	...	271
South-west tower	...	...	95
Transept	131	24·3	...
Campanile	...	...	120

Total length 380 feet.

The Cathedral establishment includes a dean, four canons, five
minor canons, seven lay vicars, ten choristers, and four Wyke-
hamical prebends. The average yearly income is £5100.

Among the more notable bishops may be named—Ralph de
Neville, Lord Chancellor, 1222-45 ; Richard de la Wych, or St.
Richard, 1245-53 ; Adam Moleynes, Henry VI.'s councillor,
1445-9 ; Lancelot Andrewes, the sycophantic favourite of James
I., 1605-9 ; Brian Duppa, 1638-41 ; and Francis Hare, the
adversary of Hoadley, in the famous Bangorian controversy
1731-40.

The EPISCOPAL PALACE is situated to the west of the cathedral, and consists of a spacious mansion whose two wings are connected by an open corridor. The CHAPEL is of the age of Henry III., with windows of a later date. Remark the timber ceiling of Bishop Sherbourne's REFECTORY, painted in compartments with scrolls and armorial bearings by the Bernardis.

The MARKET CROSS, at the point of junction of the four great Cistercian thoroughfares, was built by Bishop Storey about 1480, and considerably defaced by Waller's troopers. The dial was given, in 1724, by Dame Elizabeth Farrington. "Its vaulted roof is supported by a thick central pillar, and by a series of arches octagonal in form, and highly ornamented with coats of arms and other ornaments." It is altogether an interesting and a picturesque structure, which the townsmen keep in excellent repair.

The GUILD HALL, situated in the priory park, near the end of North Street, was formerly a chapel belonging to a monastery of Grey Friars. Behind the magistrates' seats may be seen the ancient Early English sedilia. A circular mound in the garden was, perhaps, the Calvary of the ancient priory.

A rapid visit to the Parochial Churches of the city must now be undertaken.

ST. PETER THE GREAT, in the Early Decorated style, was erected about 1850, and underwent additions in 1881. Until 1841 the north transept of the cathedral formed the parish church. Within the precincts of this parish, and in the cathedral cloisters, lies *William Chillingworth*, d. 1644, the famous author of "The Religion of Protestants a safe way to Salvation." When his funeral procession arrived at the grave, it was met by his impetuous opponent, the Presbyterian Cheynell, who flung Chillingworth's immortal work upon his coffin "to rot," he said, "with its author, and see corruption!"

ALL SAINTS', IN THE PALLANT, is of great antiquity. Some portions may be Early Norman. Hayley, the poet, was baptized here, November 25, 1745.

The church of ST. ANDREW, in East Street, was built *temp.* Henry VII. At a depth of 4 feet beneath it lies a Roman tessellated pavement. Collins was buried here in 1756.

ST. MARTIN'S, in St. Martin's Lane, was rebuilt about forty years ago, in a style which may be denominated Modern Gothic. The east window, with its stained glass, is good.

ST. OLAVE'S, in North Street, recently restored, occupies the site of a Roman building, and is, perhaps, the oldest Christian church in England. Roman bricks were employed in its construction, and the small door on the south side may even be of Roman work.

ST. PANCRAS' CHURCH stands at a small distance beyond the East Gate. It was nearly demolished during Waller's siege of the city in 1642, and not rebuilt until 1750. ST. BARTHOLOMEW'S was destroyed at the same time. There is nothing of interest in the present building.

The CHAPEL, dedicated to St. John, stands on the site of the Black Friars', near the East Gate. It was built in 1813 from the designs of James Elmes.

[The patrons and annual incomes of these benefices are as follows :—All Saints, R., £45, Archbishop of Canterbury ; St. Andrew, R., £30, Dean and Chapter of Chichester ; St. Martin, R., £57, the same patrons ; St. Olave, R., £56, the same : St. Pancras, R., £95, Simeon's Trustees ; St. Peter the Great, V., £300, Dean and Chapter ; St. Peter the Less, R., £56, the Dean ; St. Bartholomew, P. C., £65, the Dean ; St. Paul's, P. C., the Dean and Chapter ; St. John's, Trustees.]

ST. MARY'S HOSPITAL is a picturesque Decorated pile, which the tourist must not fail to visit. It was founded in 1229, and replaced a nunnery originally established in 1173. The revenues are apportioned among a *custos* or warden, six women, and two men, whose rooms are constructed in the side walls of the Refectory or Long Hall. The CHAPEL, which contains some excellent carved work, is divided from this hall by an open oaken screen. The arched roof and its huge timbers, resting on low stone walls, deserves examination.

Some houses in the upper part of South Street were built, it is said, by Wren. The Philosophical Society have their Museum of Local Antiquities and Natural History in this street, which communicates with the Cathedral Close by the CANONS' GATE, built by Bishop Sherbourne, whose arms are sculptured above the entrance.

The OTTER MEMORIAL COLLEGE (for training schoolmasters), founded by Bishop Otter, and erected in 1849-50, from Butler's designs ; and the entrenchment on the Goodwood road, known as the BROYLE (from *bruillum*, a coppice), have each a special interest for different classes of tourists.

[HINTS FOR RAMBLES.—1. To Tangmere and Boxgrove Church. Visit Halnaker House ; cross to Goodwood and return by East Lavant.—2. Through Appledram, Donnington, and Sidlesham, to Selsey. Return by way of Pagham and North Mundham.—3. By the Portsmouth road to Bosham. Keep northwards to Funtington. Thence to West Stoke and Mid Lavant.—4. Keep across the hills to Cocking, and thence by way of Heyshot and Graffham into the Guildford road. Return through Boxgrove.—5. By road to Arundel. Visit Arundel Castle and Leominster. Return from Arundel Station by rail.—By rail to Barnham Station. Visit Bognor and South Bersted. Cross the country to Oving and Tangmere (north), and return by the Brighton road.]

BRANCH ROUTE—CHICHETSER to PULBOROUGH.

If we leave Chichester by the Guildford road we shall reach, at 2 miles from the cathedral city, the highway which diverges to Brighton. TANGMERE (population, 221) lies at some small distance beyond us. Its Early English Church, dedicated to St. Andrew, consists of a nave and chancel. Part of the paving of the latter is a curious combination of bricks, stones, plain and ornamented aisles. The Duke of Richmond is patron of the rectory, which is valued at £282.

A cross road leads us from this little village through BOX-GROVE (population, 755), into the Guildford road, 4 miles from Chichester.

BOXGROVE CHURCH is not one of the least interesting in the country. It embodies portions of Boxgrove Priory, founded in 1117 by Robert de Haiâ, Lord of Halmacro, for three Benedictine monks, and dedicated to the Virgin and St. Blaise. Roger St. John, who married the Lord of Halmacro's heiress, added three more, and his sons increased the number to fifteen. When suppressed by King Henry VIII. there were but nine monks, and their annual revenues were estimated at £189, 19s.

The present parish church is supposed to have been the original choir. Some portions of the ancient nave (apparently of a still earlier date) may be traced in the broken arches west of the church. The Chapter House is attached externally to the north transept. Its Norman doorway probably led to a cloister which extended to the Refectory and the habitations of the monks. A gap, generally inhabited by browsing sheep, now separates the Refectory from the Church. Marks of a piscina may just be discerned.

The CHURCH consists of a low tower, nave, and chancel, side aisles, and north and south transept, and a space westward of the tower which has been characterized as the most ancient part of the whole building. Its length is 124 feet; width of the nave, 24 feet; of each of the aisles, 13 feet 6 inches. The east window is Early English, of three large lights, and very fine.

The interior contains six tombs of great antiquity, but which it is almost impossible to identify with any degree of satisfaction. Two of the three placed against the south wall of the south aisle probably contain the dust of Olive and Agatha, daughters of William de Albini, Earl of Arundel, and Queen Alice the Fair. Other two tombs *may* enshrine the remains of *Thomas de Poynings*, d. 1429, and his wife *Philippa*, Countess of Arundel. The Delawarr SACELLUM, or SHRINE, dated 1532, is very curious and beautiful. Its length is 14 feet, its height 12 feet, and it bears the inscription—" Of y^r charite pray for ye souls of Thomas La Ware and Elyzabeth hys Wyf." It is richly carved in stone, and profusely ornamented.

The pulpit is of carved oak. The font is ancient. The Duke of Richmond is patron of the vicarage, which is valued at £750.

About half a mile to the left lie the scanty remains of HAL-NACRE or HALNAKER HOUSE, built by Sir Thomas West, Lord Delawarr, who also fashioned for himself "a poor chapell" at Boxgrove Church. The walls were castellated. The gateway, furnished with a portcullis, was furnished with small octangular towers, leading into a square court. The surrounding Park is enriched with noble groups of Spanish chesnut, in whose shadow a large herd of deer disport.

We cross from this point westward into GOODWOOD PARK (Duke of Richmond), to which the tourist has at all times ready access. The mansion can only be seen during the family's absence. Of the luxuriantly wooded park (1214 acres) much might be said and written in commendation; with respect to the house it is otherwise. The architects were Sir William Chambers (who built the south wing) and Wyatt. The centre is 160 feet long, and ornamented with a double colonnade; each of the two receding wings is flanked by towers, and 106 feet in length.

[The COLLECTION of PICTURES is large, but contains few *chefs d'œuvres*. The HALL is adorned by some fine Vandykes—Charles I., Henrietta Maria in all her fatal beauty, and their five children; Charles II. by Sir *Peter Lely*; Louise de Querouailles, Duchess of Portsmouth, *Kneller*; her son, Charles, first Duke of Richmond, and his wife Anne, *Kneller*; Sir William Waller, by *Lely*; and the Duchess of Richmond. Sir *Thomas Lawrence*.

The DRAWING-ROOM, 35 feet by 23, is hung with Gobelin tapestry (the gift of Louis XV. to Duke Charles), representing the adventures of Don Quixote. The chimney-piece, sculptured by Bacon with the story of Venus and Adonis, cost £150. Here are preserved in a cabinet "a worked shirt of Charles I., and some silver articles used during the infancy of Charles II."

The DINING-ROOM, 45 feet by 23 feet, where the allied Sovereigns were banqueted on their visit to England in 1814, contains a bust of Wellington, by *Turnelli*; and Nollekens' busts of William Pitt and the Marquis of Rockingham. The MUSIC ROOM contains a fine picture of a ruined sea-port by *Salvator Rosa;* portraits of the Marquis of Montrose, Henry Carew the song writer, and witty Pettigrew, by *Vandyck;* the Duke of Monmouth, *Kneller;* and specimens of Lely and others. In the ANTE-ROOM may be noticed four portraits by *Sir Joshua*, and a William Pitt, by *Gainsborough.*

The LIBRARY presents to our notice the third Duke of Richmond, by *Romney;* and the fourth Duke, by *Jackson.* The BILLIARD ROOM, Lord Anson, by *Romney;* and some tolerable landscapes by the two Smiths of Chichester. Here, too, is hung the highly curious "Cenotaph of Lord Darnley," removed from the Chateau D'Aubigny, where it was accidentally discovered. In the right hand corner an inscription indicates the subject of the picture :—"Tragica et lamentabilis internecio serenissimi Henrici Scotorum Regis." Other inscriptions record that the picture was begun in October 1567 (seven months after the murder), and completed in the following January. It has been ascribed to Levinus Venetianus. Small designs representing the scene of the murder, the murdered man's body beneath a tree in the orchard, the battle of Carberry Hill, and the city of Edinburgh, surround a large oval composition in which King James, the Earl and Countess of Lennox (Darnley's parents), and others are pictured kneeling before Darnley's corpse, which is deposited at the base of an altar.

The walls of the STONE STAIRCASE are enriched with *Hogarth's* picture of "The Lady's Last Stake;" the Judgment of Paris, *Guido;* Marriage at Cana, *Paolo Veronese;* the Madonna, *Parmegiano;* Antiochus and Stratonice, *Barry;* Duke of Monmouth, *Lely;* and specimens of the Smiths of Chichester, Hudson, and Romney. The LONG HALL contains two views of London from the terrace and gardens of Richmond House, Whitehall, by *Canaletti.*

The PARK is finely ordered in its alternations of the artistic and the natural; from the ascent in the rear of the house some good prospects may be enjoyed. About 150 cedars of Lebanon remain out of 1000 planted by the third Duke of Richmond in 1761. There is a noble avenue of chestnuts, and some glorious cypresses in the High Woods, near the house, where, also, is preserved the remarkable Brito-Roman slab discovered at Chichester in 1731 (together with the remains of the stone wall of a temple), when the foundations for the Council Chamber were excavated. It is a slab of grey Purbeck marble, and was thus inscribed. [The letters in italics indicate those which have been conjecturally supplied.]

> "*N*eptuni et Minervæ temptum
> *Pro* salute *domus* divinæ
> *Ex* anchoritate *Ti*beriis Claudii
> Cogidubin r. leg. aug. in Brit.
> *Collegium* fabror. et qui in eo
> *A sacris* sunt d. a. d. donante aream
> *Pudente* pudentini fil."

*** In explanation of this inscription it may be added that the "collegium fabrorum" was probably a company of smiths or shipwrights of Chichester, who would naturally regard Neptune and Minerva as their patrons. Cogidubnus was highly rewarded for his fidelity to the Roman alliance, and, according to the Roman fashion, assumed the name of his patron, the Emperor Tiberius Claudius. The site of the temple, whose foundation stone was laid by Cogidubnus, was given by Pudens, son of Pudentinus, who is supposed to be the British Christian, a disciple of St. Paul's, referred to in conjunction with Claudia in the second epistle to Timothy, c. iv., v. 21, and also named by Martial.]

The GOODWOOD RACE COURSE, on the high ground, 1 mile north-east of the house, commands a magnificent landscape. The *Goodwood races*, a well-known aristocratic gathering, were established in 1802. Other points of different degrees of interest, either in the Park or its immediate vicinity, are *Cairney Seat*, so named from an old retainer of the Richmonds ; the *Pheasantry*, in a leafy hollow of the chalk ; the *Stables*, which are complete in every detail ; the great *Lebanon Cedar*, 25 feet in girth ; the pleasant rustic villa at *Molecomb* ; the circular camp of the *Trundle*, enclosing 5 acres, which crowns the summit of St. Roche's Hill (locally Rock's Hill), 702 feet above the sea-level.

Goodwood, or Godinwood, derived its name from its Saxon owner, Godwinus. It was purchased from the Comptons, in 1720, by the first Duke of Richmond, the son of Madam Carwell (Louise de Querouailles) and Charles II.

About 2 miles from Boxgrove, to the right of the main road, and at some short distance from it, lies EARTHAM (population, 103). Hayley resided here until 1800, when he disposed of his estate to Huskisson, the statesman, whose life was the first sacrifice to "the railway giant." He enlarged the house, and made considerable improvements in the vicinity. The Early English CHURCH consists of a chancel, nave, and north aisle. The chancel arch is Norman, and very fine. A beautiful sculpture by Flaxman commemorates *Thomas Hayley*, d. 1800, the poet's only child. There is a tablet in the north aisle to Huskisson's memory, but the unfortunate statesman was buried at Liverpool.

The vicarage, valued at £187, is in the patronage of the Lord Chancellor.

We next reach UP WALTHAM (population, 67)—where there is an Early English CHURCH, with an apsidal chancel—and turning to the right, ascend the slopes of Sutton Hill. From its crest we command a panorama of wood, and dale, and glen, and village, which we treasure up as one of " things of beauty," which are " joys for ever." Passing through SUTTON (population,

389. *Inn :* The White Horse) we wind through a pleasant blooming lane to BIGNOR (population, 203), on an excursion into Roman England. For it is neither BIGNOR PARK nor BIGNOR CHURCH that draws us hither into the depths of the Weald, but the remains of a Roman villa, of more than ordinary interest, first excavated in 1811. Bignor is the "Ad decimam" of the *itinerary* of Richard of Cirencester, that is, a station at the *tenth* milestone from Regnum,—"a halting-place which was probably established at this point of the Roman road on account of the vicinity of the great villa ; just as a modern railway ' lord' procures a station in the neighbourhood of his own residence."

The remains are now protected from the weather by some wooden huts. The fields where they are situated have been long known as the Berry field, and the Town field ; " the former no doubt because it had been the site of a principal mass of buildings (from the Anglo-Saxon *beorh*), and the other because it was an old tradition among the inhabitants of the parish that the town of ' Bignor' once stood there."

In July 1811, a ploughman, at work in the Berry field, struck his share against what proved to be part of a beautiful Roman pavement, which had evidently belonged to a large and handsome room. A series of careful excavations, under the superintendence of Lysons, the antiquary, brought to light the pavements and foundations of a Roman villa of considerable magnitude. They were traced in fact to an extent of about 600 feet in length, and nearly 350 feet in breadth. The principal household buildings formed about half that length. They stood round an inner court, which was nearly a rectangular parallelogram, about 150 feet by 100 feet. Its aspect was, in its length, nearly north-west and south-east. Round this court ran a beautiful *crypto-porticus*, or covered gallery, 10 feet wide, with a fine tessellated pavement. At the north angle there was a small square room, with an " extremely elegant tessellated pavement." On the north-east side were placed the chief apartments. The first apartment was here discovered in 1811, and presented two divisions (as in a London front and back drawing-room), which may probably have been separated by movable hangings. In each division may be noticed a circular compartment, one 16 feet in diameter, the other 17 feet 6 inches ; the larger pictorially illustrated with dancing nymphs,—the smaller with the rape of Ganymede. " This pavement so completely resembles one at Avenches in Switzerland, executed about the reign of Titus, that this Sussex villa has been assigned to the same period"—(*Murray*). There is a stone cistern or fountain in the centre of the larger room, 4 feet in diameter, and 1 foot 7¾ inches in depth, which appears to have been filled by a jet d'eau. "To judge by the remains, the walls had been beautifully painted in fresco, fragments of which were lying about, the colours perfectly fresh. A fragment or two of small Doric columns were found among the rubbish of this apartment"—(*Wright*, Wanderings of an Antiquary).

The next room exhibits another handsome pavement, which had been adorned at the angles with figures symbolical of the Four Seasons. That of Winter remains: a woman's head shrouded in drapery, a leafless branch at her side: colour and expression of no ordinary degree of merit. A third room boasts of a yet more fanciful decoration; the pavement, divided into two apartments, is ornamented with Cupids, dressed as gladiators—*retiarii*, with their short swords and entangling nets; *secutores*, helmeted and greaved; and *rudiarii*, the veteran "masters of the ceremonies." Here you see the athletes making ready for the coming fight; there, the struggle has commenced. Here, the rudiarius comes to the succour of the wounded retiarius; there, he lies disarmed, "butchered to make a Roman holiday." A semicircular division in the north angle of the pavement presents a charming female head, adorned with a wreath of blossoms, and enriched by a light azure halo. There are some remains of small Doric columns.

Another room, 14½ feet by 17 feet, contains a *caminus*, or *focus*—an open fire place—instead of the hot-air-hypocaust.

The Bath-room is at the south-west corner of the Crypto-porticus, and contains extensive portions of the bath. Adjoining it are large rooms with hypocausts for heating the sudatorium. "Other large rooms adjoin the south corner at the extremity of the south-east end of the inner court, in the middle of which end was the grand entrance into this inner court from a much larger outer court. This outer court seems to have been surrounded with bare walls, although tracings of buildings were found in various parts of the interior. The walls of this outer court seem to have been continued so as to surround the whole edifice, which perhaps, externally, presented merely the appearance of a great irregular square-walled enclosure. It must have been a princely residence, and it is evident that the luxurious comforts of the interior were no less studied than the beauty of the scenery around"—(*Wright*).

A few fragments of pottery are preserved at the villa; and at Bignor Park there is shewn a gold-ring, set with an exquisite intaglio, which depicts a warrior holding his shield before him.

☞ The Bignor remains are exhibited to the tourist on payment of a small fee. Application must be made to Mr. Tupper at the neighbouring farm. It is understood that their owner would be glad to dispose of the site and its relics, and suggestions have been made for the removal of the latter to the British Museum. Let us hope that they will be suffered to remain *here*, on the land which of old they occupied as portions of the royal villa of some haughty proprietor or august legate; and that so the tourist's imagination may be inspired to people the surrounding hills with the stalwart soldier-colonists sent forth by imperial Rome,—to hear the soft voice of Lydia or Aglaia repeating the graceful love-songs of Tibullus,—to see the social life of Roman England seething, and toiling, and whirling all around him, where now in the grassy valley only murmurs the music of the winds!

We return now to Bignor (¼ mile west), and visit the uninteresting CHURCH, small in itself, but "a world too large" for the congregation which ordinarily assembles there. The churchyard boasts of two noble yews. Lord Leconfield is the patron of the rectory, which is valued at £143.

BIGNOR PARK (S. H. Hawkins, Esq.) was originally "an appendage to the Castle of Arundel, and used for fatting deer driven in from the forest"—(*Horsfield*). The present house, commanding rich and extensive views of the lofty sweep of the South Downs and the brown leaf masses of the Weald, was begun in 1826, and occupies the site of an old Tudor mansion. Charlotte Smith, the author of "The Old Manor House," died 1806, and Mrs. Dorset, author of the "Peacock at Home," were the daughters of Nicholas Turner, Esq., who long enjoyed this picturesque estate, and they resided here for many years. In her "Sonnets," Charlotte Smith has duly celebrated the charms of this neighbourhood and of the valley of the Arun.

[From Bignor the tourist may diverge south-east to BURY HILL, where there is a large tumulus, and whence a fine prospect may be obtained; or he may keep away southward to DALE PARK (C. Fletcher, Esq.), which commands some exqui-

L

site views of the surrounding country. SLINDON PARK (Countess of Newburgh) lies to the south-west of Dale Park, from which it is separated by the village of SLIN- DON (population, 599). It was erected by Sir Garret Kempe, *temp.* Elizabeth, on the site of a mansion originally built—as early as the thirteenth century—by an archbishop of Canterbury, and reported to be the scene of the death of the great Stephen Langton. SLINDON CHURCH, Early English, contains the effigy of a knight under a niche in the chancel.]

Returning through SUTTON and BARLAVINGTON (popula- tion, 128), into the Guildford road, we speedily reach, at 2½ miles south of Petworth, the small parish of BURTON (population, 28), chiefly included within the ring-fence and palings of BURTON PARK (S. Biddulph, Esq.), formerly the seat of the Gorings. The present building retains some portions of "a new, spacious, and splendid structure," designed by Giacomo Leoni, which was nearly destroyed by fire in 1826. The park includes 210 acres. It is abundantly wooded and well watered. The ponds are stored with carp, trout, and pike, and haunted by wild fowl. An oak, near the house, is 25 feet in girth.

BURTON CHURCH contains some memorials, in Sussex marble, for members of the Goring family. Divine service is now per- formed in the parish church at COATES, a small building con- taining some interesting relics of the Goring family, who were the former lords of the manor.

[At DUNCTON (population, 272), on the northern slope of the chalk hills, the re- mains of a Roman hypocaust were discovered in 1815, about 140 yards north-east of the church. It probably belonged to a Roman public military bath.]

Keeping north from Burton we cross (2 miles from Petworth) the branch line of the London, Brighton, and South Coast Railway to Midhurst and Petersfield, and crossing the Rother (here little more than a brook) soon see before us the demesne of Petworth Park.

BRANCH ROUTE—CHICHESTER, *via* MIDHURST, TO HASELMERE.

We leave the cathedral city by the direct Guildford road, which runs through a country of singularly romantic character After passing the Broyle, to our right lies WEST HAMPNETT (population, 637), or Hamplonette, whose workhouse or "Union" exhibits considerable remains of the ancient Elizabethan Place-

House, built by Richard Sackville. The ceiling of the Great Staircase is covered with an allegory of St. Cecilia. To the aforesaid *Richard Sackville*, and *Elizabeth* his wife, there is a curious mural monument in the chancel of St. Peter's church, with "one of the worst representations of the Trinity that can possibly be conceived." The Duke of Richmond is the patron of the vicarage.

At 2 miles from Chichester we pass MID LAVANT (population, 284), and beyond it, EAST LAVANT (population, 421). Pennant derives the word "Lavant" from the Celtic TELEVAN, and says it indicates "a place alternately covered with water, or left dry at the recess of the tides." Hence he infers that "the harbour of Chichester formerly flowed higher up the country, and washed even the walls of the city." The Lavant is now a small rivulet, which empties itself into Chichester Harbour. It rises in Charlton Forest.

MID LAVANT CHURCH is as commonplace in character as most of the churches built after the Restoration generally prove. It contains a marble effigy of Dame *Mary May*, d. 1681. The Duke of Richmond is patron of the curacy.

EAST LAVANT CHURCH consists of a nave and chancel, and contains a brass for *Thomas Cawse*, and a slab of Sussex marble, inscribed in Longobardic characters,—" *Pries çi passes par ici. Pour l'alme Luci de Mildebi.*"

The rectory, valued at £460, is in the patronage of the Duke of Richmond.

At Mid Lavant a road branches off across the downs, overlooking in its course the rich masses of Goodwood Park, while another keeps to the left along the base of the hill, and passes WEST DEAN (population, 669). WEST DEAN PARK (Rev. L. V. Harcourt) is a luxuriantly wooded demesne, sheltered by an environment of pleasant hills. The mansion has a frontage of 300 feet, in a quasi-Gothic style, and was built by Lord Selsey in 1804. Near Chilgrove, in this parish, Roman sepulchral urns have been occasionally found.

WEST DEAN CHURCH, dedicated to St. Andrew, is partly Early English, and consists of a nave, chancel, transept, and west tower. A stately monument on the right side, with a full-length figure recumbent, and two effigies in a devotional attitude, commemorates three of the Lewknor family—uncle, son, and nephew. Dates of decease, 1616, 1602, —. There are some other noteworthy memorials of the Selseys, Peacheys, and Lewknors. The Dean and Chapter of Chichester present to this vicarage.

Either at West Dean or East Dean (*dene*, a valley), some authorities place the first interview between King Alfred and the learned Asser (see p. 37).

At SINGLETON (population, 603) both roads unite, and the highway winds through a richly-wooded valley, until, climbing the northern range of the South Downs, it reaches the village of COCKING (population, 482), situated in a narrow gap, from which, on either side, the green slopes of the hills ascend with, so to speak, a billowy swell. The Early English CHURCH here has a nave, chancel, and south aisle. There was a cell here in connection with the abbey of Seez and with the college of Arundel.

[A pleasant excursion may be made from this point through HEYSHOT (population, 432), GRAFFHAM, and LAVINGTON (population, 170), to Burton, and thence northward to Petworth. The road runs along the crest of the Downs, and commands, as may be imagined, a landscape of peculiar charm and beauty. Hills, shrouded in leafy woods, rise before us as we ascend, and beneath us sweeps the long valley of the Rother from Pulborough, where it breaks through the chalk-range to the very borders of Hampshire. Beyond, rises the elevated ridge of the lower greensand, and far away, against the misty skies, swells the undulating outline of the Surrey hills. Everywhere, a quiet village, an ancient grange, a gray old church-tower, a gabled manor-house, recalls some interesting association or picturesque tradition.

HEYSHOT CHURCH is an uninteresting Perpendicular building. GRAFFHAM CHURCH, partly Early English and partly decorated, is dedicated to St. Giles.]

At 2 miles north of Cocking, and in a country whose characteristics are sufficiently indicated by its name, lies MIDHURST (population, 1500. *Inns* : Angel, New Inn, Eagle), on an ascent rising gently from the bank of the Rother, which is navigable from hence to Pulborough, where it meets the Arun. It is a quiet, old-world town, with little trade, but in the centre of some delightful scenery. On ST. ANNE's HILL, across the river, remain the ruined foundations of the old castle of the Bohuns. A strong CHALYBEATE SPRING wells out unheeded from the turfy depths of a pleasant little dell, near Coster's Mill. At GREAT TODHAM are traces of an old Jacobean manor-house. The MIDHURST GRAMMAR SCHOOL (on the Petworth road), founded by Gilbert Hannam in 1672, bears a good reputation, and is connected with Winchester College. Here Sir Charles Lyell, the geologist, was educated. MIDHURST CHURCH, Perpendicular in style, is dedicated to St. Dennis, and consists of a nave, chancel, south aisle, and low embattled tower. The Montague sepulchral chapel, south of the chancel, has recently been deprived of its most remarkable monument (see EASEBOURNE). The Earl of Egmont is patron of the benefice, a perpetual curacy, valued at £170.

FROM MIDHURST TO PETWORTH—EAST.

[COWDRAY PARK (800 acres) lies to the east of Midhurst. The Petworth road runs quite through it. Its wooded knolls and ferny hollows, its grassy glades and broad stretches of crisp green turf, are the very luxuries of beauty. An avenue of Spanish chesnuts is especially grand in its full and vigorous leafiness; and there are everywhere nooks of greenery and shadowy dells, which boon to poet and artist will offer a fresh and genial inspiration.

The ruins of Cowdray, the great house of the great Montagues, are not extensive, but they are interesting. The arms of Sir Anthony Browne, Henry VIII.'s favourite, and the standard-bearer of England, adorn the entrance-gateway. Traces of the paintings which enriched the walls are visible; the windows of the hall and chapel are almost entire; within the quadrangle lie, half-consumed, the bucks carved in wood which formerly ornamented "the Buck Hall." We may stand here amid the ivy-shrouded ruins, and reproduce in imagination the stately mansion which, raised by Sir William Fitzwilliam, Earl of Southampton,—stepson of Sir Anthony Browne —about 1530, was embellished with Roberti's paintings and Groupe's statues; with the genius of Holbein, and the fancy of Pellegrini; with curious antique fittings and furniture; a noble quadrangle, a richly decorated chapel—all consumed or scathed by fire on the night of Tuesday, September 24, 1793. Its owner, George, eighth and last Viscount Montague, was at the time on the continent, and before the news of the destruction of his ancestral mansion reached him, was drowned in a rash attempt to pass the falls of Schaffhausen in Switzerland.

Cowdray now devolved upon his sister, who had married W. S. Poyntz, Esq. This gentleman built a cottage ornée about 1 mile from the ruins, which he named COWDRAY LODGE, and which, with the demesne, was sold in 1843 to the Earl of Egmont.

Queen Elizabeth passed five days at Cowdray in 1591, on a visit to Lord Montague, who had attended her at West Tilbury with 200 horsemen. The "Close Walk," where she exhibited her regal magnificence to the dazzled eyes of her courtiers, and where she brought down with a cross-bow three or four deer which were driven past her covert, still flourishes in leafy luxuriance.

Beyond the park gate, and on the right of the road to Petworth, stands EASE-BOURNE CHURCH, a Perpendicular building, dedicated to St. Margaret. The south aisle was a nun's chapel, attached to a nunnery founded by John de Bohun, temp. Henry III., of which some remains are extant. An ancient monument in the chancel, with the effigy of a knight carved in oak, commemorates Sir David Owen, son of Owen Tudor, d. 1541-2. The stately tomb of the Montagues will not fail to attract the visitor's attention. Upon an altar-tomb adorned with two female figures in robes of state, rises another tomb, where recumbent lies the effigy of Sir Anthony Browne, Lord Montague, d. 1592, in armour and ruff. The female figures represent his two wives, Lady Jane and Lady Magdalen.

The perpetual curacy of Easebourne, valued at £180, is in the patronage of the Earl of Egmont. Population of the parish, 1076.

LODSWORTH (population, 661) lies about 2 miles north-east of Easebourne, on the left of the road to Petworth. Its ancient church may be interesting. It is said that on the right side stands "an open cloister of timber-work." At TILLINGTON (population, 982), we reach the borders of Petworth Park. A family of the true Saxon name of Aylings have held land here upwards of 800 years. The small church is mainly Decorated, and consists of a nave, chancel, south aisle, and "a light and lofty tower, constructed, in 1807, at the sole expense of the Earl of Egmont." There is a brass for *William Spencer*, d. 1593, "a gentleman of great wisdome, pietie, and discretion," and his wife, d. 1592. Another tablet commemorates *William Cox*, D.D., precentor of Chichester Cathedral, *temp.* Charles I., and his wife, who expressed a wish to be buried here, in the hope of a better consort hereafter—"hic, ope melioris consortii, recondi voluit."

Lord Leconfield is the patron of the rectory.

The road from Midhurst to Petworth is one of great variety, and unusual beauty. It keeps in a broad open valley, whose north boundary is a ridge of the greensward, its south, the western range of the South Downs. The river Rother winds through meadow and coppice on the right, at some points approaching closely to the main road.]

FROM MIDHURST TO PETERSFIELD—WEST.

[The road to Petersfield passes through the villages of Stedham, Trotton, Terwick, and Rogate, before it crosses the boundaries of Hampshire. STEDHAM CHURCH, dedicated to St. James, dates from the reign of Edward I. The font is Norman. The tower was built in 1677. Population, 538. TROTTON (population, 484), is situated on the banks of the river Rother. It was originally a portion of the possessions of the Camoys family, and Thomas, Lord Camoys, early in the fifteenth century, built the bridge over the Rother, and the CHURCH, which he dedicated to St. George. There are two good brasses in the chancel, for *Marguerite de Camoys*, d. 1310, and on a large altar-tomb for *Thomas, Lord Camoys*, d. 1419, and his wife, *Elizabeth*, the widow of Hotspur, and the witty lady Kate, so vividly presented by Shakspeare in the second part of Henry IV.

Otway, the dramatist, was born at Trotton, March 3, 1651. His father was curate of the parish, and it was here that the author of "Venice Preserved" passed his boyish years,—

> "Wild Arun, too, has heard thy strains,
> And echo, midst my native plains,
> Been sooth'd by pity's tale"—(*Collins*).

At TERWICK (population, 97) there is nothing to delay the tourist. ROGATE (population, 1117) has a small Norman Church, dedicated to St. Bartholomew. DURFOLD ABBEY, in this parish, was founded for Præmonstratensian canons in 1169, by Henry Hoese or Hussey, Lord of Harling. A portion of the monastic edifice is embodied in the modern house. About ¼ mile south of the village is HABEN BRIDGE, and near it, on a knoll above the Rother, are the remains of a moated castle, which may have been erected by one of the Camoys family.

In this neighbourhood is DUNFORD HOUSE, the estate presented by his friends and admirers to Richard Cobden, whose "plain unadorned eloquence" contributed largely to the repeal of the Corn Laws, and whose exertions in concluding the recent Commercial Treaty with France have received so large a meed of public approval.]

We now resume our route to Haselmere. WOOLBEDING (population, 320) lies about ¼ mile on our left. Its situation on the north bank of the Rother is very delectable. The manorial mansion is "an elegant modern residence," in pleasant grounds. The marble fountain was removed from Cowdray. The CHURCH is ancient, contains a Norman font, and some coloured glass in the chancel from Mottisfont Priory, which is of some little interest.

After crossing the greensward ridge we reach, at 5 miles from Midhurst, the pleasant village of FARNHURST (population, 768), the centre of much changeful and certainly romantic scenery. Its Early English CHURCH has a small nave, chancel, and shingled spire. The perpetual curacy, valued at £111, is in the patronage of the Earl of Egmont.

Deep in the oak groves of VERDLEY (east of the village) are the ruins of an old hunting castle, appendant to the lordship of Midhurst. It was a quadrangular building, nearly twice as long as broad—that is, 60 feet by 33. It was reduced to its present condition some 30 years ago, when the roads were repaired with its materials! The spot, however, should be visited for its solitary beauty.

Nearly 3 miles north-west, on the slope of the hill which here overlooks the boundaries of Surrey and Sussex, stands LINCH-MERE (population, 339). The CHURCH is utterly uninteresting, but at no considerable distance from it lie the remains of SHUL-BREDE PRIORY, founded by Sir Ralph de Ardenne, early in the thirteenth century, for five Augustinian canons, and suppressed by the Bishop of Chichester in 1525. The "prior's chamber" is still in tolerable preservation, and its walls are covered with rude but characteristic frescoes. One of these mediæval pictures represents the nativity of the Saviour, and introduces certain animals bearing testimony to that event in Latin phrases, which have a certain resemblance of sound to their natural cries. Thus the cock crows "Christus natus est," the duck quacks "Quando, quando?" The raven croaks a reply, "In hâc nocte," a cow bellows "Ubi, ubi?" and the lamb bleats out "Bethlem." The whole is surmounted by the inscription "Ecce virgo concipiet, et pariet filium, et vocabitur nomen ejus Emmanuel."

☞ The road now winds along the hills for about 2 miles (from Farnhurst), and crosses the Sussex boundary into Surrey, whence it proceeds to GUILDFORD ; but for a description of the country through which it passes, the tourist must be referred to our "Guide to the History, Antiquities, and Topography of Surrey." Our exploration of Sussex is nearly ended, and that portion of the road from CHICHESTER (whither we now return) to PORTSMOUTH, which lies within this pleasant county, we shall describe, for obvious reasons, under the head of "Hampshire."

INDEX.

M

Patching, 132
Pan Hill, 76
Pett, 8
Petworth, 121-126
Pevensey, 29
Peverels, Seat of, 101
Piddinghoe, 92
Plumpton, 79
Polegate, 33
Poling, 133
Pope's Oak, West Grinstead, 113
Portslade, 106
Poynings, 100
Preston, 98; Viaduct, 80
Preston, near Arundel, 133
Puck Church Parlour, 44
Pulborough, 120

RICHMOND'S, DUKE OF, SEAT, 156
Ringmer, 60
Rivers of Sussex, xix
Roar Glen, 9
Robertsbridge, 10
Rogate, 166
Rotherfield, 66
Rother River, 166
Rottingdean, 91
Rudgwick, 140
Rusper, 104
Rustington, 133
Rye, 28

ST. BOTOLPH'S, 109
St. Leonard's, 1; Forest, 108
St. Pancras's Priory, 51
Salehurst, 11
Saxon composition of words of places, xi
Seaford, 43
Selsea, 143
Seven Sisters, 37
Sevington, 37
Sheffield Park, 75
Shermanbury, 101
Shoreham, New, 106
Shurley Chapel, 67
Silver Hill, 11
Singleton, 154
Slaugham, 96
Sompting, 130
Southease Churches, 92
Southover Church, 54; House, 59
Southwick, 106

Shernfold Place, 22
Stanmer Park, 80
Stedham Church, 166
Steyning, 109
Stoke, 139
Stopham, 121
Storrington, 116
Street Place, 79
Sullington, 116
Sutton, 158

TARRING, EAST, 92; West, 180
Tangmere, 155
Terwick, 166
Three Bridges Station, 96
Ticehurst, 12
Tillington, 166
Tortington, 141
Trotton, 166

UCKFIELD, 67
Udimore, 27
Up Waltham, 158

WADHURST, 21
Wakehurst Place, 77
Walberton, 141
Waldron, 63
Walshes Manor House, 66
Waltham, Up, 158
Warbleton, 64
Warminghurst, 130
Washington, 115
Weald, the, x
West Dean, 163
Westfield, 9
Westham, 33
West Tarring, 130
Wiggonholt, 119
Willingdon, 33
Wilmington, 41
Winchelsea, 23
Wiston, 111
Withyham, 71
Wivelsfield, 94
Woodmancote, 100
Woolbeding, 167
Worth, 97
Worthing, 127

YAPTON, 141

IMPERIAL HOTEL

(NEAREST FIRST-CLASS HOTEL TO THE RAILWAY STATION)

ABERDEEN.

Personally Patronised by their
Royal Highnesses
The Duke of Edinburgh,
The Duke of Connaught,
Prince Leopold,

Princess Beatrice,
Prince and Princess Christian,
Prince Frederick Charles of
Prussia,
and other distinguished Visitors.

The only one in Aberdeen expressly built from the Foundation
as a First-Class Hotel, and for which purpose the
entire Building is expressly occupied.

THE IMPERIAL HAS LATELY BEEN ENLARGED AND REFURNISHED.

THE IMPERIAL HOTEL is well known for its home comforts, and is without exception *the* only First-class Hotel in Aberdeen.

Address—The Manager.

PALACE HOTEL,
Union Street, ABERDEEN
(One Hundred Yards from the Railway Station).

THE PALACE

Is one of the largest, most recently erected, and best appointed Hotels in Scotland.

THE Management is under the direct and constant supervision of the Proprietor, who has had a long practical experience, and as *Chef de Cuisine* has had the honour of serving personally many of the

Royal and Imperial Families of Europe.

Selected Vintage WINES *at Moderate Charges.*

The Hotel 'Bus awaits arrival of all through Trains.

CHARLES MANN, *Proprietor.*

ABERDEEN.
THE FORSYTH HOTEL
90 TO 104 UNION STREET.
First-Class, combined with Moderate Charges.

M. & E. WALKER.

¡FLIES DRESSED TO PATTERN.

WILLIAM GARDEN,

GUNMAKER, FISHING ROD AND TACKLE MANUFACTURER,

122½ UNION STREET, ABERDEEN.

Large Stock of Salmon, Trout, and Loch Flies to choose from.

AMMUNITION OF EVERY DESCRIPTION.

Guns, Fishing Rods, and Reels repaired or made to order.

ABERFELDY.

BREADALBANE ARMS HOTEL,

One minute's walk from the Station.

SITUATED at the entrance to the Glen and Falls of Moness, and Birks of Aberfeldy, this Hotel is the best centre from which to visit the most magnificent scenery in Scotland.

Coaches run daily in connection with Loch Tay Steamers.

Post Horses and Carriages of all descriptions.

Salmon and Trout Fishing on a beautiful stretch of the Tay, and Trout Fishing on Loch-na-Craig, both with use of Boat Free.

OMNIBUS AWAITS ALL TRAINS.

Orders by Post or Telegraph punctually attended to.

ALEXANDER NICOL, *Lessee.*

ABERFOYLE.

BAILIE NICOL JARVIE HOTEL.

JAMES BLAIR, Proprietor.

THIS Hotel has recently been greatly altered and enlarged. It is situated at the Starting-Point of the New Road for the Trossachs and Loch Katrine, and a short distance from the terminus of the Strathendrick and Aberfoyle Railway. In the neighbourhood are the Famous Trouting Waters of Lochs Ard and Chon, on which fishing can be had from Mr. Blair, who keeps during the season excellent Boats and Boatmen for the use of Anglers and Pleasure Parties.

Post and Telegraph Offices within two minutes' walk of the Hotel.

¡POSTING IN ALL ITS BRANCHES.

BALLATER.

INVERCAULD ARMS HOTEL

UNDER NEW MANAGEMENT

In connection with the Invercauld Arms Hotel, Braemar.

POSTING IN ALL ITS BRANCHES. A COACH TO BRAEMAR DAILY ON AND AFTER 1st MAY

(*By Special Appointment Posting Master to the Queen.*)

M'GREGOR.

BANAVIE.

LOCHIEL ARMS HOTEL.

THIS Hotel is now under *new Management*, after *extensive Alterations and Improvements. Over* 100 *Beds can be made up. Principal Starting-place for Mr. MacBrayne's Steamers for Inverness.*

New Ladies' Drawing Room.　First-Class Billiard Room.

POSTING.　　　　FAMILIES BOARDED.

POST AND TELEGRAPH OFFICE.

GUIDES FOR THE ASCENT OF BEN NEVIS.

CHARGES STRICTLY MODERATE.

JOHN MENZIES, *Proprietor,*

Recently Lessee of the Caledonian Hotel, Inverness.

BATH.

CASTLE HOTEL

THE OLDEST ESTABLISHED and most CENTRAL for Families, Private and Commercial Gentlemen.

JOHN RUBIE, Proprietor.

GRAND
PUMP ROOM HOTEL
BATH

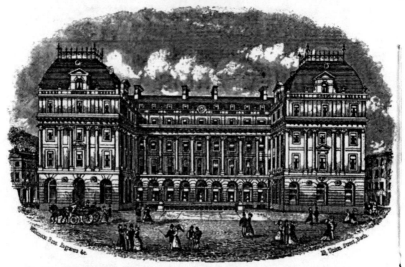

IS situated in the centre of the City, and connected with the finest suite of Mineral Water Baths in Europe,

IMMEDIATELY OPPOSITE THE GRAND PUMP ROOM AND ABBEY,

AND THE RECENTLY DISCOVERED MAGNIFICENT ROMAN BATH.

This Handsome Hotel is replete with every Accommodation, and is especially adapted for those requiring the use of the Bath Waters.

The Wines are carefully selected, and the Cuisine is under an experienced Chef.

FOR PARTICULARS APPLY TO

C. W. RADWAY, *Lessee.*

BERWICK-ON-TWEED.

KING'S ARMS HOTEL

AND POSTING HOUSE.

FOR FAMILIES AND COMMERCIAL GENTLEMEN.

The Hotel Omnibus meets the Trains.

JOHN CARR, *Proprietor.*

BETTWS-Y-COED.

ROYAL OAK HOTEL.

THIS Celebrated Hotel has an unrivalled situation, and is very suitable as a centre from which the most beautiful scenery in North Wales may be visited. It is near the Station, to which it has a private road. The coaches for Llanberis, Beddgelert, and Bangor, start daily from the Hotel.

AN OMNIBUS MEETS EVERY TRAIN.

FISHING TICKETS FOR ALL THE NEIGHBOURING RIVERS.

Billiards. Lawn Tennis. Archery.

POSTING. FIRST-CLASS STABLING.

David Cox's celebrated Signboard Picture.

E. PULLAN, *Proprietor* (Ten Years Proprietor of the Crown Hotel, Harrogate).

BLAIR-ATHOLE.
ATHOLE ARMS HOTEL.
Adjoining the Railway Station.

NOW one of the largest and best appointed Hotels in the Highlands.

THE SITUATION is unequalled as a centre from which to visit the finest Scenery of the PERTHSHIRE HIGHLANDS, comprising KILLIECRANKIE ; LOCHS TUMMEL and RANNOCH ; GLEN TILT ; BRAEMAR ; the FALLS OF BRUAR, GARRY, TUMMEL, and FENDER ; DUNKELD ; TAYMOUTH CASTLE and LOCH TAY ; the GROUNDS of BLAIR CASTLE, etc.

This is also the most convenient resting-place for breaking the long railway journey to and from the North of Scotland.

TABLE D'HÔTE daily during the season in the well-known magnificent DINING HALL, with which is connected *en suite* a spacious and elegantly furnished DRAWING ROOM.

Special terms for Board by the week, except during August.
Tariff on Application.

THE POSTING DEPARTMENT is thoroughly well equipped.

Experienced Guides and Ponies for Glen Tilt, Braemar, and Mountain Excursions.   **D. & P. T. MACDONALD,** *Proprietors.*

BOURNEMOUTH.
NEWLYN'S ROYAL EXETER HOTEL.

Patronised by the Royal Families of Europe.

THIS First-Class Hotel is situated in the most sheltered and picturesque part of Bournemouth, South Cliff, within one minute's walk of the Pier, and receives the highest patronage. *Cuisine* as at the Clubs.

Proprietor, HENRY NEWLYN,

Many years Manager of the Junior Athenæum and Guards' Clubs, London.

"Remarkably quiet and select, with the most refined comforts of a private house. —*Court Journal,* 22d June 1878.

BRAEMAR.
THE INVERCAULD ARMS,

The finest Hotel situation in Scotland.

Recently re-erected after Plans by J. T. WIMPERIS, Esq., Sackville St., London.

MAGNIFICENT DINING HALL, ELEGANT LADIES' DRAWING ROOM, AND NUMEROUS SUITES OF APARTMENTS.

POSTING IN ALL ITS BRANCHES.

BY SPECIAL APPOINTMENT POSTING-MASTER TO THE QUEEN

Coaches during the Season to Blairgowrie, Dunkeld, and Ballater.

Excellent Salmon Fishing in connection with the Hotel.

Letters and Telegrams Punctually attended to.

A. M'GREGOR.

FIFE ARMS HOTEL

BRAEMAR, BY BALMORAL.

𝔅𝔶 𝔖𝔭𝔢𝔠𝔦𝔞𝔩   𝔄𝔭𝔭𝔬𝔦𝔫𝔱𝔪𝔢𝔫𝔱.

Patronised by the Royal Family and the Court.

**Coaches daily between Braemar and Ballater, and
Braemar, Blairgowrie, and Dunkeld.**

POSTING IN ALL ITS BRANCHES.

LAWN TENNIS.

PARTIES BOARDED BY THE WEEK UNTIL
1st AUGUST.

MR. M‘NAB has leased from the Earl of Fife, K.T.,
seven miles of his Lordship's Private Salmon Fishings,
which gentlemen staying at the Hotel can have.

BRIDGE OF ALLAN.

QUEEN'S HOTEL.

A. ANDERSON begs to intimate that he has taken over the Business of this First-Class Old Established Hotel, and hopes, by strict attention and Moderate Charges, to merit a share of the patronage so kindly bestowed in former years.

Hotel 'Bus meets all Trains.

BRIDGE OF ALLAN.

CARMICHAEL'S HOTEL.

TEMPERANCE.

Within easy access of Callander, the Trossachs, and Lochlomond.

POSTING IN ALL ITS BRANCHES.   HOTEL 'BUS ATTENDS ALL TRAINS.

BRIGHTON GRAND AQUARIUM.

THE largest and most complete Marine and Fresh Water Aquarium in the World. The Collection of Fishes and other aquatic Animals in this magnificent Establishment is unequalled for variety and the number and size of the specimens exhibited.

Sea Lions, and baby Sea Lion, born in the Aquarium, May 1877; Porpoises, Royal Sturgeons, baby Sturgeons, Telescope Fish, Sea Horses, Herring, Mackerel, Sterlet, Mud Fish (Gambia), Electric Eels (Amazon), Groups of Alligators and Crocodiles, Sea Birds (Northern Divers), and thousands of other rare Specimens, many of which are not to be seen in any other Aquarium. The Aquarium Band at intervals daily. Concerts or Entertainments every afternoon and evening. ' Organ Recitals twice daily.

Admission—Daily, 1s.   Schools Half-Price.   **Evening, 6d.**
Periodical Tickets.—One Month, 5s.; Three Months, 7s. 6d.

Note.—From 1st May to 31st October Excursionists are admitted at Sixpence each upon presentation of Railway Ticket.   J. WILKINSON, *Sec. and Manager.*

BUXTON, DERBYSHIRE.

GROSVENOR PRIVATE HOTEL,

BROAD WALK.

THIS High-Class House (carried on many years by the late Mr. Brian Bates) stands in the most charming, convenient, and central situation in the Town, adjoining and overlooking the celebrated Gardens, and close to the Mineral Wells and Baths.

Comfortable Smoking Room.

Reduced Terms from October 1st to April 30th.

THE

BUXTON HYDROPATHIC ESTABLISHMENT AND WINTER RESIDENCE:

(MALVERN HOUSE)

DERBYSHIRE.

Overlooking Pavilion and Public Gardens.

WITHIN four minutes' walk of Celebrated Mineral Baths and Railway Stations. The Establishment has been Re-decorated and Handsomely Furnished.

TABLE D'HOTE, 6 O'CLOCK.

FOR TERMS, ETC., APPLY TO THE PROPRIETOR.

CALLANDER.

THE M'GREGOR HOTEL.

ALEXANDER M'NAUGHTON, Proprietor

(For Ten Years Waiter at the Alexandra Hotel, Oban).

TOURISTS and Families visiting the above long-established and First-Class Hotel will have every comfort and attention, and the Charges will be found strictly moderate.

Salmon and Trout Fishing on several Lochs, also on three miles of the River Teith.

Letters and Telegrams for Rooms promptly attended to.

CARDIFF.

THE ANGEL HOTEL.

THIS beautifully-situated first-class House is built on the site of the old Cardiff Arms Hotel and Gardens. Cardiff Castle, the residence of the Marquis of Bute, being on the north side, the Park and Gardens on the south, and commanding uninterrupted views from nearly all the rooms. The Hotel has been fitted up and furnished with all that experience can devise to ensure the comfort of Visitors; it is within seven minutes' walk of all the Railway Stations, and Tram Cars pass every few minutes to all parts of the Town.

Magnificent Coffee Room and elegant Suites of Rooms.

BLAND & SAVOURS, *Proprietors.*

B

CALLANDER AND THE TROSSACHS.

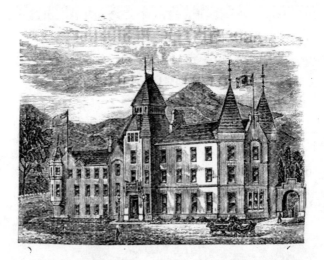

DREADNOUGHT HOTEL,

CALLANDER.

THIS old-established and favourite Hotel adjoins the Callander Railway Station, and is the most convenient and comfortable place for Tourists to and from Oban and the Trossachs to break their journey.

Large Posting Establishment. Coaches to the Trossachs.

Fishing on the River and Lochs free to Visitors.

Accommodation for over 100 sleepers, moderate charges.

Tariff.—Table d'Hote Breakfast, 2s. 6d. ; Dinner, 4s. ; Tea, 1s. 6d. ; Bedroom, 2s. 6d. and upwards; Attendance per day, 1s. 6d. ; Private Parlour, 5s. and upwards ; Table d'Hote Dinner at 6.30.

F. KLEFFEL, *Manager.*

CARLISLE.

THE COUNTY AND STATION HOTEL,

WHICH affords every accommodation for Families and Gentlemen, is Fireproof, and connected with the Platform of the Railway Station by a covered way. Porters in attendance on arrival of Trains.

A Ladies' Coffee Room.

CHEPSTOW,

BEAUFORT ARMS HOTEL.

An Old-Established First-class Family Hotel, within two minutes' walk of the Railway Station, Castle, and River Wye.

Ladies' Coffee Room 60 feet by 30. Gentlemen's Coffee and Billiard Rooms.

Omnibuses and Carriages meet all trains.

The **BEAUFORT ARMS HOTEL**, Tintern Abbey, conducted by the same Proprietress. **E. GARRETT.**

CHESTER.

THE GROSVENOR HOTEL.

FIRST-CLASS. Situated in the centre of the City, close to the CATHEDRAL and other objects of interest.

A Large Coffee Room and Ladies' Drawing Room for the convenience of Ladies and Families.

Open and close Carriages, and Posting in all its Branches.

Omnibuses attend the Trains for the use of Visitors to the Hotel. Tariff to be had on application. A Night Porter in attendance.

DAVID FOSTER, *Manager.*

CHRISTCHURCH.

CHISTCHURCH HOTEL.

NEWLYN'S FAMILY HOTEL.

" Charming Views from the Balcony of the Hotel."

Opposite the old Priory Church and Ruins.

Omnibuses to and from the Station. Excellent Boating in the Harbour.

GOOD FISHING.

CLIFTON.
CLIFTON-DOWN HOTEL,
Facing the Suspension Bridge.

THE popularity of this Hotel has compelled the Proprietors to extend the accommodation by the addition of several Bedrooms, Ladies' Drawing Rooms, a Suite of Apartments for Wedding Breakfasts, Ball Suppers, &c. &c. Visitors will find all the comforts of home, with fixed and moderate charges. The situation of the Hotel is unrivalled, being on the Downs, and within ten minutes' walk of the new Clifton-Down Railway Station.

N.B.—From this Hotel the following Trips are easy, returning to the Hotel the same day: Chepstow Castle, the Wynd Cliff, Tintern Abbey, Wells Cathedral, Glastonbury Tor, Bath, Weston-super-Mare, Clevedon, Portishead, Cardiff, Newport, and Channel Docks. HARRY F. BARTON, *Manager.*
Clifton Hotel Company (Limited).

CLIFTON, GLOUCESTERSHIRE.
"LYNDHURST,"
22 PEMBROKE ROAD, CLIFTON.
Private Boarding House—Notice of Removal.

MRS. J. M. HANCOCK has REMOVED from ARLINGTON HOUSE to the above, a newly-erected Residence, with lofty and well-ventilated Rooms, and modern sanitary arrangements.
TERMS ON APPLICATION.

COLWYN BAY, NORTH WALES.
POLLYCROCHAN HOTEL
(Late the Residence of Lady Erskine).

THIS First-class Family Hotel is most beautifully situated in its own finely-wooded park in Colwyn Bay, commanding splendid land and sea views; there are miles of delightful walks in the adjacent woods. It is within a few minutes' walk of the Beach and ten minutes' of Colwyn Bay Station, and a short drive of Conway and Llandudno.

Sea-Bathing, Tennis, Billiards, Posting.

J. PORTER, *Proprietor.*

CONISHEAD PRIORY
Hydropathic Mansion, by Ulverston, Furness.
LADIES' & GENTLEMEN'S TURKISH, SEA, & LAKE WATER BATHS.

Summer Terms, from 1st April to 30th September, from
£2:12:6 per Week.

Winter Terms, from 30th September to 1st April, from
£2:9s. per Week.

Resident Physician—Dr. ALEXANDER W. GORDON PRICE, University of Edinburgh.

Manager—Mr. GRANT, to whom Letters should be addressed, and from whom Terms
and Prospectuses may be obtained on application.

THE Magnificent and Historical Mansion of Conishead Priory, built at a cost of about
£140,000, standing on its own beautifully-wooded grounds, on the western shore
of Morecambe Bay, is, on high medical authority, stated to be one of the best Hydropathics in the kingdom, both for Summer and Winter residence.

Excursions can be made from the Priory, either by coach or rail, to any part of the
English Lake District, returning in the course of the day ; and special arrangements
have been made for excursion parties on extremely moderate terms. The Directors
have also liberally provided for amusements.

"One of the finest of old English mansions."—*Scotsman.* "Justly described as the
Paradise of Furness."—*Black's Guide.* "The furnishings and appointments throughout
are of the best."—*Bradford Observer.* "The architectural character of Conishead
Priory gives this establishment a more magnificent building than usual, indeed no
place of the kind at all approaches it in this respect."—*Newcastle Chronicle.* "Here
the hawthorn scents the air ; there a gigantic rhododendron lavishes all its beauties ;
sycamores and oaks, and firs abound."—*Christian World.*

The PRIORY OMNIBUS waits the arrival of every Train at Ulverston.

Passengers for the PRIORY by the London and North-Western Railway change Carriages
at Carnforth Junction. Passengers by the Midland Railway may require to change
at Helliefield.

COMRIE.

ROYAL HOTEL.

THIS Hotel is pleasantly situated on the main road between Crieff and Lochearnhead.
Places of interest are numerous in the vicinity, viz. GLENARTNEY, GLENLEDNOCK,
LOCH TURRET, SPOUT ROLLO; also within fifteen minutes' walk is the famous "DEIL'S
CAULDRON." Walks and other places of interest are numerous.
The Hotel has recently been enlarged and is now replete with every comfort for
FAMILIES and TOURISTS, who can be Boarded on the most moderate terms.
CAPITAL TROUT FISHING is to be had in the rivers Earn, Ruchil, and Lednock.
A COACH runs daily from the Hotel for Crieff Station; also the CALEDONIAN
COACHES call at the Hotel on their route from Crieff to Lochearnhead, and *vice versa*,
four times daily.
UNDER PERSONAL ATTENTION. CHARGES STRICTLY MODERATE.
POSTING ESTABLISHMENT COMPLETE.   D. HAMILTON, *Proprietor.*

CONNEMARA.

Was Opened on Wednesday, the 12th September 1883,

FOR TOURISTS AND SPORTSMEN,

RENVYLE HOUSE HOTEL.

**Fourteen Miles from Clifden, Four Miles from Letterfrack
Thirty from Westport.**

GOOD Sea Bathing, Sea and Trout Fishing, Seal and Mixed Shooting
—but game to be the property of the proprietor. The situation of
this Hotel is the finest in the country, close to the sea-shore, with fine
white sands. Beautiful Drives in the neighbourhood. Cars, Boats, and
Ponies to be had on hire, also Stabling. Salt Sponge Baths, and with
Seaweed. The freshness of the breezes and mildness of the climate render
it one of the best places for restoring health. A delightful retreat, suitable
either for Summer or Winter residence.

MRS. BLAKE, *Proprietor,*
Renvyle, Letterfrack, Galway.

CAUTION.—Let nothing prevent your coming on.

CONWAY.

THE CASTLE HOTEL.

FIRST-CLASS. Beautifully situated in the Vale of
Conway, and very central for Tourists in North
Wales.

ST. ANN'S HILL
HYDROPATHIC ESTABLISHMENT.
COUNTY CORK.

Founded by the late DR. BARTER *in the year 1843.*
(2½ miles from Blarney Station and 7 miles from the city of Cork.)
Resident Physician—J. B. FITZSIMONS,
M.D., Q.U.I.; L. AND L.M., R.C.S.I.; L.M. ROTUNDA HOSPITAL, DUBLIN;
L.M., COOMBE HOSPITAL, ETC. ETC.

Leave Train at Blarney Station for St. Ann's Hill.

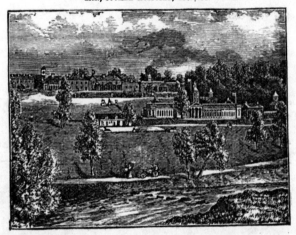

Postal Address—St. Ann's Hill, Cork.

THIS celebrated Health Resort is a favourite with both Invalids and Tourists, being picturesquely situated amongst wooded hills, commanding a bird's-eye view of the groves and castle of Blarney, and occupying a central position within easy reach of the chief objects of interest in the south of Ireland; is only three hours by rail from the Lakes of Killarney, and two hours from Youghal, the entrance to the Blackwater (Irish Rhine), where Sir Walter Raleigh's house is to be seen; and is within walking and driving distance of many other places interesting to the antiquary, the artist, and the historian.

THE BATHS,
As they should be in the Birthplace of the improved Turkish Bath in Western Europe, are amongst the finest in the kingdom, comprising separate spacious Turkish Baths for Ladies and Gentlemen, Pine, Electric, and all other baths and Hydropathic Appliances. Local electricity in its various forms and Waldenburg's compressed air apparatus are applied in suitable cases.

Attached to the establishment are Circulating Library, Reading Room, Covered Lawn-Tennis Court, three grass Tennis Grounds, Theatre, Cinder Tennis Court, American Bowling Alley, Billiard Rooms for both ladies and gentlemen, &c.

Good Trout-Fishing preserved for the use of Visitors. Foxhounds meet in the immediate neighbourhood. Postal and Telegraph Office in the Establishment.

SPECIAL TOURIST TICKETS for Two MONTHS at REDUCED RATES are issued at Kingsbridge, Dublin, on production of a written order from the Secretary at St. Ann's Hill, who will forward the same, or Prospectus, on application.

Terms from £2 : 2s. to £2 : 17 : 6 per week.

CORK.

STEPHENS' COMMERCIAL HOTEL

(Opposite the General Post Office, Cork)

POSSESSES first-class accommodation for Tourists, Commercial Gentlemen, and Families.

It is very centrally situated—close to the Banks and Theatre.

Charges extremely Moderate.

MRS. STEPHENS, PROPRIETRESS,
From the West of England.

EXTRACT from a "Tour through Ireland," published in the *North Briton*, 1864:—

"When we arrived in Cork we took up our quarters at Stephens's Commercial Hotel, where we obtained excellent accommodation."

EXTRACT from the *Glasgow Chiel*, 27th December 1884.

"When you go to Cork, stop at Stephens's capital Hotel—everything done well."

CRIEFF.

THE DRUMMOND ARMS HOTEL.

First-Class. Renovated and Refurnished. Under new management. Families boarded by Week or Month. Large Posting Establishment.

The Hotel Omnibus meets every Train.

W. C. S. SCOTT, PROPRIETOR.

CRIEFF.

STEWART'S HOTEL.

UNDER NEW MANAGEMENT.

POSTING IN ALL ITS BRANCHES.

THE above Hotel has been entirely Refurnished, both in Hotel and Stable Yard, and will be found replete with every convenience.

Good Trout-fishing in River Earn from April to September, and first-class Salmon-Fishing on to the end of October. Tickets for Angling to be had in Hotel.   DUNCAN FORBES, *Proprietor.*

DERBY.

THE ST. JAMES'S HOTEL,

IN the centre of the Town, facing the Post Office and Corn Market, is new, with every convenience for Families and Commercial Gentlemen. A Large Hall for Meetings, Wedding Breakfasts, Concerts, &c. Hot and Cold Baths. Stock Rooms.

THE STABLING IS PERFECT AND EXTENSIVE.

J. WAGSTAFF, Proprietor.

DUBLIN.

SHELBOURNE HOTEL.

SITUATED in the most central and fashionable part of Dublin, and is the great Tourist Hotel of Ireland. Contains magnificent Public Rooms, Elevator, Telegraph Office, &c. &c. First-Class. Charges Moderate.

JURY & COTTON, *Proprietors.*

DUBLIN.

JURY'S HOTEL, COLLEGE GREEN.

The most Central Hotel in the City.

Superior Accommodation.   Tariff extremely Moderate.
Table d'Hote at 3 and 6.30 p.m. daily.

LADIES' COFFEE, DINING, AND DRAWING ROOMS.

HENRY J. JURY, *Proprietor.*

DUBLIN.

THE WICKLOW HOTEL
(FAMILY AND COMMERCIAL),

6, 7, & 8 WICKLOW STREET,
Off Grafton Street, Dublin.

THE very centre of the City. Quiet, clean, comfortable, and homely. Most moderate charges.   RICHARD O'BRIEN, *Proprietor.*

(Late Manager Stephen's Green Club.)

DUNBLANE.

STIRLING ARMS HOTEL.

Beautifully situated on the river Allan, close to Station.

CHARGES STRICTLY MODERATE.

MRS. MARSHALL, *Proprietress.*

DUNKELD.

UNDER ROYAL 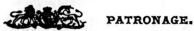 PATRONAGE.

FISHER'S ROYAL HOTEL.

COACH TO BRAEMAR AND BALMORAL DURING THE SEASON.

Seats secured only at the Hotel.

POSTING IN ALL ITS BRANCHES.

DUNKELD.
THE DUKE OF ATHOLE'S ARMS HOTEL.

D. ROBERTSON, *Proprietor* (late GRANT's).

THIS Hotel, from its situation close to the beautiful Bridge of Dunkeld, commands an unrivalled view of the magnificent scenery on either side of the river Tay. The Apartments, both Public and Private, are elegantly furnished and well aired.

Her Majesty the Queen, in her Journal of her Life in the Highlands, has been graciously pleased to take notice of this Hotel as being very clean, and having such a charming view from the windows. The Empress of the French, with her Son, the Prince Imperial, also visited this Hotel, and was pleased to express her entire approval of all the arrangements. EVERY ATTENTION IS PAID TO THE COMFORT OF VISITORS. *Job and Post Horses, with Careful Drivers. An Omnibus awaits the arrival of all the Trains free of Charge.* Seats can be secured at this Hotel for the Braemar Coach.

DUNOON, ARGYLL HOTEL.

UNDER NEW MANAGEMENT.

MR. D. S. MUNNINGS, for many years manager of the Royal Clyde Yacht Club and Marine Hotel, at Hunter's Quay, begs to intimate that he has been appointed as manager of the Argyll Hotel, and that it will be his constant endeavour to secure every comfort and attention to Tourists and others favouring him with their patronage.

The Argyll has first-class accommodation for Tourists and Families. The Bedrooms are large and well lighted. The Charges are strictly moderate. Special terms by week or month. Steamers to all places of interest on the Clyde call daily at Dunoon, which, as a centre or headquarters for the Tourist, is unrivalled, combining as it does cheapness of transit with great natural beauty of position.

Inquiries addressed to

D. S. MUNNINGS, *Manager.*

DUNOON, McCOLL'S HOTEL,

Adjoining the Castle Hill, West Bay.

MR. McCOLL (late lessee of the Argyll Hotel, Dunoon) begs to intimate to his numerous friends that he has purchased Lismore Lodge (late residence of H. E. C. Ewing, Esq., Lord-Lieutenant of Dumbartonshire), and has opened it as a FIRST-CLASS FAMILY AND COMMERCIAL HOTEL. This House is beautifully situated, and commands a magnificent view of the Firth of Clyde. Every attention having been paid to the fitting up of the house, it will be found to possess all the comforts of a home. Tourists will find this a very convenient resting-place, as all the Steamers for the favourite routes touch here at convenient hours. Hot, Cold, and Spray Baths. Private entrance to West Bay Shore for Sea-bathing. Spacious and Airy Bedrooms. Private Sitting and magnificent Drawing Room. Splendid Dining Room. Croquet Lawn. Charges moderate. Table d'Hôte daily. *This is the only Hotel in Dunoon with Ladies' Drawing-Room and Private Pleasure Grounds.*

EDINBURGH.

THE

COCKBURN HOTEL

Adjoining the Station and overlooking the Gardens.

JOHN MACPHERSON, PROPRIETOR.

OPPOSITE

THE

SCOTT

MONUMENT

AND

PRINCES

STREET

GARDENS.

(One of the finest Hotels in Europe.)

THE

ROYAL HOTEL

DONALD MACGREGOR, Proprietor,

53 PRINCES STREET, EDINBURGH.

The Royal Hotel is within a hundred yards of Railway Terminus, and occupies the finest position in the City.

PLACES OF INTEREST SEEN FROM HOTEL:—Arthur's Seat, over 800 feet high. Assembly Hall. Calton Hill. Edinburgh Castle. East and West Princes Street Gardens. Free Church College and Assembly Hall. Royal Observatory. Sir Walter Scott's Monument. Salisbury Crags. St. Giles's Cathedral. Parliament House. The Royal Institution. The Royal Scottish Academy and National Gallery. The Antiquarian Museum. From tower of Hotel are seen the Firth of Forth, Bass Rock, the Lomond, Corstorphine, and Pentland Hills, and a part of four or five of the neighbouring counties.

Charges Moderate. Rooms from 2s. 6d. Passenger Elevator. Night Porters.

CAUTION.—*Visitors intending to put up at the Royal must be careful to see that they are taken there, as mistakes have occurred causing great disappointment.*

EDINBURGH.
WINDSOR HOTEL,
100 PRINCES STREET.
(Opposite the Castle.)
A. M. THIEM, PROPRIETOR.

THIS 'old-established Hotel, one of the finest in Edinburgh, entirely rebuilt and refurnished in the most elegant manner, offers superior accommodation and comfort. The Proprietor is especially cognisant of the needs of the Nobility and Gentry, and spares no pains to render their sojourn with him agreeable.

ROXBURGHE HOTEL,
CHARLOTTE SQUARE.

FIRST-CLASS FAMILY HOTEL.

In Connection with the above is CHRISTIE'S PRIVATE HOTEL. Apartments *en suite*, and Board on Moderate Terms.

J. CHRISTIE, *Proprietor.*

BEDFORD HOTEL,
83 PRINCES STREET, EDINBURGH.

Recently leased by Mme. Dejay (late of Dejay's Hotel), and under her own personal superintendence. Unsurpassed for comfort, economy, and quietness.

Most moderate Terms.   *Cuisine à la française.*
Coffee Room and Ladies' Drawing Room.
This Hotel is situated in the best part of Princes Street, and commands a good view of the Castle. *On parle français.*

DARLING'S REGENT HOTEL,
20 WATERLOO PLACE, EDINBURGH.
(PRINCES STREET.)

Nearly opposite the General Post Office, and only a few minutes' walk from General Railway Terminus.

This is admitted to be one of the best Temperance Hotels in Scotland.
Special Terms for Board during the Winter Months.

EDINBURGH.
CALEDONIAN HOTEL,

115, 116, & 117 PRINCES STREET, AND 1, 3, & 5 CASTLE STREET.

Established 50 Years.

(Exactly opposite the Castle.)

R. B. MOORE. LATE J. BURNETT.

THE ROYAL ALEXANDRA HOTEL,
124 PRINCES STREET, EDINBURGH.

MISS BROWN begs to announce that she has REMOVED from Shandwick Place to more Convenient Premises, No. 124 PRINCES STREET, where she will carry on business under the present name,

THE ROYAL ALEXANDRA HOTEL,

and hopes to merit a continuance of the patronage already bestowed upon her.

EDINBURGH.
THE TREVELYAN TEMPERANCE HOTEL,
3 CALTON STREET.

Plain Breakfast or Tea, 1s. Bed and Attendance, 1s. 6d.

Recommended by the Rev. Alexander Wallace, D.D., Glasgow, and Rev. Wm. Reid, D.D., Edinburgh.

DUNCAN M'LAREN, *Proprietor.*

FERGUSON'S
EDINBURGH ROCK.

1 MELBOURNE PLACE

(NEAR CASTLE).

ELGIN.

STATION HOTEL.

THIS first-class Family and Commercial Hotel occupies one of the best sites in the town, close to the Railway Stations, about five minutes' walk from the Cathedral, and within easy drive of the beautiful and romantic Pluscarden Abbey and other places of interest in the neighbourhood. The Bedroom accommodation is first-class. Large Coffee Room, Drawing Room, Private Sitting Rooms, &c. &c. Also Billiard, Smoking, and Hot and Cold Bath Rooms.

Hiring.   Table d'Hote daily.

WILLIAM CHRISTIE, *Lessee.*
Also of the Station Hotel, Lossiemouth.

EXETER.
ROUGEMONT HOTEL.
Devon and Exeter Hotel Co., Limited.

(OPENED IN 1879.)

THE LARGEST AND ONLY MODERN HOTEL
IN THE CITY.

Omnibus and Hotel Porters meet all Trains.

NIGHT PORTER. TABLE D'HOTE, 7 O'CLOCK.

T. W. HUSSEY, MANAGER.

EXETER.
ROYAL CLARENCE HOTEL,
FACING THE GRAND OLD CATHEDRAL.
THE MOST CENTRAL & MOST COMFORTABLE HOTEL. MODERATE TARIFF
Patronised by the Best Families.
LADIES' COFFEE ROOM, BILLIARD ROOM, AND BATH ROOM.
Omnibuses and Cabs meet every Train.
J. HEADON STANBURY, *Proprietor.*

EXETER.
GARDNER'S
HALF MOON HOTEL,
HIGH STREET.
(Old Established.)
FAMILY AND COMMERCIAL.
Is situated in the most central part of the City. Families and Commercial Gentlemen
will find this House replete with every comfort, and the charges moderate.
Ladies' Coffee Room and Superior Billiard Room. 8 spacious and well-lighted Stock Rooms
Omnibuses belonging to the Hotel meet all Trains. A Night Porter.

C

FORT-WILLIAM.
THE ALEXANDRA HOTEL,
PARADE, FORT-WILLIAM.

THIS *Recently-Built First-Class Hotel* is delightfully situated on the outskirts of the town, facing the sea, and commanding magnificent views of the surrounding mountains.

Parties Boarded by the Week or Month.   *Every Comfort, with Moderate Charges.*

Visitors to the *Alexandra* conveyed by Omnibus *Free of Charge* to and from all the steamers during the season.

N.B.—MR. M'BRAYNE'S STEAMERS CALL DAILY FOR NORTH AND SOUTH.

MRS. DOIG, *Proprietrix.*

GATEHOUSE OF FLEET, N.B.
MURRAY ARMS HOTEL

HAS comfortable accommodation for Families and Tourists at very moderate terms. The Drives, Walks, and Scenery in the neighbourhood are unsurpassed in the South of Scotland, embracing as they do the scene of Scott's "Guy Mannering."

Good River and Loch Fishing can be had. A 'Bus from the Hotel meets Trains twice daily at Kirkcudbright.

POSTING.   LETTERS, ETC., PROMPTLY ANSWERED.

GEORGE McMICHAEL, Proprietor.

THE SHANDON HYDROPATHIC

BEAUTIFULLY SITUATED ON THE GARELOCH, near HELENSBURGH.

Terms, from £3 : 3s, per week, or 10s. 6d. per day.

THE FINEST HYDROPATHIC RESIDENCE IN THE KINGDOM.

WELL sheltered, salubrious climate, Highland Scenery, within easy drives to Lochlong and Lochlomond. The Conservatory, Vineries, Gardens, and Policies, with five miles of Enclosed Gravel Walks, are unrivalled. Large Sea-Water Swimming, Turkish and other Baths, with every Modern luxury. Pleasure Boats, &c. Post and Telegraph Offices at the Entrance Lodge.

Numerous Trains from Glasgow connecting with Steamers at Craigendoran Pier on North British Railway, or at Greenock on Caledonian and Glasgow and South-Western Railways.

Apply to the Manager, West Shandon, by Helensburgh.

GIANT'S CAUSEWAY.

CAUSEWAY HOTEL AND ELECTRIC TRAMWAY.

THIS beautifully situated Hotel is now worked in connection with the GIANT'S CAUSEWAY ELECTRIC TRAMWAY. It is the most central spot for Tourists visiting the district. Most comfortable, and Charges Moderate. Guides, Boats, and Posting at fixed rates. Electric Tram Cars run to meet all Trains. Orders to view the Electric Generating Station obtained here.

Postal and Telegraph Address—Bushmills: A. SHERIDAN, Manager.

Note.—Ask for through Railway Tickets to the Giant's Causeway.

GLASGOW.

NORTH BRITISH IMPERIAL HOTEL.

HAVING renewed the Lease of these Premises, and completely refurnished and redecorated the entire Hotel, I am now in a position to offer to parties patronising this Establishment an increase in the comfort formerly enjoyed at this House.

The convenience for Travelling cannot be surpassed, having an entrance to the platform of the Queen Street Station—the main departure platform for the Trossachs and Waverley and East Coast Route to London.

JAMES CUTHBERT, PROPRIETOR.

GLASGOW.

ALEXANDRA HOTEL
BATH STREET.

THIS New and Elegant Hotel, one of the finest in the City, offers superior Accommodation for Families and Gentlemen. The Proprietor respectfully states that this Establishment embraces every Luxury and Comfort calculated to add to domestic happiness. *Nearest first-class Hotel to all the different Railway Termini.* CHARGES STRICTLY MODERATE.

JOHN MACRAE, Lessee & Manager.

TARIFF ON APPLICATION.

HIGH-CLASS TEMPERANCE HOUSE.

GLASGOW.
PHILP'S COCKBURN HOTEL,
141 BATH STREET.

THIS large new Hotel is especially planned and constructed with every Modern Improvement to meet the requirements of a First-Class Hotel. Situation unsurpassed. In an elevated and quiet but central and convenient part of the City; within easy access of the different Railway Stations and Steam-Ship Landings. Street Cars pass within a few yards to all parts of the City.

Passenger Elevator.

Turkish Baths and Billiard Rooms.

The home of Americans in Glasgow.

BED AND ATTENDANCE FROM 2s. 6d.

LIBERAL BOARD TERMS.

N.B.—In connection with the COCKBURN HOTEL, EDINBURGH, and Philp's Glenburn Hydropathic, Rothesay.

Agent for Cook's system of Scottish Tours

TO THE HIGHLANDS AND ISLANDS OF SCOTLAND.

GLASGOW.
MACLEAN'S HOTEL,
ST. VINCENT STREET, GLASGOW.

THE Accommodation is unsurpassed, and consists of luxurious Drawing, Dining, Coffee, Reading, Billiard, and other Public Rooms, 104 Bedrooms, etc., etc. The situation is close to the centre of the City, within half a mile from the various Railway Stations, Wharves, etc., and in the quiet West and Residential district close to Blythswood Square. From its elevated situation it commands extensive Views of Glasgow and the surrounding Country.

The Proprietor has resolved to maintain a Moderate Scale of Charges, a Tariff of which will be supplied on application.

Arrangements made for Boarding Families at Reduced Rates.

A Hydraulic Elevator on the Premises.

THE BATH HOTEL,

152 BATH STREET, GLASGOW.

The most comfortable First-class Hotel in Glasgow. Very Moderate Charges.

P. ROBERTSON, Proprietor.

GLASGOW.

ANDERSON'S STEEL'S HOTEL.

CORNER OF QUEEN STREET AND ARGYLE STREET.

The most central Hotel in Glasgow.

Ladies' Coffee Room. Over 90 Apartments.
Breakfast and Lunch from 1s. 6d. to 2s. 6d.   Dinner from 3s.
Bed and Attendance from 2s. 6d.

WM. ANDERSON, *Proprietor.*
Late of Café Royal Hotel, Edinburgh.

GLASGOW.

HIS LORDSHIP'S LARDER AND HOTEL,

10 ST. ENOCH SQUARE, GLASGOW.

(*Opposite St. Enoch Station Booking Office.*)

TO exercise economy consistent with comfort, Visitors cannot do better than live at this most central House. Breakfast, Dinner, Tea, and Bedroom included, from 7s. to 8s. per day.

T. WHITE, *Proprietor.*

THOS. CURTIS, *Manager.*

SMITH, SONS,

AND

LAUGHLAND,

SILK MERCERS, FAMILY DRAPERS,
COMPLETE OUTFITTERS,
GENERAL WAREHOUSEMEN,

Carpet Merchants and Household Furnishers,

78 to 82 UNION STREET,
GLASGOW,

Have always a Large, Choice, fully Assorted Stock; and Novelties
are added to each Department as they appear.

HOLTON'S
BALMORAL TEMPERANCE HOTEL
(Opposite Caledonian Railway Station),
BUCHANAN STREET, GLASGOW.

THIS old-established, large, and commodious Hotel comprises accommodation of a
most complete description, and from its position is well suited for Tourists and
Travellers generally. Under Mr. Holton's personal superintendence visitors may
rest assured of every attention.
Bed and Service, 2s. 6d.   Breakfast, 1s. 3d. to 2s.   Dinner, 2s. and 2s. 6d.
Tea, 1s. 3d. to 2s.   Private Parlours, 3s. per day.
Hot and Cold Baths.   Billiards.
Tram Cars to all parts of the City.

GLOUCESTER.
SPREAD EAGLE HOTEL.

THIS Old-Established First-Class Family Hotel will be found by Visitors replete with
every comfort.   Well-ventilated Bed and Sitting Rooms *en suite.*   Headquarters
Bicycle Touring Club.   Handsome Coffee Room.   Hot and Cold Baths.   All the latest
sanitary arrangements complete.   First-rate *Cuisine* and choice Wines, &c.   Good
Stabling and Loose Boxes for Hunters, &c.   An Elegant and Spacious Ballroom to be
let for Balls, Concerts, Dinners, Meetings, Sales, &c.   Tariff on application.   Posting.
Flys, &c., on hire.   *The Hotel Omnibus meets all Trains.*
A NIGHT PORTER ALWAYS IN ATTENDANCE.
HENRY CHARLES GROGAN, *Proprietor.*

GOLSPIE.

ROYAL SUTHERLAND ARMS HOTEL.

BEAUTIFULLY situated within a mile of Dunrobin Castle, the Grounds of which are open to the Public. Free Trout Fishing on Loch Brora for parties staying at the Hotel. Five minutes' walk from sea-shore. Horses and Carriages on Hire. An Omnibus meets Trains. Charges moderate.　　　　　JAMES MITCHELL, *Proprietor.*

THE ISLAND OF GUERNSEY.
GARDNER'S

ROYAL HOTEL,

FAMILY & COMMERCIAL HOUSE, ESPLANADE, GUERNSEY.
ESTABLISHED 50 YEARS.

THIS Hotel is situated in the most commanding part of the Island, facing the spacious harbours and the approaches thereto, also having a full front view of the adjacent islands of Sark, Herm, Jersey, and Alderney. Visitors should be especially careful on landing to ask for the "Royal." Table d'Hôte. Billiards for the use of visitors staying in the hotel only.　　　JAS. B. GARDNER, *Proprietor.*

HARROGATE.

"THE GRANBY,"
HIGH HARROGATE,
FACING THE STRAY.

THIS First-Class Family Hotel stands in its own extensive grounds, and is beautifully situated in the best part of Harrogate. Good Lawn-Tennis Court. Great alterations have lately been made in the House, and Visitors will find in it every convenience. Carriages to the Wells and Baths every morning free of charge. Ten minutes' walk from the Station. For Terms, &c., apply

W. H. MILNER, *Proprietor.*

HARROGATE.

ROYAL HOTEL.
WILLIAM KEIGHLEY, Proprietor.

THIS first-class Family Hotel is most pleasantly and healthily situated, and is replete with every comfort for families. Within five minutes' walk of the Railway Station.

BILLIARD ROOM.

HARROGATE WELLS.
BÁRBER'S GEORGE HOTEL.

VISITORS to Harrogate will find many advantages in making their temporary residence at this Hotel, it being situated within three minutes' walk of the Sulphur and Cheltenham Springs, seven minutes' walk from the Railway Station, and in the immediate vicinity of the Public Baths, Concert Rooms, &c. The sheltered situation of the Hotel makes it admirably adapted for Visitors in Spring and Autumn. Terms per day:—Board and Lodgings, in Public Rooms, 6s. 6d. each; ditto, ditto, in Private Rooms, 7s. 6d. each; Private Sitting Rooms, 3s. to 5s. each; Attendance, &c., 1s. 3d. each. Beds charged extra if for less than three nights. Horses' Hay, 10s. 6d. per week. Ostler extra. Billiard Room. Stabling for Hunters and Carriage Horses.

N.B.—No fees given to Conductor to recommend this Hotel. NOTE.—Harrogate being a health resort, the patrons of this Hotel are not expected to use Wine, &c., unless they require it.

HIGH HARROGATE.
GASCOIGNE'S
FIRST-CLASS FAMILY AND COMMERCIAL HOTEL.

STANDING in its own grounds, in the most fashionable part of |High Harrogate. Seven minutes' walk from the Station. A Carriage leaves the Hotel for Wells each morning, free of charge. Private Sitting Rooms on application. Billiards. Terms moderate. An Omnibus meets every Train.   J. S. DAVIES, *Proprietor.*

In order to prevent disappointment *please note Address.*
SOUTH ASPECT.

HELENSBURGH.

THE Finest Watering-Place in the West of Scotland. Trains and Boats to Loch Lomond and Trossachs, and Steamer every morning to Dunoon at 8.45, in time to meet the "Iona" for the Highlands by that most celebrated Route—Ardrishaig, Crinan, and Oban, to Staffa and Iona. The alterations and improvements at the QUEEN'S HOTEL are now completed, and the Suites of Apartments for Families cannot be surpassed. The view of the Clyde and Lake is most magnificent. Tourists conveniently arranged. A magnificent Coffee Room. Smoking and Billiard Room.

All Charges strictly Moderate.

Omnibuses and Carriages to all Steamers and Trains.

A. WILLIAMSON, *Proprietor.*

HUNTER'S QUAY, HOLY LOCH.
ROYAL MARINE HOTEL.

HEADQUARTERS of ROYAL CLYDE YACHT CLUB. Situated close to Hunter's Quay, at which Pier Steamers call several times a day, and is within ten minutes' walk of Kirn Pier. The Hotel has lately been considerably enlarged, and is most comfortably furnished, offering superior accommodation for Families and Gentlemen. Charges strictly moderate. Visitors boarded by day or week. Coaches pass daily by Loch Eck Route to and from Inveraray. There is frequent communication between Dunoon and Sandbank by brakes. Hot, Cold, Spray, and Douche Baths. Carriages and Boats for hire.   OSCAR TROEGER, *Manager.*

ILFRACOMBE HOTEL.

THE ILFRACOMBE HOTEL, on the verge of the Atlantic. Five Acres of Ornamental Grounds. Six Lawn-Tennis Courts. 250 Rooms.

Table d'Hôte at Separate Tables daily from 6 to 8 o'clock.

There is attached to the Hotel one of the largest Swimming Baths in England. Also Private Hot and Cold Sea and Fresh Water Baths, Douche, Shower, &c.

Every information will be afforded by the Manager,

ILFRACOMBE, NORTH DEVON.

THE attractions of Ilfracombe, and the places of interest in the neighbourhood, point to it as the natural centre to be chosen by the Tourist who desires to see with comfort all the beauties of Coast and Inland Scenery which North Devon affords. There is also easy access into South Devon and Cornwall. The means of communication with Ilfracombe by Railroad and Steamboat are most complete.

Tourist Tickets to Ilfracombe for two months are issued at all principal Stations.

THE ROYAL BRITANNIA HOTEL, ILFRACOMBE.

GOOD PUBLIC ROOMS. MODERATE TERMS.

ADDRESS—THE MANAGER.

ILFRACOMBE.

ROYAL CLARENCE
FAMILY AND COMMERCIAL HOTEL.

REPLETE with every Home comfort. A spacious Ladies' Coffee Room, with large number of Bedrooms, has recently been added.   Moderate Charges.   Tariff on application.

First-Class Billiard Room.   Omnibus meets every Train.

CHARLES ED. CLEMOW, *Proprietor.*

In connection with Anderton's Hotel, Fleet Street, London.

ILKLEY, YORKSHIRE.

MIDDELTON HOTEL,

FACING THE MOORS.

THIS First-Class-Family HOTEL stands in its own extensive grounds on the banks of the picturesque River Wharfe, six miles from the famous Bolton Woods.

HOT AND COLD BATHS, TENNIS COURTS.

BILLIARD AND SMOKE ROOMS.

TABLE D'HOTE DAILY AT 6.45—SEPARATE TABLES.

TARIFF ON APPLICATION TO

Manageress.

ILKLEY, NEAR LEEDS.

TROUTBECK HYDROPATHIC ESTABLISHMENT
AND SANATORIUM.

Physician—THOMAS SCOTT, M.D., M.R.C.S.E.
Proprietor and Manager—JOHN DOBSON.

TROUTBECK is beautifully situated on an eminence overlooking the Valley of the Wharfe, adjoining the Moor, and close to the Tarn. This Establishment is a handsome erection in the Elizabethan style, capable of accommodating seventy persons, built expressly for the purpose of carrying out the Hydropathic System to its fullest extent, and is justly famed for being one of the most compact and comfortable in Ilkley, every attention having been paid to render it at all times a most attractive residence for Invalids seeking health, as well as for Visitors who desire merely relaxation and change.

For full Prospectus, address—JOHN DOBSON, as above.

INNELLAN.

ROYAL  HOTEL.

JOHN CLARK, in returning thanks to his friends and the Public for past patronage, begs to announce that the new additions to this already large and commodious Hotel are now finished, and include one of the largest and most handsome Dining Rooms and Ladies' Drawing Rooms of any Hotel on the Firth of Clyde, also Parlours with suites of Bedrooms on each flat.

The Hotel is within three minutes' walk of the Pier, and, being built upon an elevation, commands a sea-view of the surrounding country, including Bute, Arran, the Cumbraes, Ayrshire, Renfrewshire, and Dumbartonshire, making the situation one of the finest in Scotland. The grounds of the Hotel are laid out in walks and interspersed with shrubs and flowers, and are quiet and retired for families. There are also beautiful Drives in the vicinity. The Dining Room has a large Fernery, with water fountain which plays daily during the summer, making it cool and refreshing during the hot weather.

Steamers call at the pier nearly every hour for the Highlands and all parts of the coast. Tourists arriving at the Hotel the night before can have breakfast at *Table d'Hôte* at 9 A.M., and be in time to join the "Iona" at 10 A.M. for the North, calling at Innellan on her return at 4 P.M.

The Cuisine and Wines are of the finest quality. Large Billiard Room attached. Hot, Cold, and Spray Baths.

Horses and Carriages kept for Hire. Families Boarded by the Day or Week.

INVERNESS.

IMPERIAL HOTEL.

The most central First-class Hotel in Town, and opposite to the Railway Station.

Large Dining		Two-Tabled
Saloon		Billiard Room,
accommodating		
90 Guests.		Hot and Cold
Ladies'		Baths, and over
Drawing Room.		40 Bedrooms.

The Hotel Omnibus attends all Steamers, and Porters await the arrival of Trains.

ONLY THE BEST WINES KEPT.

W. MACBEAN, *Proprietor.*

INVERNESS.

THE ROYAL HOTEL.

Opposite the entrance to the Railway Station.

J. S. CHRISTIE begs to solicit the attention of the travelling Public to this large well-known First-class Hotel, which has been greatly enlarged, and now comprehends, besides extensive First-class Bedroom accommodation, a SPACIOUS and LOFTY LADIES' and GENTLEMEN'S DINING SALOON, with handsome DRAWING ROOM *en suite*, and several elegant and handsomely furnished SUITES of PRIVATE ROOMS; also SMOKING ROOM, HOT, COLD, and SHOWER BATH ROOMS, etc.

Though immediately *opposite* and within a *few yards* of the Railway Station entrance, the Hotel is entirely removed from the bustle, noise, and other disturbing influences which usually affect the comfort of Hotels situated in close proximity to the Railway.

Table d'Hôte daily, and Dinners à la Carte.

The Porters of the Hotel await the arrival of all trains, and an Omnibus attends the Caledonian Canal Steamers. Posting.

D

THE VICTORIA HOTEL, INVERNESS.

Opposite the Castle.

Only First-class Hotel Fronting the River.

COMMANDING from every window a delightful view of the Caledonian Valley and surrounding Country. Handsome Coffee Room and Drawing Room. Every accommodation for Commercial Gentlemen. Parlours and Billiard Room. Bright and Airy Bedrooms. Nearest First-class Hotel to the Canal Steamers, and within Three Minutes of Railway Station and Post Office. A 'Bus awaits the Steamers, and Boots attends the Trains.

INVERNESS.

THE HIGHLAND RAILWAY COMPANY'S

STATION HOTEL.

FREQUENTLY PATRONISED BY THE ROYAL FAMILY.

A PRIVATE entrance from the platform under cover. The Hotel Porters attend the Trains, and an Omnibus the Caledonian Canal Steamers.

POSTING.   VERY MODERATE TARIFF.

E. CESARI, *Manager.*

WHEN YOU ARE

IN

THE HIGHLANDS

VISIT

MACDOUGALLS',

DERWENTWATER LAKE.
JEFFERY'S
"Blencathra" Family & Commercial Temperance Hotel
(*opposite the Wesleyan Chapel*),
SOUTHEY STREET, KESWICK.

FIVE MINUTES' WALK FROM THE STATION.

PLEASANTLY situated, commanding extensive views of Mountain Scenery, recently enlarged and Refurnished. Hot and Cold Baths. Posting in all its branches.
A 'BUS MEETS ALL TRAINS.

JOHN H. JEFFERY, *Proprietor.*

KILLARNEY LAKES.

By Her Most Gracious Majesty's Special Permission.

THE ROYAL VICTORIA HOTEL
Patronised by H.R.H. THE PRINCE OF WALES ;
by H.R.H. PRINCE ARTHUR ;
and by the Royal Families of France and Belgium, and Leading American Families, &c.

THIS Hotel is situated on the Lower Lake, close to the water's edge, within ten minutes' drive of the Railway Station, and a short distance from the far-famed Gap of Dunloe.

TABLE D'HOTE DURING THE SEASON.

Postal Telegraph Office.

Hotel open throughout the year.   Boarding terms from October to June.

JOHN O'LEARY, *Proprietor.*

KILLARNEY LAKE DISTRICT.
THE MUCKROSS HOTEL,
COMBINED with strictly moderate charges, contains all that is necessary to promote the comfort and convenience of Visitors. It is situated in the most central and beautiful part of the Lake District, and within fifteen minutes' drive of the Railway Station, at which the hotel 'bus attends. Surrounded by pleasant walks and drives, many objects of great interest and beauty, this Hotel will be found a most desirable place to spend a few days or weeks.

Angling.—The Proprietor has arranged for the use of Visitors good Salmon Fishing. There is also good Salmon and Trout Fishing on the lakes, which are FREE, and Anglers can have boats from the Proprietor without charge.

Tariff and other particulars on application.

Please be particular to observe the 'bus you enter bears the name, THE MUCKROSS HOTEL.

LAKES OF KILLARNEY.

"THE LAKE HOTEL.'

Patronised by the Duke of Saxe-Coburg-Gotha (brother of the late Prince Consort), the Marquis of Lorne, Prince Napoleon, the Khedive of Egypt, the Duc de Nemours, and other members of the ex-Royal Family of France.

It is essential to apprise Tourists that there is at Killarney but one establishment called "THE LAKE HOTEL."

IT is situate in the Bay of Castlelough, on the Eastern Shore of the Lower Lake, in the centre of the varied scenery of the Lake, and within ten minutes' drive of the Railway Station. Forty of the Bedrooms and Sitting Rooms face the Lake.

The waters of the Lake approach the Hall Door, and hence the distinctive title, "THE LAKE HOTEL."

Boats and Vehicles of every description supplied at fixed and Moderate Prices.

No Gratuities allowed to Drivers, Boatmen, etc., as they are paid ample wages by the Proprietor.

The Lake Hotel Omnibus attends the arrival and departure of the Trains.

The Hotel has lately come under new Proprietorship and Management. It is newly fitted up, and nothing has been left undone to meet the views of Tourists with regard to comfort and economy.

NOTICE OF THE PRESS—*From Bradshaw's "Tourists' Hand-Book."*

"In point of situation, that of 'THE LAKE HOTEL' is, beyond question, the very best in the Lakes of Killarney. It occupies the centre of the circle described by the great mountain ranges of Mangerton, Toro, Eagle's Nest, Purple Mountain, Glena, Toomies, Dunloe Gap, and Carranthual, and concentrates in one view all that is *graceful, picturesque, and sublime* in the scenery of Killarney."—*Bradshaw's "Tourists' Hand-Book," page* 382.

LOCH TAY, PERTHSHIRE.

KILLIN HOTEL,

BY CALLANDER AND OBAN RAILWAY.

THIS HOTEL is situated on the banks of the Lochay, at the head of Loch Tay, amongst some of the finest scenery in Scotland. The new Steamer "Lady of the Lake" is now sailing on Loch Tay between Kenmore and Killin, with Coaches in connection at both ends. The drive to the Pier is unsurpassed, crossing a new bridge over the river Lochay, and then through the old Avenue, passing Finlarig Castle and the Mausoleum of the Breadalbane family.

Parties staying at this Hotel can make daily tours through the Trossachs and back by Loch Lomond, Loch Awe and back by Oban ; also Loch Etive and back.

ENGLISH CHURCH, POST AND TELEGRAPH OFFICE CLOSE BY.

Lawn-Tennis and Croquet Green has just been added for Visitors staying at the Hotel.

Trout Fishing and Pleasure Boats Free of Charge.

POSTING ESTABLISHMENT COMPLETE.

Coaches from Hotel meet North and South Trains.

ALEXANDER STUART, *Proprietor.*

KINGSTOWN.

ROYAL MARINE HOTEL,
KINGSTOWN.

FIRST-CLASS FAMILY HOTEL.

Faces Dublin Bay and Kingstown Harbour.

Two minutes from Royal Mail Packet Pier.

FOURTEEN MINUTES FROM DUBLIN BY RAIL.

LUGGAGE PER MAIL SHOULD BE LABELLED "KINGSTOWN."

KIRKBY-LONSDALE, WESTMORELAND.

WILMAN'S ROYAL HOTEL.
FIRST-CLASS FAMILY AND POSTING HOTEL.

KIRKBY-LONSDALE is pleasantly situated on the Banks of the Lune, noted for its picturesque and varied scenery, within driving distance of the Lakes, Clapham Caves, and other places of interest.

BILLIARD ROOM.

An Omnibus meets all trains at Kirkby-Lonsdale Station, London and North-Western Railway. Also morning and evening trains at Arkholme on the Midland.

KIRKMICHAEL.

KIRKMICHAEL HOTEL,
PERTHSHIRE.

THIS Hotel has lately been considerably enlarged, and is most comfortably furnished, offering superior accommodation for families and gentlemen, and is beautifully situated on the banks of the River Ardle in the Perthshire Highlands. The Hotel is distant 14 miles from Blairgowrie and half-way between the Spital of Glenshee and Pitlochry.
POSTING IN ALL ITS BRANCHES.

Coach from Kirkmichael daily at 9.30 A.M. and Blairgowrie 2.30 P.M. *Telegraphic* communication. JAMES DEWAR, *Proprietor.*

LLANDUDNO.

THE IMPERIAL FAMILY HOTEL.

(CENTRE OF BAY.)

IN consequence of the EXTENSIVE PATRONAGE which this Hotel has enjoyed since it was opened in 1872, it has been found necessary to ADD A NEW WING. APARTMENTS *EN SUITE.*

ELEGANT BILLIARD SALOON FOR THREE TABLES.

An Omnibus attends all Trains. EXCELLENT STABLING. *Tariff on Application.*

JOHN CHANTREY, *Proprietor.*

LLANDUDNO.

MOON'S PRIVATE HOTEL.

Two Minutes' Walk from Station.

TOURISTS, Families, and Gentlemen visiting this Fashionable Seaside Resort, will find the above Hotel replete with all that can be desired.

Good Bedrooms, Private Sitting Rooms, Coffee Room, Ladies' Coffee Room, and Smoke Room.

Charges Moderate, either by Day or Week.

MRS. MOON, *Proprietress.*

LLANGOLLEN.

EDWARDS' HAND HOTEL.

Unequalled for the Beauty of its Situation on the Banks of the Dee.

Several Bedrooms and Sitting Rooms have been added to the House to suit the requirements of Families visiting this delightful Neighbourhood.

TABLE D'HOTE, 6.30. BILLIARDS.

Omnibuses from this Hotel meet all Trains.

THE LOCH AWE AND DALMALLY HOTELS,

ARGYLESHIRE.

THE scenery round these well-known Hotels is certainly the finest in the Highlands. Situations unsurpassed. The great centres for tourists. Numerous delightful Excursions by coach, rail, and steamer.

Capital Salmon and Trout Fishing, Boating, Tennis, Billiards, etc.

DUNCAN FRASER, *Proprietor.*

LOCH EARN HEAD.

LOCH EARN HEAD HOTEL,

BALQUHIDDER, PERTHSHIRE.

12 miles by rail from Callander.

(Under Royal Patronage. Twice visited by the Queen.)

THIS Hotel, which has been long established, has excellent accommodation for Families and Tourists, with every comfort and quiet, lies high and dry, and charmingly sheltered at the foot of the Wild Glen Ogle (the Kyber Pass). It commands fine views of the surrounding Hills and Loch, the old Castle of Glenample, the scenery of the Legend of Montrose, in the neighbourhood of Ben Voirlich, Rob Roy's Grave, Loch Voil, Loch Doine, and Loch Lubnaig, with many fine drives and walks. Posting and Carriages. Boats for Fishing and Rowing free. A 'Bus to and from the Hotel for the Trains during Summer. Coaches to and from Crieff daily in Summer.

R. DAYTON.

The Callander and Oban Railway is now open. Parties breaking the journey here can proceed next morning with greater comfort.

LOCH FYNE.

CAIRNDOW HOTEL,
HEAD OF LOCH FYNE.

PARTIES staying at the Hotel can have excellent Salmon and Trout Fishing, free of charge, on the River Kinglass and Loch Restal. See pages 188 and 184 of *The Sportsman's and Tourist's Guide.* The Tarbet, Inveraray, and Oban Coaches pass the Hotel daily during the season.

HORSES AND CARRIAGES ON HIRE.

WILLIAM JONES, *Proprietor.*

LOCHLOMOND.

COLQUHOUN ARMS HOTEL, ARDLUI.

Under New Management.

THIS Hotel is situated at the Head of Lochlomond. During the season Coaches in connection with the Lochlomond Steamers, and Callander and Oban Railway, start from this Hotel, where seats may be secured. Carriages for Hire. Fishing on river Falloch and Lochlomond free. Boats for Hire. Parties boarded by week or month. Moderate Charges.

J. BRODIE, *Proprietor.*

LOCHLOMOND.

TARBET HOTEL,

(OPPOSITE BEN-LOMOND)

A. H. MACPHERSON, Proprietor,

IS the finest and most commodious Hotel on the Lake, and commands the best View of Ben-Lomond. Large additions, comprising Bedrooms, Billiard Rooms, and Ladies' Drawing Room, have just been made to the Hotel.

Boarding by the Week or Month.

Coaches direct for the far-famed Glencroe, Inveraray, and Oban, will commence running on 1st June.

Tourists *en route* for Trossachs and Callander can leave per 10 A.M. Steamer, next morning, in connection with the Steamer down Loch-Katrine.

Fishing on Lochlomond free.

Small Boats on the Lake, and Guides to Ben-Lomond, to be had at the Hotel.

LOCHLOMOND.

INVERSNAID HOTEL.

THE landing-place for Loch Katrine, The Trossachs, Aberfoyle, &c. This Hotel has been considerably enlarged.—The additions comprising Large Dining Rooms, several Bedrooms, Drawing Room, Billiard Room, &c. All newly furnished.

The scenery surrounding is unsurpassed.

Carriages can be had on hire, and there are also excellent boats and boatmen to be had for the use of Anglers or Excursionists on the Loch.

Arrangements can be made by Parties for Board by the Week or Month.

ROBERT BLAIR, *Proprietor.*

LOCHLOMOND.

BALLOCH HOTEL, FOOT OF LOCHLOMOND.

THE above Hotel is beautifully situated at the foot of the "Queen of Scottish Lakes," and within two minutes' walk of the Railway Station. Visitors will find every comfort, combined with moderate charges.
First-class Billiard Room, Smoking Room, Hot and Cold Baths, &c.
Parties purposing to proceed by first Steamer up Lochlomond would do well to arrive at the Hotel the previous evening.
Visitors staying at the Hotel have the privilege of walking through the Grounds and Flower Gardens of Mr. Campbell of Tullichewan Castle, and also permission to visit "Mount Misery," which commands 17 miles of the most beautiful portion of Lochlomond—23 islands being comprised in the view. Trout and Salmon Fishing. Posting in all its branches. Boats for the Lake. MRS. M'DOUGALL, *Proprietrix.*

CRIANLARICH HOTEL,

NEAR LOCH LOMOND.

JOSEPH STEWART begs to inform the public that he has lately entered on a lease of this Hotel, which has been improved, comfortably fitted up, and furnished anew. The River Fillan and Loch Dochart—in the immediate vicinity, abounding in fine trout—offer excellent sport for parties residing at the Inn, for whose accommodation a boat is kept, free of charge. The Railway Station is within one minute's walk from the Hotel. Charges strictly moderate. Coaches in connection with Callander and Oban Railway, and Loch Lomond Steamers, start from this Hotel daily.

DALLAS'S
DRUMNADROCHIT HOTEL,
GLEN URQUHART, INVERNESS-SHIRE.

THIS old-established and well-known Hotel has been entirely rebuilt on a first-class scale, having now Thirty large Bedrooms, splendid Coffee and Drawing Rooms, besides Parlours, Smoking Room, Bath Room, and all conveniences. The House was specially built for an Hotel, and is newly and elegantly furnished in the most modern style, and Families and Visitors are now afforded first-class accommodation, combined with comfort and quiet, at moderate charges.

The Walks and Drives around Drumnadrochit are unrivalled for beauty, variety, and extent, while in the immediate vicinity is scenery made famous by Phillips, Millais, Shirley Brooks, John Bright, and others. Within convenient distances are Urquhart Castle, Falls of Dhivach, Dog Falls, and the famous Glen Affric and Strathglass.

Visitors staying at the Hotel have liberty to fish in Loch Ness, and other Fishing can be had in the neighbourhood.

Posting complete in all Departments, and Conveyances, on Intimation, will meet all Steamers.

LETTERS AND TELEGRAMS CAREFULLY ATTENDED TO.

J. SIMPSON, *Lessee.*

Drumnadrochit Post and Telegraph Office within Two Minutes' walk of Hotel.

MR. MACBRAYNE'S STEAMERS CALL AT TEMPLE PIER DAILY.

LONDON.

UPPER NORWOOD.

NEAR THE CRYSTAL PALACE.

THE QUEEN'S HOTEL.

THIS unique establishment stands unrivalled for the exquisite picturesqueness and beauty of its situation, its commanding and central position, and the commodiousness and completeness of its general arrangements. Delicate Persons, to whom a light bracing air, charming scenery, close vicinity to the Crystal Palace and its amusements, and quiet seclusion, would be an invaluable boon, will find, in this establishment, their wishes fully realised. New stables have lately been added to the Hotel, giving every accommodation for gentlemen's horses and carriages.

"THE QUEEN'S HOTEL, at Upper Norwood, is like a Private Royal Residence, managed with marvellous quietness, and is replete with all domestic comforts and appliances, being a veritable home for individuals as well as families. Lately there have been added some new rooms of magnificent proportions, suitable for balls, wedding breakfasts, public dinners, &c. Ladies and gentlemen can make use of a most delightful coffee-room for meals, overlooking the beautiful grounds. For gentlemen there are billiard and smoking rooms, and also a private club. It deserves the special attention of the nobility and gentry, and their families, who may be seeking the means of restoration to health, both of mind and body, without going far from London."—From the *Court Journal.*

SPECIAL NOTICE OF WINTER ARRANGEMENTS AND TERMS AT THE ABOVE HOTEL

The Patrons of this establishment are respectfully informed that Tourists, Families, and others are received on most reasonable terms for the Winter months—which season has many enjoyments for Visitors at the QUEEN'S HOTEL, owing to its elevated, dry, and salubrious situation, and its convenient vicinity to the Crystal Palace and the Winter Garden, whilst it commands by Rail easy access to the West End, the City, &c.

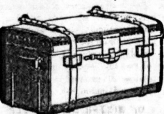

H. KIMPTON, TAILOR, 105 STRAND.

The Stock of Suitings, Trouserings and Overcoatings, for the present and coming Season, in great variety, is now complete, at

H. KIMPTON'S TAILORING ESTABLISHMENT,

105 STRAND, OPPOSITE EXETER HALL, LONDON.

VISITORS TO LONDON.

TRANTER'S TEMPERANCE HOTEL,

7, 8, & 9 BRIDGEWATER SQUARE, BARBICAN, LONDON, E.C.

MOST CENTRAL FOR BUSINESS OR PLEASURE.

Close to Aldersgate Street, Metropolitan Railway Station, and near St. Paul's Cathedral and General Post Office.

Homely, Highly Respectable, and Select; Bed 1s. 6d. to 2s. 6d.
Breakfast or Tea from 1s. to 1s. 9d.   **NO charge for attendance.**
HOT AND COLD BATHS.   ESTABLISHED 1859.

VISITORS' GUIDE TO LONDON—What to see, and How to see it in a Week; and Tariff Card free on application.

BY SPECIAL APPOINTMENT TO HER MAJESTY AND H.R.H. THE PRINCE OF WALES.

TURKEY, PERSIAN, & INDIAN CARPETS.

IMPORTED BY THOS. BONTOR & CO., LATE

WATSON, BONTOR, & COMPANY,

Carpet Manufacturers to the Royal Family,

35 & 36 OLD BOND STREET, LONDON, W.

EXHIBITION MEDALS, 1851, 1862; DUBLIN, 1865; AND AMSTERDAM, 1883.

Superior Brussels, Velvet, Saxony, and all other Carpets in the Newest Designs.

E

MALVERN.
THE FOLEY ARMS HOTEL
(Patronised by the Royal Family).

"THE first time we visited Malvern, when shown into an upper chamber in the 'FOLEY ARMS,' we were literally taken aback. We can hardly say more than that the prospect struck us as far finer than from the terrace over the Thames at Richmond, etc., etc."—*Extract from article in "Blackwood," August 1884.*

COFFEE ROOM FOR LADIES AND GENTLEMEN.
EDWARD ARCHER, *Proprietor.*   MISS YOUNGER, *Manager.*

MALVERN.
THE ABBEY HOTEL,
IN EXCELLENT SITUATION.

MOST COMFORTABLE FAMILY HOTEL.

Coffee Room for Ladies and Gentlemen.

Thoroughly well warmed by New Apparatus during the colder months of the year.

L. ARCHER, *Proprietor.*   MISS COGHLAN, *Manager.*

SMEDLEY'S
HYDROPATHIC ESTABLISHMENT,
MATLOCK.

Railway Station—Matlock Bridge.
Postal and Telegraph Address—Matlock Bank.

Physicians.
WILLIAM B. HUNTER, M.D., etc. | GEORGE TENNANT, M.B., etc. (Resident).

FOUNDED by the late John Smedley upwards of thirty years ago, this Establishment has gone on increasing until, from an origin the most insignificant, it has become one of the largest in the Kingdom. Additions are still in progress, but gradually and quietly, so as to avoid interference with the comfort of the Residents.

The Turkish and Russian Baths are specially adapted in Ventilation and Management to the requirements of invalids, and the diet, meal hours, and general arrangements of the house have special regard to the same without being unnecessarily restrictive.

An Hydraulic Lift gives access to the greater part of the bedroom flight. The heating, ventilation, and sanitary arrangements are under constant and skilled supervision, and amusements are provided to the utmost compatible with the primary purpose of the place.

For fuller particulars see Prospectus, to be had on application to the Matron.

MATLOCK BATH, DERBYSHIRE.

(On the Main Midland Line.)

TYACK'S NEW BATH HOTEL,

Adjoining the New Pavilion, Public Gardens, Concert Room, etc.

THIS first-class old-established Family House, acknowledged to be one of the most homely and comfortable Hotels in the kingdom, is beautifully situated on the highest and most open part of the valley, surrounded by its own extensive Pleasure Grounds, commanding the finest views of the grand and picturesque scenery for which Matlock Bath (the Switzerland of England) stands unrivalled. Matlock is the most central place for day excursions to the most interesting parts of Derbyshire. A Public 'Bus to Haddon and Chatsworth daily.

A Public Dining Room and Drawing Room. Private Sitting Rooms. Coffee, Smoking, and Billiard Rooms. A large natural Tepid Swimming Bath, 68 degrees. TABLE D'HÔTE daily at 6.30 p.m. Excellent Stabling and Coach Houses. Posting, &c.

An Omnibus to and from each Train.

LAWN TENNIS AND CROQUET. GOOD FISHING.

Places of interest in the vicinity:—Buxton, Chatsworth, Haddon Hall, Castleton, Dovedale, Wingfield Manor, Hardwick Hall, &c.

MATLOCK BATH.

THE ROYAL HOTEL

(Adjoining the Pavilion and Gardens),

HAVING been rebuilt and newly furnished, now contains accommodation for 150 guests. Public Dining and Drawing Rooms. Table d'Hôte at 6.30. Hot, Cold, and Shower Baths. Natural Tepid Swimming Bath in the Hotel. Billiards, Bowls, Lawn Tennis, etc.

Omnibus meets all Trains.   Tariff Moderate.

W. H. IVATTS, *Manager.*

MATLOCK BATH.

WALKER'S BATH TERRACE HOTEL.

Pleasantly situated near the New Pavilion and Public Gardens.

FOR FAMILIES AND TOURISTS.

ESTABLISHED 1798.   *TERMS MODERATE.*

MELFORT.

CUILFAIL HOTEL,

PASS OF MELFORT, NEAR OBAN.

ADVICE TO ANGLERS.

When tired an forfouchen,	Take yer rods an yer reels,
When houstin' and coughin',	Throw the doctor his peels,
When ill wi' the bile	An come doon to Cuilfail
Or the wee deevils blue—	Wi' yer friens leal and true.

FIRST-CLASS Trout Fishing free—Season, 1st of April to end of September. The Hotel has been greatly enlarged and comfortably furnished; and splendid Billiard Room, Hot and Cold Baths, and all conveniences connected with Hotels. Families boarded by the week or month. The Lochs are well stocked with Trout, and the Hotel-keeper gets a fresh supply of Loch Leven and the Great American Brook Trout annually from the Howietoun Fishery, Stirling, for keeping up the stock of Trout, and improving the Fishing. Gentlemen can rely on getting good sport. Boats and steady boatmen are kept for the use of Anglers. There is excellent deep-sea fishing, and delightful sea-bathing. The scenery about is magnificent, including the famous Pass of Melfort, which is within a few minutes' walk from the Hotel. Postal delivery daily. Route by Caledonian Railway to Oban, thence Coach daily, or by Steamer "Columba," to Ardrishaig, thence Coach daily.　　Lawn Tennis.

Address—JOHN M'FADYEN,

CUILFAIL HOTEL,

KILMELFORD,

By LOCHGILPHEAD, N.B.

Telegraph Office—Kilmartin, N.B.

THE
WAVERLEY HYDROPATHIC ESTABLISHMENT,
MELROSE.

ONE hour from Edinburgh, one and a half from Carlisle. Terms from £2 : 2s. per week. Summer, from £2 : 9s. Billiards, Bowling, Lawn Tennis, Trout Fishing in Tweed included. First-class Table.

For Prospectus apply to the Manager.

MELROSE.

THE ABBEY HOTEL, ABBEY GATE.

THIS is the only Hotel which is built on the Abbey Grounds, at the entrance to the far-famed ruins of Melrose Abbey. An extensive addition having been built to the Establishment, consisting of Private Sitting Rooms, Bedrooms, Billiard Room, &c. &c., it is now the largest Hotel in Melrose, and only two minutes' walk from the Railway Station.

First-class Horses and Carriages to Abbotsford and Dryburgh Abbey.

An Omnibus attends all trains to convey Visitors' Luggage to and from the Hotel. 　·　　GEORGE HAMILTON, PROPRIETOR.

MELROSE, CLEAVER'S KING'S ARMS HOTEL.

Two Minutes' walk from Railway Station and Abbey.

TOURISTS and Visitors coming to this Hotel are cautioned against taking a cab at the Railway Station, and are requested either to take the King's Arms Omnibus (which attends all trains) or walk down to the Hotel, where Carriages of every description can be had for Abbotsford, Dryburgh, etc.

MOFFAT, DUMFRIESSHIRE.

THE MOFFAT HYDROPATHIC AND PENSION,

One of the largest and best establishments of the kind in the kingdom, is beautifully situated amidst magnificent mountain scenery.

The BATHS—comprising large SWIMMING, TURKISH, SPRAY, VAPOUR, etc.—are of the most perfect construction, and free to all Visitors.

Commodious BILLIARD, SMOKING, and READING ROOMS.

SEPARATE DINING ROOM FOR CHILDREN.

SPECIAL ATTENTION is paid to the CUISINE.

(Wines may be used at Table or not, at Visitors' discretion.)

For Terms apply to

Mr. FARQUHARSON, Resident Manager and Secretary.

MOFFAT SPA.

ANNANDALE ARMS HOTEL.

TOURISTS and Visitors to this famous Watering-Place will find at the ANNANDALE ARMS first-class accommodation, combined with Moderate Charges. Commercial Gentlemen will find every attention to their convenience and interests. 'Buses meet the Trains at Moffat Station. A Summer Excursion Omnibus runs along the route, passing "Craigieburn Wood," Bodesbeck, Grey Mare's Tail—to St. Mary's Loch, every Tuesday, Thursday, and Saturday, in connection with a Coach to Selkirk.

OMNIBUSES PLY TO THE WELL EVERY MORNING.

Carriages of all kinds.   Job and Post Horses on Hire.

ROBERT NORRIS, *Proprietor.*

MONMOUTH.

VALLEY OF THE WYE.

THE KING'S HEAD HOTEL
AND POSTING HOUSE.

THIS old-established Hotel, situate in Agincourt Square, the centre of the town, is replete with every accommodation for Families and Tourists, at Moderate Charges.

A SPACIOUS LADIES' COFFEE ROOM,
AND A SUPERIOR BILLIARD ROOM.

An Omnibus meets every Train.

JOHN THOMAS, PROPRIETOR.

OBAN.

THE CRAIG-ARD HOTEL.

FIRST-CLASS.

THIS Hotel is unrivalled for situation and view; built expressly for summer visitors; commanding extensive views of the beautiful bay of Oban and other romantic scenery in the neighbourhood. The hotel is situated on an elevated plateau near the steamboat wharf, to which a new and convenient approach has been lately added.

The Wines and Cuisine are of the first quality.

Omnibus awaits arrival of all Trains and Steamers.

D. C. MACMILLAN, *Proprietor.*

OBAN.

THE ALEXANDRA

FIRST-CLASS HOTEL,

ON THE ESPLANADE, OBAN.

———

Stands within its own Grounds, and commands the Finest
View in Oban.

———

Omnibus waits arrival of Trains and Steamers.

L. G. M‘ARTHUR, *Proprietor.*

OBAN.

KING'S ARMS HOTEL

HAS a commanding sea view; is adjacent to the railway station and
steamboat wharf; and possesses home comforts, combined with
moderate charges.

LADIES' DRAWING ROOM.   BILLIARD, SMOKING, and BATH ROOMS.

Parties boarded on moderate terms.

Tariff on application.   *Table d'Hôte daily.*

Boots waits the arrival of Trains and Steamers.   Boat kept for fishing.

ALEX. M'TAVISH, PROPRIETOR.

OBAN.

SUTHERLAND'S GREAT WESTERN HOTEL.

LEADING HOTEL IN OBAN.

REPLETE WITH EVERY COMFORT.   BEST SITUATION.

An Omnibus attends the arrival and departure of Trains and Steamers.

Visitors conveyed to and from the Hotel free of Charge.

OBAN.

GRAND HOTEL.

Overlooking the Bay; commanding a beautiful and extensive
view of the surrounding Mountain and Lake Scenery.

Parties Boarded on the most Moderate Terms.

Omnibus awaits arrival of Trains and Steamers.

CHARGES STRICTLY MODERATE.

LETTERS AND TELEGRAMS PUNCTUALLY ATTENDED TO.

WILLIAM HOWE, *Proprietor.*

ANGUS'S

IMPERIAL HOTEL,

OBAN.

Immediately opposite the Steamboat Pier.

74 OXFORD—PENZANCE.

OXFORD.

RANDOLPH HOTEL,
IN THE CENTRE OF THE CITY.

THE only modern built Hotel in Oxford, close to the Colleges and
Public Buildings, and commanding a fine open view down
Beaumont Street, St, Giles's Street, and Magdalen Street, opposite

THE MARTYRS' MEMORIAL.

*Handsome Suites of Apartments. Drawing Room, Billiard Rooms, and
every modern comfort and convenience.
Excellent Wines imported direct from abroad.*

CHARGES MODERATE.

GOOD STABLING AND LOOSE BOXES.

Visitors at this Hotel will meet with every attention and
consideration.

ADDRESS—THE MANAGER.

OXFORD.

THE CLARENDON HOTEL.

PATRONISED by H.R.H. the Prince of Wales, H.R.H. Prince Leopold, Their
Imperial Majesties The Emperor and Empress of Brazil, The Princess Frederick
Charles of Prussia, and Prince Louis Lucien Bonaparte.
Situate in the most central part of the city, near the principal Colleges and places
of interest to Visitors. Families and Gentlemen will find the Hotel replete with every
comfort. SPACIOUS COFFEE AND BILLIARD ROOMS.

PRIVATE SITTING AND BEDROOMS (en suite). LADIES' COFFEE ROOM.
Guides always in Attendance. Fashionable Open and Close Carriages.
Job and Post Horses. Good Stabling and commodious Coach Houses.
JOHN F. ATTWOOD, *Proprietor.*

PENZANCE.

MOUNT'S BAY HOTEL,
ON THE ESPLANADE.

THIS old-established Hotel commands a better view of Mount's Bay than any other
Hotel in Penzance, as all the windows in the front and at side have an
Uninterrupted and unsurpassed View of all the Bay and St. Michael's Mount.
THE HOTEL IS HEATED WITH HOT WATER. HOT AND COLD BATHS.
Choice Wines, etc. Post Horses and Carriages.
TABLE D'HOTE. PORTER MEETS EACH TRAIN. CHARGES MODERATE.
Terms and View on Application.
MRS. LAVIN, *Proprietress.*

PENZANCE.

QUEEN'S HOTEL.

ON THE ESPLANADE.

THIS magnificent Hotel has a frontage of over 170 feet, all the rooms of which overlook the sea. Penzance stands unrivalled for the variety and quiet beauty of its scenery, whilst the mildness of its climate is admirably adapted to invalids. Apartments *en suite.* Ladies' Drawing and Coffee Rooms, Billiard and Smoking Rooms, Hot and Cold Baths. Table d'Hôte.

An Omnibus meets every Train.

POSTING IN ALL ITS BRANCHES.

ALEX. H. HORA, *Proprietor.*

PERTH.

SALUTATION HOTEL.

AT this old-established and well-known Hotel (under new management) Tourists, Commercial Gentlemen, and Families will find comfort and attention, combined with strictly moderate charges. Special terms for cyclists.

BILLIARD ROOM WITH FIRST CLASS TABLES.

HOTEL 'BUS AWAITS THE ARRIVAL OF TRAINS.

Orders by Letter or Telegram receive prompt attention.

W. CARGILL, *Proprietor.*

PITLOCHRIE.
FISHER'S HOTEL,
FIRST-CLASS FAMILY HOTEL
AND
POSTING ESTABLISHMENT.

PARTIES wishing to see the magnificent Scenery in this part of the Scottish Highlands will find this Hotel (to which large additions have been made) most convenient, for in One Drive they can visit the

Falls of Tummel, the Queen's View of Loch Tummel;
The Far-Famed Pass of Killiecrankie;
Glen Tilt; The Falls of Bruar, &c.

Pitlochrie is on the direct route to Balmoral Castle, by Spittal of Glenshee and Braemar; and to Taymouth Castle and Kinloch-Rannoch, by Tummel Bridge.

Salmon and Trout Fishing on the Rivers Tummel and Garry, and on the Lochs in the neighbourhood.

EXCURSION COACHES
leave the Hotel daily during the summer season for Pass of Killiecrankie, Falls of Bruar, Queen's View on Loch Tummel, Kinloch-Rannoch, Glen Tilt, &c. Seats secured at the Hotel. Fares moderate.

Job and Post Horses and Carriages of every kind,
By the Day, Week, or Month.

ORDERS BY TELEGRAPH FOR ROOMS, CARRIAGES, OR COACH SEATS, PUNCTUALLY ATTENDED TO.

The Royal Hotel, Plymouth.

Two Lines of Railway from London and the North of England to Plymouth; viz.—Great-Western and London and South-Western.

EXTENSIVE POSTING ESTABLISHMENT.

Re-decorated. Re-furnished. Spacious General Coffee Room.
Retiring Room for Ladies.
Good Smoking Room for Gentlemen staying in the Hotel.

S. PEARSE, PROPRIETOR.

PORTREE HOTEL.

DONALD M'INNES, *Proprietor.*

THIS well-known and first-class Hotel is now under the experienced management of
MR. M'INNES, who will be in constant attendance to look after the comfort of his
patrons. The House is of modern construction,and admirably adapted for the purposes of
a first-class Family and Commercial Hotel. The accommodation is superior and most
ample, consisting of about sixty Apartments, including elegant Sitting Rooms, nice airy
Bedrooms, commodious Coffee and Smoking Rooms, well-lighted Bathrooms, &c.

The TARIFF has been drawn up on the most moderate scale. Special terms made
with Parties staying a week or longer.

First-Class carriages always on hire, and well-appointed Conveyances leave daily for
Coruisk, Quiraing, and other Places of Interest in Skye.

Post and Telegraph Offices Next Door.

PRESTON, LANCASHIRE.

Half-way between London and Edinburgh, and London and Glasgow.

THE VICTORIA HOTEL.

Close to the Railway Station. Established 47 Years.
Night Porter. Charges Reasonable.

GOOD STABLING AND COACH-HOUSES.

MISS BILLINGTON, *Proprietress.*

RIPON, FOUNTAINS ABBEY.

UNICORN HOTEL AND POSTING HOUSE.

PATRONISED BY H.R.H. PRINCE OF WALES.

ONE of the Oldest Established Hotels in the North of England, and
the principal in Ripon. To meet requirements it has been lately
much enlarged and improved.

Orders by Post punctually attended to.

R. E. COLLINSON, WINE AND SPIRIT MERCHANT, *Proprietor.*

ROSSLYN.

THE ROYAL HOTEL.

THIS, the only First-Class Hotel in Rosslyn, affords every comfort to visitors.
Superior Bedroom accommodation. Parties boarded per day, week, or month, on
very moderate terms. The Hotel is beautifully situated, and only two minutes' walk
from that venerable pile of ancient and beautiful architecture, viz. ROSSLYN CHAPEL;
also the ruins of Rosslyn Castle, and classic HAWTHORNDEN.

FIRST-CLASS DINNERS AND PICNIC PARTIES CONTRACTED FOR.

*Luncheon Bar and Restaurant in connection with the Hotel, and superior
Bowling Green 38 yards square.*

PHILP'S
GLENBURN HYDROPATHIC ESTABLISHMENT,
ROTHESAY, BUTE.

 BEAUTIFULLY situated, over-
looking the charming Bay
of Rothesay, bounded by the
Kyles of Bute and the lofty mountains of Argyle—possesses probably the greatest attractions of
any similar establishment in Scotland.   Large   Recreation   Hall,
Smoking and Billiard Rooms,
recently erected.   The Baths—
Turkish, including Salt Water,
and every modern appliance—
finest in Britain.

Resident Physician—DR. PHILP (formerly of Conishead Priory).
For Prospectus, apply to Manager,
or Philp's COCKBURN HOTELS, Edinburgh and Glasgow.

ROTHESAY, ISLE OF BUTE.
(Opposite the Pier.)
THE BUTE ARMS HOTEL.
(UNDER NEW MANAGEMENT.)
THIS Old-Established and First-Class Hotel affords excellent accom-
modation for Families, Tourists, and Commercial Gentlemen.
Charges Strictly Moderate.
PARTIES BOARDED BY THE WEEK OR MONTH.
ROBERT SMITH, *Proprietor.*

SETTLE.
CRAVEN DISTRICT and NEW ROUTE to SCOTLAND.
THE GOLDEN LION HOTEL,
ESTABLISHED OVER TWO CENTURIES.
THIS old-established Hotel is Now Open under New Management, and thoroughly
renovated and refurnished throughout, without regard to cost, by Messrs. Gillows
and Co., and offers every accommodation for Visitors, combined with the comforts of
home. Private Sitting Rooms, spacious Coffee Room, Commercial Room, Smoke Room,
and every accommodation for Private Families and Commercial Gentlemen. The Tariff
is strictly moderate and uniform.   Post Horses, Conveyances.   Omnibus attends all
Trains both at Settle and Giggleswick Stations.
A. G. WOOLISCROFT, *Manageress.*

SALISBURY.

THE WHITE HART HOTEL.

The Largest and Principal Hotel in the City.

AN old-established and well-known first-class Family Hotel, nearly opposite Salisbury Cathedral, and within a pleasant drive of Stonehenge. This Hotel is acknowledged to be one of the most comfortable in England.

A Ladies' Coffee Room, a Coffee Room for Gentlemen, and first-class Billiard and Smoking Rooms.

Carriages and Horses of every description for Stonehenge and other places of interest. Excellent Stabling. Loose Boxes, etc.

Posting-Masters to Her Majesty.

Tariff on application to H. T. BOWES, *Manager.*

SKIPTON.

THE MIDLAND HOTEL.

Opposite the Railway Station.

BREAK your journey, and stay at the above Hotel, and visit Bolton Abbey and Woods, Malham and Gordale Scar, Kilnsay, and other places of interest in the neighbourhood. Horses and Carriages for hire. Picnic Parties arranged for. This well-appointed Hotel offers superior accommodation to Families and Gentlemen, containing spacious Coffee, Private Sitting, and Smoking Rooms. Visitors will meet with home comforts and attention. Private Bowling Green attached.

JOHN THROUP, *Proprietor.*

SKIPTON.

THE DEVONSHIRE HOTEL.

AN old-established First-class Family and Commercial Hotel, in the centre of the Town. Parties visiting "BOLTON ABBEY" will find this Hotel within an easy distance; with comfort, superior accommodation, and moderate charges combined. Conveyances of all kinds on hire.

Billiards and Bowling Green.

AN HOTEL OMNIBUS MEETS THE TRAINS.

Mrs. EDMUND WRIGLEY, *Proprietrix.*

F

THE
HIGHLAND SULPHUR SPA,
STRATHPEFFER, ROSS-SHIRE.

THE Sulphur Waters of Strathpeffer are among the strongest of
the Sulphur Waters of Europe, and are unrivalled in Britain
in the treatment of Chronic Rheumatism, Gout, Diseases of the
Skin, and Affections of the Liver and Kidneys. *See Dr. Manson's
Pamphlet on Strathpeffer* (5th Edition).

There are Four Hotels, besides a number of handsome Villas, at
the Spa, thus affording ample Accommodation. The varied Scenery
of the district is unsurpassed in Scotland. Post and Telegraph
Offices. There is a resident Physician, Dr. Fox from the London
Hospital, who has made the Waters a special study.

Splendid Pavilion for Balls, Concerts, etc.

These Waters are in themselves more potent as a Curative Agent in
the Spring and Autumn, while the Hotels' and Lodging Houses' Charges
are comparatively lower than during the height of the Season.

For further Particulars, apply to THE MANAGER.

THE BEN WYVIS HOTEL,
STRATHPEFFER SPA, ROSS-SHIRE, N.B.

VISITORS to this popular Watering-place will find this Hotel
replete with every comfort, combined with charges *strictly
moderate.* It stands within its own grounds, which comprise
Bowling, Croquet, and Lawn-Tennis Greens, is surrounded with
grand scenery, and commands a splendid view of Ben Wyvis, the
ascent of which can be accomplished from the Hotel in a few hours.

The BEN WYVIS HOTEL, which contains Public and Private
Apartments *en suite*, Billiard Room, &c., is within two minutes'
walk of the Mineral Wells and Baths, and of Post and Telegraph
Offices.

The Hotel is within two minutes' walk of the new Strathpeffer
Station, and is a convenient point from which to visit Skye, Loch
Maree, Dunrobin, &c. &c.

Orders for Apartments and Carriages punctually attended to.

APPLY TO THE MANAGER.

STIRLING.

ROYAL HOTEL.

THIS old-established First-Class Hotel is conveniently situated for Families, Tourists, and Commercial Gentlemen, being within three minutes' walk of the Railway Station. Carriages of every description kept at the Hotel. *Omnibus awaits all Trains.*

A. CAMPBELL, *Proprietor.*

STRATHPEFFER.

SPA HOTEL,

STRATHPEFFER.

AN Old-Established Family Hotel, beautifully situated, and commanding some of the finest views in Strathpeffer. The Spa Hotel is well known as a FIRST-CLASS House, is noted for the excellence of its Cuisine, and is unrivalled for cleanliness and comfort.

PARTIES BOARDED BY THE DAY OR WEEK.
Charges Strictly Moderate.

MRS. EDWARDS, *Proprietrix.*

TAYNUILT.

TAYNUILT HOTEL.

THIS Hotel is situated near Loch Etive, within two minutes' walk from the Taynuilt Station on the Callander and Oban Railway. Visitors have the privilege of Salmon and Trout Fishing on the River Awe.

JAMES MURRAY, *Proprietor.*

Post Horses, Carriages, &c.

TORQUAY.

GREAT WESTERN HOTEL.

THE best Views, elegantly Furnished, and the most moderate Tariff. Visitors taken at fixed charges by the week. Every modern accommodation. Luggage to and from Hotel free of charge.

Unrivalled for Scenery, Comfort, and Convenience.

E. A. SAUNDERS, *Proprietor.*

TARBERT HOTEL,
ISLE OF HARRIS.
SALMON & SEA-TROUT FISHING FREE. SEA-FISHING.
ROBERT HORNSBY

BEGS respectfully to call the attention of Tourists, Anglers, &c., to his Hotel, where they will find every comfort and good sport. Parties living in the Hotel can get good Salmon and Sea-trout Fishing, or they can have Boats for Sea-Fishing. Various Lochs in connection with the Establishment. Post Horses and Carriages are kept for hire. The scenery of Harris is magnificent, including a view of St. Kilda, and the climate is extremely healthy.

The Steamer DUNARA CASTLE, from Glasgow, calls every week; and the Steamer CLYDESDALE, also from Glasgow, every fortnight.

The Lochs of the Island of Scalpa can be fished by residing at this Hotel, and Excursions can be arranged to all the outlying Islands.

The Shootings of the Island of Scalpay, &c., also Seal Shooting, are attached to the Hotel.

Yachts supplied with Stores and Fresh Vegetables.

Reading Parties taken in by the Week or Month.

TROSSACHS.
STRONACLACHER HOTEL.
(HEAD OF LOCH KATRINE.)

DONALD FERGUSON begs to intimate that he has lately completed extensive alterations and additions to his Hotel, and that it will be his constant endeavour, as heretofore, to secure every comfort and attention to Tourists and others favouring him with their patronage. It is the best Fishing-Station, and Boats, with experienced Boatmen, are always in readiness. During the Season Coaches run to and from Inversnaid in connection with Steamers on Loch Katrine and Loch Lomond.

Carriages and other Conveyances kept for Hire.

TYNDRUM HOTEL
PERTHSHIRE.

JOSEPH STEWART of Crianlarich Hotel begs to intimate that he has taken a lease of the above first-class Hotel, and hopes by strict attention and moderate charges to merit a share of patronage.

Fishing on Lochs Nabea and Dochart and River Fillan free of charge.

POSTING IN ALL ITS BRANCHES.

YORK.
HARKER'S YORK HOTEL,
ST. HELEN'S SQUARE.

THIS long-established First-Class Hotel occupies the best Situation in the City, being nearest to the Minster and the Ruins of St. Mary's Abbey ; is free from all noise of Trains, and surrounded by the patent wooden pavement.   P. MATTHEWS, *Proprietor*,

Also of the North-Eastern Family Hotel.

YORK.
MATTHEWS' NORTH-EASTERN FAMILY HOTEL
(LATE ABBOTT'S)

CONTAINS every appointment of a Modern First-Class Hotel for Families and Gentlemen. Situated within three minutes' walk of New Railway Station, and free from the noise of trains.

The Hotel Porters meet all trains day and night to convey Visitors' luggage, and will be found under the Portico at the entrance to the Station.

P. MATTHEWS, *Proprietor*,
Also of Harker's York Hotel.

HYDROPATHY.
DR. RAYNER'S ESTABLISHMENT AND WINTER RESIDENCE,
GREAT MALVERN.

For the scientific application of Warm and Cold Water Treatment, and for Persons requiring rest and change.   Complete system of Hydropathic, Galvanic, and Medicated Baths, including Droitwich Brine.

For Prospectus apply to T. RAYNER, M.D., Great Malvern.

THE

BRAEMAR, DUNKELD, BLAIRGOWRIE, AND GLENSHEE COACHES

WILL COMMENCE RUNNING ON 1st JULY,

Leaving BRAEMAR at 8 A.M., DUNKELD at 9 A.M., BLAIRGOWRIE at 11 A.M., every lawful day.

FIFE ARMS HOTEL, BRAEMAR, *April* 1885.

LONDON & SOUTH-WESTERN RAILWAY,
WATERLOO STATION, LONDON.

The Shortest and Quickest Route to the South-West and West of England, EXETER, BARNSTAPLE, BIDEFORD (" Westward Ho !"), ILFRACOMBE, NORTH and SOUTH DEVON, BUDE *via* HOLSWORTHY, TAVISTOCK, LAUNCESTON, PLYMOUTH, DEVONPORT, WEYMOUTH, BOURNEMOUTH, SOUTHAMPTON, PORTSMOUTH, STOKES BAY, and ISLE OF WIGHT.   The only throughout Railway to Ilfracombe.

Fast Expresses at Ordinary Fares, and Frequent Fast Trains.

All Trains convey Third-Class Passengers.

CHEAP TOURIST AND EXCURSION TICKETS.

Through Tickets in connection with the London and North-Western, Great Northern, and Midland Railways.   Regular Mail Steam-Ships, *via* Southampton, to and from the CHANNEL ISLANDS, JERSEY, and GUERNSEY.   Also Fast Steam-Ships for HAVRE, ROUEN, and PARIS, ST. MALO, CHERBOURG, GRANVILLE, and HONFLEUR.   The Company's Steam-Ships are not surpassed in Speed or Accommodation by any Channel Vessels.

CHARLES SCOTTER, *General Manager.*

GREAT WESTERN RAILWAY.

TOURIST ARRANGEMENTS.

FIRST, SECOND, and THIRD CLASS TOURIST TICKETS, available for two months, and renewable, with exceptions, up to Dec. 31st, are issued during the Summer months of each year, AT THE PRINCIPAL STATIONS ON THIS RAILWAY, to the Watering and other places of attraction in the WEST OF ENGLAND, including :—

CLEVEDON.	LYNTON.	TORQUAY.	ST. IVES.
WESTON-SUPER-MARE.	EXETER.	PLYMOUTH.	PENZANCE.
MINEHEAD.	DARTMOUTH.	DEVONPORT.	SCILLY ISLANDS.
BARNSTAPLE.	DAWLISH.	TRURO.	DORCHESTER.
ILFRACOMBE.	TEIGNMOUTH.	FALMOUTH.	WEYMOUTH, & THE
FOWEY.	NEWTON ABBOT.	NEW QUAY.	CHANNEL ISLANDS.

To North and South Wales, including—

DOLGELLY.	LLANDUDNO.	BANGOR.	TINTERN.
BARMOUTH.	PENMAENMAWR.	CARNARVON.	SWANSEA. TENBY.
ABERYSTWITH.	BLEONAW. FESTINIOG.	HOLYHEAD.	PEMBROKE.
RHYL.	BETTWS-Y-COED.	CHEPSTOW.	NEW MILFORD.
To BUXTON.	WINDERMERE.	EDINBURGH.	WHITBY.
ISLE OF MAN.	SCARBOROUGH.	GLASGOW.	MATLOCK.
To BRIGHTON.	ST. LEONARDS.	ISLE OF WIGHT.	MARGATE.
EASTBOURNE.	HASTINGS.	RAMSGATE.	DOVER.

And to WATERFORD. CORK.   LAKES OF KILLARNEY. DUBLIN, ETC.

Passengers holding 1st or 2d Class Tourist Tickets to the principal stations in the West of England can travel by the 11.45 a.m. Fast Train from Paddington, which reaches Exeter in four hours and a quarter, and Plymouth in 6 hours and 10 minutes ; or by the 3.0 p.m. Fast Train from Paddington, which reaches Exeter in the same time, and Plymouth in 5 hours and 55 minutes.

Tourists by the GREAT WESTERN LINE—THE BROAD GAUGE ROUTE TO THE WEST OF ENGLAND—pass through the most picturesque scenery in Devonshire and Cornwall, extending from Exeter to Plymouth, Falmouth, St. Ives, Penzance, and the Land's End ; while the Broad Gauge Carriages running in the Fast Express Trains to and from the West of England, for which they have been specially built, are THE FINEST RAILWAY CARRIAGES IN ORDINARY USE IN THE KINGDOM.

Holders of Tourist Tickets are allowed to break their journey at several stations en route, and visit at their leisure places of interest in the vicinity. The holders of 1st and 2d Class ordinary tickets between London and Exeter, and places west thereof, are also allowed, both in summer and winter, to break their journey at Bath, Bristol, Taunton, or Exeter, and proceed the next day, —an arrangement which conduces largely to the comfort of invalids and others to whom a lengthened railway journey is objectionable.

FAMILY CARRIAGES (with lavatories and other conveniences), containing compartments for servants, can be engaged on payment of not less than Four First-Class and Four Second-Class Fares. Application for these carriages should be made to the Superintendent of the Line, Paddington, some days before the proposed date of the journey, in order to prevent disappointment.

For particulars of the various Circular Tours, Fares, and other information see the Company's Tourist Programmes, which can be obtained at the Stations and Booking Offices.   J. GRIERSON, General Manager.

LONDON & NORTH-WESTERN AND CALEDONIAN RAILWAYS

West Coast Royal Mail Route between England & Scotland

Via PRESTON AND CARLISLE.

TRAIN SERVICE—1st, 2d, and 3d Class by all Trains.

STATIONS.	WEEK-DAYS.							SUNDAYS.		
	a.m.	a.m.	a.m.	a.m.	p.m.	p.m.	ngt†	p.m.	p.m.	nght
London (Euston)....dep.	5.15	7.15	10.0	11.0	8.50	9.0	12.0	8.50	9.0	12.0
Birmingham (New St.).. „	7.25	8.50	11.30	12.55	10.25	10.25	3.5	10.25	10.25	3.5
Liverpool (Lime Street) „	9.40	10.55	1.45	3.0	11.50	12.50	2.35	10.45	12.50	2.35
„ (Exchange) .. „	10.15	11.40	2.20	3.25	..	..	..	..	..	..
Manchester (Exchange) „	10.0	11.5	1.45	3.5	12.25	1.20	..	12.25	1.20	..
„ (L. and Y.).. „	..	11.10	1.45	3.25	..	..	..	..	..	..
Moffat ....arr.	2.42	4.27	6.47	..	..	..	11.2	..	..	11.2
Edinburgh (Princes Street) „	4.15	5.50	8.0	10.0	6.45	7.50	12.52	6.45	7.50	12.52
Glasgow (Central Station) „	4.25	6.0	8.0	10.15	6.55	8.0	1.15	6.55	8.0	1.15
Greenock .... „	5.50	7.15	9.5	11.42	7.50	*9.48	2.50	7.50	9.48	2.50
Stirling .... „	5.39	..	8.25	10.40	7.21	*8.43	1.57	7.21	8.43	1.57
Oban .... „	9.47	..	..	4.45	12.25	..	6.17	12.25	..	6.17
Perth .... „	6.50	..	9.35	11.50	8.15	*9.55	3.45	8.15	9.55	3.45
Dundee .... „	7.30	..	10.30	1.0	9.0	*12.0	4.45	9.0	12.0	4.45
Aberdeen .... „	10.10	..	..	3.20	11.40	*2.15	8.35	11.40	2.15	8.35
Inverness .... „	..	..	..	8.0	1.30	*6.20	..	1.30	6.20	..

No connection to places marked (*) on Saturday nights. † Not on Saturday nights from London.

UP TRAINS.	p.m.	a.m.	a.m.	a.m.	p.m.	p.m.		a.m.	p.m.	
INVERNESS ....dep.	10.0	..	..	10.10	..	1.30	..	10.10	..	..
Aberdeen .... „	a.m.	..	8.55	12.30	..	4.40	..	12.30	..	..
Dundee .... „	7.40	..	11.10	3.30	..	6.40	..	3.10	..	..
Oban .... „	..	..	6.10	12.35	..	4.0	..	..	..	..
Perth .... „	8.30	..	12.0	4.4	..	7.30	..	4.4	..	..
Stirling .... „	9.30	..	1.5	5.5	..	8.30	..	5.5	..	..
Greenock .... „	9.0	..	1.10	5.0	8.5	..	..	..	..	..
Glasgow (Central Station) „	10.0	10.5	2.15	6.0	9.5	..	..	6.0	9.5	..
Edinburgh (Princes Street) „	10.0	10.25	2.25	6.10	9.10	..	..	6.10	9.10	..
Moffat .... „	10.30	12.10	3.50	..	..	..	..	..	..	..
Manchester (Exchange) arr.	4.35	6.0	8.55	..	..	3.35	..	13.30	3.45	..
„ (L. and Y.).. „	4.5	5.25	8.45	12.22	..	..	..	..	..	..
Liverpool (Lime Street) „	4.35	5.50	9.10	12.10	..	3.45	..	12.10	3.55	..
„ (Exchange) .. „	4.2	..	8.45	..	..	..	..	..	..	..
Birmingham (New St.).. „	6.15	9.10	11.25	2.10	6.10	6.10	..	2.10	6.10	..
	p.m.	p.m.			a.m.	a.m.			a.m.	
London (Euston) ....arr.	8.0	11.20	4.35	4.5	7.15	7.45	..	4.5	8.0	..

Through Guards and Conductors travel by the principal day and night Express Trains.

DRAWING-ROOM SALOONS, without extra charge, fitted with Lavatory accommodation, and furnished with every modern convenience, are run between London and Edinburgh and Glasgow by the train leaving Euston at 10 a.m., returning from Edinburgh and Glasgow by 10 a.m. Up Express. Carriages with Lavatories are also run on all the principal Express and Fast Trains between England and Scotland.

IMPROVED SLEEPING SALOON CARRIAGES, lighted with gas, comfortably heated, and provided with Pillows, Sheets, Blankets, Rugs, Lavatories, etc., are attached to the Night Trains from and to London, Edinburgh, Glasgow, Greenock, Stranraer, Perth, etc., the charge for each Berth being 5s. in addition to the ordinary First-Class Fare. Separate apartments are reserved for ladies travelling alone. Saloons, Family Carriages, Reserved Compartments, and all other conveniences necessary to ensure comfort on the journey, can be arranged upon application to Mr. G. P. NEELE, Superintendent of the L. & N.-W. line, Euston Station, London; Mr. IRVINE KEMPT, General Superintendent, Cal. Rail., Glasgow; or to any of the Station-Masters at the Stations on the West Coast Route.

1ST, 2D, AND 3D CLASS TOURIST TICKETS
Available from date of issue up to and including 31st December 1885,
ARE (DURING THE SEASON) ISSUED FROM

LONDON and all Principal Stations in ENGLAND
TO CHIEF TOURIST RESORTS & PLACES OF INTEREST IN SCOTLAND,
And also from the same places in Scotland to English Stations.
For full particulars see the "West Coast Tourist Guide" (with Maps, price 3d.), which can
be obtained at all Stations.

BREAK OF JOURNEY.—Passengers may break their journey, either going
or returning, at Rugby, Birmingham, Stafford, Crewe, Warrington, Wigan, Preston,
Lancaster, Carnforth, Oxenholme (to enable them to visit Windermere and the other
Lakes), Shap, Penrith, Carlisle, and at any intermediate Station on the direct route between Carlisle and their destination in Scotland. Passengers may also break their journey
at Kenilworth, as also at Leamington (for Stratford-on-Avon) and at Lichfield. Tourists
breaking the journey when travelling in the outward direction are required to produce
both the outward and return halves of their tickets.

TOURIST TICKETS issued by the West Coast Route to Stirling, Oban,
Perth, Dundee, Aberdeen, Inverness, and other Stations north of Larbert, entitle the
Passengers either to travel direct to the North, or first to visit Edinburgh and then
Glasgow, travelling by the Caledonian Line throughout, thus:—To Edinburgh, via
Carstairs: from Edinburgh (Princes St.) to Glasgow, via Caledonian Line; from Glasgow
to the North, via Caledonian Line, and vice versa on return. Tickets are also issued
entitling the holders to travel via Carstairs and Edinburgh, break the journey at the
latter place, and proceed thence to Larbert, starting from the Waverley Station,
Edinburgh, and travelling via Linlithgow, returning by the same route. Passengers
must state at the time of booking by which route they elect to travel, and obtain Tickets
accordingly. Passengers holding Tourist Tickets to Montrose, Brechin, Aberdeen, and
Stations north of Guthrie, may travel via Forfar or via Dundee, in either direction.

DINING.—The Down and Up Day Expresses wait 20 minutes at PRESTON to
enable Passengers to dine, and Hot Dinners are provided, 2s. 6d. each—No fees.
Special Dinners will be provided for Family Parties, on notice being given to the
Conductor at Crewe on the Down journey, and at Carlisle on the Up journey.

LUNCHEON-BASKETS are supplied to Passengers in the Trains at the
Euston, Rugby, Stafford, Crewe, and Preston Stations, at the following charge:—Baskets
containing half a chicken, with ham or tongue, or a portion of cold beef, salad, ice,
bread, cheese, butter, etc., with either half a bottle of claret, two glasses of sherry, or
a pint bottle of stout, 3s. HOT LUNCHEONS, consisting of fillet of beef or mutton
chop, fried potatoes, bread, etc., can be supplied to Passengers in the Trains at Crewe,
Rugby, and Stafford, on giving notice to the guard of the train at the preceding
stopping stations. The charge for the hot luncheon is 3s. with wine or beer, and 2s. 6d.
without. Luncheon-Baskets are provided at Perth for the convenience of Passengers
travelling by the West Coast Route.

OMNIBUSES FOR USE OF FAMILY PARTIES travelling by
the West Coast Route.—The L. and N.-W. Ry. Co. provide, when previously ordered,
Omnibuses capable of carrying six persons inside and two outside, with the usual
quantity of luggage, to meet trains at Euston Station. The Omnibuses will also be
sent to the hotels or residences of parties leaving London by L. and N.-W. Ry. on
application being made to the Station-Master at Euston, stating the train by which
it is intended to leave Euston. The charge for the use of an Omnibus will be as
follows:—For distances under six miles, 1s. per mile; for distances six miles and
over, or when two horses are used at the request of a Passenger, 1s. 6d. per mile,
driver and reasonable quantity of luggage included. Passengers from Scotland, by the
West Coast Route, travelling by the Limited Mail or other Through Scotch Trains
from Perth, Glasgow, Edinburgh, and Stations South, can secure these Omnibuses
to meet the Trains on arrival at Euston Station, by giving notice to the respective
Station-Masters before starting. The Omnibuses can generally be obtained on arrival
of the Train at Euston, even though not previously ordered.

FAMILY LUGGAGE.—Arrangements have been made in London and other
large towns for carting to the Station, at low rates, the luggage of Families travelling by
the L. & N.-W. Ry., and also for forwarding such luggage by Passenger Train in advance.

THE LIMITED MAIL TRAINS travel by the "West Coast Route," and
are in connection with the Mail Coaches to the outlying districts of the Highlands.
These Trains have been accelerated between London and Edinburgh and Glasgow; and
additional accommodation and increased facilities are afforded to Passengers travelling
by them.   May 1885.   By Order.

EAST COAST "EXPRESS" ROUTE.
GREAT NORTHERN AND NORTH-EASTERN RAILWAYS.

SPECIAL EXPRESS TRAINS
BETWEEN LONDON & EDINBURGH & GLASGOW.

LONDON TO EDINBURGH IN 9 HRS.   TO GLASGOW IN 10 HRS. 20 MINS.

ADDITIONAL SPECIAL EXPRESS TRAINS
now run between Glasgow, Edinburgh, and London, as under:

DOWN.		UP.	
KING'S CROSS ...... Dep. 10.0 A.M.		GLASGOW .... Dep. 8.40 A.M.	
EDINBURGH .... Arr. 7.0 P.M.		EDINBURGH .... ,, 10.0 ,,	
GLASGOW .... ,, 8.20 ,,		KING'S CROSS ...... Arr. 7.0 P.M.	

THROUGH WEEK-DAY SERVICE
BETWEEN LONDON AND SCOTLAND BY EAST COAST ROUTE.

DOWN.

	A.M.	A.M.	A.M.	P.M.	P.M.
King's X, Dp.	5.15	10.0	10.35	8.30*	9.0
Edinburgh Ar.	3.30	7.0	8.38	6.0	7.20
Glasgow.. ,,	5.25	8.20	10.25	7.35	9.0
Stirling .. ,,	5.5	8.25	10.26	7.28	8.43
Perth..... ,,	6.40	9.35	11.36	8.23	9.55
Dundee... ,,	6.45	10.30	12.50	9.38	12.0
Aberdeen. ,,	8.40	3.20	3.20	11.40	2.15
Inverness. ,,	..	8.0	8.0	1.30	6.20
Golspie .. ,,	..	1.17	1.17	5.14	..
Helmsdale ,,	..	2.10	2.10	5.51	..
Thurso.... ,,	..	4.45	4.45	7.50	..
Wick .... ,,	..	5.0	5.0	8.0	..

UP.

	A.M.	P.M.	A.M.	P.M.	A.M.
Wick.....Dp.	12.10	..	11.30	11.30	..
Thurso.... ,,	12.25	..	11.40	11.40	..
Helmsdale ,,	3.30	6.0	2.10	2.10	..
Golspie... ,,	4.30	7.0	2.50	2.50	..
Inverness. ,,	10.10	1.30	10.0†	10.0†	..
Aberdeen . ,,	12.30	4.40	..	..	8.55
	P.M.		A.M.	A.M.	
Dundee... ,,	4.0	6.40	7.0	7.0	11.10
Perth..... ,,	4.20	7.35	7.30	7.30	12.0
Oban ... ,,	12.35	4.0	..	..	..
Stirling... ,,	5.19	8.41	8.41	8.41	1.5
Glasgow.. ,,	6.0	8.50	8.40	8.40	1.0
Edinburgh ,,	7.30	10.20	10.0	10.15	2.50
King's X, Ar.	5.45	8.15	7.0	8.30	2.25
	A.M.	A.M.	P.M.	P.M.	A.M.

Third-Class tickets are issued by all trains, except the additional Special Scotch Express trains, from King's Cross at 10.0 A.M., and Edinburgh at 10.0 A.M.

This train service will be in force until 1st July, but from that date the night express train service will be altered and additional fast express trains run between King's Cross and Scotland by East Coast route. An additional day express will leave King's Cross at about 10.25 a.m.

* The 8.30 P.M. Express train from King's Cross is in direct connection with the "Iona" and other West Coast Steamers.

† Not run from Inverness on Saturday nights.

IMPROVED CARRIAGE STOCK
has been constructed, and is now in use, for through traffic between London and Scotland.

PULLMAN CARS & SLEEPING CARRIAGES
are attached to the night trains.

Alterations may be made in the times of the trains from month to month, for particulars of which see the East Coast Railways' Monthly Time Book.

Conductors in charge of through luggage travel with the Express trains leaving London at 10.0, 10.25, and 10.35 A.M., 8.30 and 9.0 P.M.; and Perth at 4.20 P.M. and 7.30 A.M.; and Edinburgh at 10.0, 10.15 A.M., 7.30 P.M., and 10.20 P.M.

EAST COAST ROUTE.
GREAT NORTHERN AND NORTH-EASTERN RAILWAYS.
:TOURIST TICKETS

1st, 2d, and 3d Class, are issued from 1st May until 31st October, and are *available for return, without extra payment, until 31st December 1885.* They are issued in London, at King's Cross Station (G. N. R.), Moorgate Street Station (G. N. R. Office), Victoria (L. C. & D.), 3 Trafalgar Buildings, Charing Cross, 32 Piccadilly Circus, and 285 Oxford Street, to the under-mentioned stations in Scotland :—

FARES FROM KING'S CROSS.

	1st Class s. d.	2d Class s. d.	3d Class s. d.		1st Class s. d.	2d Class s. d.	3d Class s. d.
COLDSTREAM .	96 8	76 0	50 0	PERTH ...	123 3	88 8	54 0
BERWICK ..	94 0	75 4	49 6	DUNKELD ..	127 8	90:10	54 0
MELROSE, *via*				ABERFELDY..	132 3	94 4	56 10
Hexham ..	99 6	74 9	50 0	ST. ANDREWS .	121 9	88 10	56 0
PEEBLES ...	104 9	..	50 0	DUNDEE ...	125·3	90 8	56 0
EDINBURGH..	109 6	79 9	50 0	ARBROATH ..	128 3	92 2	56 0
FORFAR ...	130 3	98 8	56 0	MONTROSE ..	133 0	94 6	56 0
GLASGOW ..	110 3	81 2	52 0	BRECHIN ..	133 0	94 6	56 0
HELENSBURGH.	112 9	82 4	52 0	ABERDEEN ..	133 6	94 9	56 0
LARBERT . . .	112 0	82 0	52 0	BALLATER ..	143 3	105 8	62 10
STIRLING...	114 3	83 10	53 6	PITLOCHRY ..	131 2	93 6	56 0
BRIDGE OF ALLAN	115 0	84 6	54 0	STRUAN ...	134 4	95 10	57 10
DUNBLANE ..	115 6	84 9	54 0	BOAT OF GARTEN	147 10	103 10	60 0
CALLANDER..	118 6	86 3	54 0	KEITH ...	147 6	103 9	60 0
CRIEFF ...	121 6	88 8	54 0	ELGIN. ...	148 6	104 3	60 0
KILLIN ...	122 7	94 7	58 6	INVERNESS ..	150 0	105 0	60 0
DALMALLY ..	129 9	96 2	62 0	NAIRN ...	150 0	105 0	60 0
LOCH AWE ..	130 3	96 8	62 6	FORRES ...	150 0	105 0	60 0
CONNEL FERRY	131 9	97 8	63 6	DINGWALL ..	150 0	108 11	63 1
TAYNUILT ..	131 3	97 2	63 0	ACHNASHEEN .	157 6	112 6	67 6
OBAN, *via* Dal-				STROME FERRY	164 9	117 4	70 0
mally ...	132 3	98 2	64 0	LAIRG..	160 0	115 0	70 0
OBAN, *via* Glas-				GOLSPIE ...	165 0	118 9	72 6
gow or Helens-				HELMSDALE..	170 0	122 6	75 0
burgh ...	130 3	101 2	63 0	THURSO ...	184 6	133 9	83 0
OBAN, Circ. Tour	131 3	102 2	63 6	WICK ...	186 9	135 4	84 0

From Victoria (L. C. & D.) and Moorgate, 8d. 1st, and 6d. 2d Class will be added to the King's Cross fares, except to Berwick.

BREAK OF JOURNEY.

Passengers may break their journey, both in going and returning, at Peterboro', also at Grantham or Doncaster to enable them to visit Lincoln Cathedral, paying the ordinary fares between those places and Lincoln, and at York to enable them to visit Harrogate, Scarboro', and the East Coast watering-places, and also at Darlington, Durham, Newcastle, Bilton, and Belford, resuming it by trains having carriages attached corresponding to the class of ticket held ; also at Berwick or any station north of Berwick on the routes by which the tickets are available. Passengers for places north of Edinburgh and Larbert may break the journey in Edinburgh and at Glasgow, and also at any station at which the train ordinarily stops. The journey can be broken both going and returning, and without restriction as to period, except that the return journey must be completed within the time for which the ticket is available. Passengers with tickets for Melrose (*via* Hexham) are also at liberty to break the journey at St. Boswell's for Dryburgh Abbey. The above facilities and arrangements, as regards passengers breaking their journey, apply equally to 1st, 2d, and 3d class.

Tourist Tickets are available by any train of corresponding class. See the Tourist Programme of the Great Northern or North-Eastern Co. for information as to break of journey, extension of time, &c. &c.

For further information apply at the Offices of the East Coast Ry. Cos. in
Edinburgh, 9 Princes Street.   Dundee, 33 Cowgate.
Glasgow, 32 West George Street.   Aberdeen, 28 Market Street.
Perth, General Station.   Inverness, 6 Academy Street.
Stirling, Spittal Square   Oban, Queen's Park Place
(Mr. A. J. Stephenson).   (Mr. A. Mitchell).

MIDLAND RAILWAY.
ENGLAND AND SCOTLAND.

AN improved service of Express and Fast Trains has been established between the Midland System and Scotland by the Settle and Carlisle Route. A Morning Express Train runs from London to Edinburgh and Glasgow, and also from Glasgow and Edinburgh to London, with a Pullman Parlour Car to and from Glasgow attached (and, commencing June 1st, a Parlour Car will also be run to and from Edinburgh). A Night Express Train runs in each direction between the same places, with Pullman Sleeping Cars attached. Additional Express Trains are also run during the Summer Months. For the convenience of Passengers to and from the West of England and Scotland, a New Service of Express Passenger Trains has been established to and from Bristol, Bath, Gloucester, Cheltenham, Worcester, and Birmingham, in connection with the Through Service between London and Edinburgh and Glasgow. The Up and Down Day Express Trains stop *half-an-hour at Normanton* to enable Passengers to dine, a spacious and comfortable Dining Room having been provided. Table d'Hôte of five Courses with Dessert, 2s. 6d. each—no fees. Passengers by this Route between London, Edinburgh, and Glasgow are conveyed in Through Carriages of the most improved description, fitted with an efficient continuous Automatic Break and all the most approved modern appliances, and Through Guards accompany the principal trains in charge of Passengers' luggage. Return Tickets between Stations in England and Stations in Scotland are available for One Calendar Month.

LIVERPOOL AND MANCHESTER.

A SPECIAL SERVICE of Express Trains has been established between LONDON and MANCHESTER and LIVERPOOL (*via* DERBY and MATLOCK). Passengers travelling by this route pass through the most picturesque portion of the Peak of Derbyshire and the Vale of Matlock. Pullman Drawing-Room and Sleeping Cars are run by this route. Passengers holding First-Class Tickets are allowed to ride in the Pullman Cars attached to the Day Express Trains *without extra payment.* A Pullman Dining Saloon Car is also attached to the Express Trains leaving London (St. Pancras) at 5 P.M. for Manchester and Liverpool; and Manchester (Central) at 5 P.M. for London. Passengers leaving London for Liverpool at 5 P.M. can change from the Dining Car into the Liverpool portion of the Train at Derby, and Passengers leaving Liverpool at 4.40 P.M. can join the Dining Car at Derby. No extra charge beyond the sum payable for the Dinner is made. *Table d'Hôte, Luncheon, &c., served* en route.

Omnibuses.—For the use of Family Parties travelling by Midland Railway the Company provide *Small Omnibuses* capable of carrying Six Persons Inside and Two outside, with the usual quantity of Luggage, to meet the Express and other principal Trains at the St. Pancras Station when *previously ordered.* These Vehicles must be *engaged* either by written application to the Station-master at St. Pancras Station, or by giving notice to the Station-master at the starting-point (if a Midland Station), or at *any Station* en route *not less than 30 miles from London,* so that a telegram may be sent to St. Pancras to have the required Vehicle in readiness. The Omnibuses will also be sent to the Hotels or Residences of *parties leaving London by Midland Railway,* or to any of the Railway Termini, on application being made to the Station-master at St. Pancras, stating the Train by which it is intended to leave St. Pancras.

Larger Omnibuses worked with a pair of horses can also be obtained on application to the Station-master at St. Pancras.

The charge for the use of a Small Omnibus is 1s. per mile, with a minimum charge of 3s.; for distances over 6 miles, when two horses are required, the charge is 1s. 6d. per mile, with a minimum charge of 6s.; and larger Omnibuses are charged 2s. per mile, minimum charge 6s. The usual weight of Luggage is allowed. In cases where Passengers take an excessive weight, a charge at the rate of 6d. per cwt. is levied upon the excess, with a minimum charge of 3d.

A Service of Omnibuses has been established between St. Pancras and Charing Cross and Waterloo Stations, for the accommodation of Passengers travelling between the Midland and South-Eastern and London and South-Western Railways, and to and from the Midland Grand Hotel, on weekdays only. The Omnibuses meet the Principal Trains, and Passengers holding Through Tickets between Stations on the Midland and South-Eastern and London and South-Western Railways, are conveyed by the Omnibuses Free of Charge.

BELFAST, BY THE SHORT SEA MAIL ROUTE via BARROW.

THE capacious New Docks of Barrow, situated within the ancient Harbour of Piel, under shelter of Walney Island, being now open for traffic, the Swift and Powerful First-class Paddle Steam Ships "DONEGAL," "LONDONDERRY," "ARMAGH," "ROE,"

RAILWAYS. 95

or other First-class Vessels, will sail between Barrow (Ramsden Dock) and Belfast (weather permitting) in connection with through Trains on the Midland and Furness Railways; and through Tickets to Belfast, in connection with the Boat, will be issued from London and all principal Stations on the Midland Railway—Return Tickets being available for One Calendar Month, and in the summer for Two Calendar Months.

Passengers to or from London, and other Stations south of Leicester, may break their Journey at Furness Abbey, Leeds, Derby, Trent, Nottingham, Leicester, Kettering, Luton, and Bedford, and they may also travel *via* Birmingham, and break the journey at that place. Passengers to or from Stations west of Birmingham may break the journey at Furness Abbey, Leeds, Derby, or Birmingham; and Passengers to or from Stations on the North-Eastern Railway at Leeds or Furness Abbey, taking care that from any of those places they proceed by Midland Trains.

BELFAST *via* LARNE.

Passengers are also booked through to Belfast by the Shortest Sea Route *via* Carlisle, Dumfries, Stranraer, and Larne.

TOURIST TICKETS.—SCOTLAND.

During the summer months 1st and 3d Class Tourist Tickets will be issued from London (St. Pancras) and principal Stations on the Midland Railway to Edinburgh, Glasgow, Greenock, Oban, Melrose, Dumfries, Ayr, Stirling, Perth, Dundee, Aberdeen, Inverness, and other principal places of interest.

Saloon, Family, and Invalid Carriages can be obtained for the use of parties travelling to and from Scotland by the Midland Route, by giving a few days' notice to the Station-master at any of the principal Stations, or to the Superintendent of the Line, Derby.

MORECAMBE AND THE ENGLISH LAKES.

MORECAMBE, WINDERMERE, AMBLESIDE, GRANGE, FURNESS ABBEY, SEASCALE, RAVENGLASS, PENRITH, KESWICK, and TROUTBECK.

Every Friday and Saturday, from April to October, Cheap Excursion Tickets to Morecambe will be issued from Leicester, Nottingham, Derby, Sheffield, Masboro', Barnsley, Normanton, Leeds, Bradford, Keighley, Skipton, and principal intermediate points, available to return on the Sunday, Monday, or Tuesday after date of issue.

For Dates, Fares, and further particulars, see Tourist Programmes and Special Handbills.

MATLOCK AND BUXTON.

Tourist Tickets are issued from principal Stations on the Midland Railway, and Lines in connection, to Matlock and Buxton.

Passengers holding Tickets to Buxton are allowed to break the journey at principal places of interest on the Line between Matlock and Buxton.

RETURN TICKETS at Low Fares will be issued from certain stations to MATLOCK and BUXTON, by any of the Through Trains, on Fridays and Saturdays, from April to October, available for Return by any *Train on the Sunday, Monday, or Tuesday after date of issue.*

First and Third Class Tourist Tickets, available for Two Months or longer, are issued during the Summer Months from principal Stations on the Midland Railway, to Scarboro', Whitby, Filey, Bridlington, Harrogate, Ilkley, and other Stations in the Yorkshire district.

Yarmouth, Lowestoft, Cromer, Cleethorpes, and other Stations on the East Coast. Brighton, Hastings, Portsmouth, The Isle of Wight, Bournemouth, and other Stations in the South of England.

Penzance, Plymouth, Torquay, Exeter, Weston-super-Mare, Ilfracombe, and other Stations in the West of England.

Monmouth, Swansea, Tenby, Severn Bridge, Upper Lydbrook, and other Stations in South Wales.

Aberystwith, Llandudno, Rhyl, Bangor, and other Stations in North Wales. Southport, Blackpool, and other Stations on the Lancashire Coast; and to Bath, Malvern, Leamington, Brecon, &c.

For further particulars, see Tourist Programmes and Hand-bills.

PLEASURE PARTIES.—CHEAP RETURN TICKETS

Are issued to parties of not less than SIX First-Class, or TEN Third-Class Passengers, desirous of taking Pleasure Excursions to places on or adjacent to this Railway.

For particulars, apply to the Station-masters, or to the Superintendent of the Line at Derby. JOHN NOBLE, *General Manager*.

DERBY, 1885.

CALEDONIAN RAILWAY.

TOURS IN SCOTLAND.

THE CALEDONIAN RAILWAY COMPANY have arranged a system of TOURS—over 100 in number—by Rail, Steamer (on Sea, River, and Loch), and Coach, comprehending almost every place of interest either for scenery or historical associations throughout Scotland, including—

EDINBURGH, GLASGOW, ABERDEEN, DUNDEE, INVERNESS, GREENOCK, PAISLEY, DUMFRIES, MOFFAT, PEEBLES, STIRLING, PERTH, CRIEFF, DUNKELD, OBAN, INVERARAY,·

The Trossachs, Loch Katrine, Loch Lomond, Loch Eck, Loch Earn, Loch Tay, Loch Awe, Caledonian Canal, Glencoe, Iona, Staffa, Skye, Balmoral, Braemar, Arran, Bute, The Firth of Clyde, The Falls of Clyde, &c. &c.

☞ TOURISTS are recommended to procure a copy of the Caledonian Railway Company's "Tourist Guide," which contains descriptive notices of the Districts embraced in the Tours, Maps, Plans, &c., can be had at any of the Company's Stations, and also at the chief Stations on the London and North-Western Railway, and which are supplied gratis to the chief Hotels, Hydropathics, Steamboats, &c., in Great Britain.

Tickets for these Tours are issued at the Company's Booking Offices at all the large Stations. The Tourist Season generally extends from JUNE to SEPTEMBER, inclusive.

The Caledonian Co. also issue Tourist Tickets to the Lake District of England, The Isle of Man, Connemara, The Lakes of Killarney, &c.

The Caledonian Railway, in conjunction with the London and North-Western Railway, forms what is known as the

WEST COAST ROUTE

BETWEEN

SCOTLAND AND ENGLAND.

DIRECT TRAINS RUN FROM AND TO

GLASGOW, EDINBURGH, GREENOCK, PAISLEY, STRANRAER, STIRLING, OBAN, PERTH, DUNDEE, ABERDEEN, INVERNESS, and other Places in Scotland,

TO AND FROM

LONDON (Euston), BIRMINGHAM, LIVERPOOL, MANCHESTER, PRESTON, PENRITH (for Lake District), LEEDS, BRADFORD, and other Places in England.

Sleeping and Day Saloon Carriages. Through Guards and Conductors.

The Caledonian Company's Trains from and to Edinburgh, Glasgow, Carlisle, &c., connect on the Clyde with the "Columba," "Iona," "Lord of the Isles," "Ivanhoe," and other steamers to and from Dunoon, Innellan, Rothesay, Largs, Millport, the Kyles of Bute, Arran, Campbeltown, Ardrishaig, Inveraray, Loch Goil, Loch Long, &c. &c.

A full service of Trains is also run from and to Glasgow, to and from Edinburgh, Stirling, Oban, Perth, Dundee, Aberdeen, and the North; and from and to Edinburgh, to and from these places.

For particulars of Trains, Fares, &c., see the Caledonian Railway Co.'s Time Tables.

The Caledonian Company's large and magnificent

NEW CENTRAL STATION HOTEL, GLASGOW,

Is under the Company's own Management.

GENERAL MANAGER'S OFFICE,   JAMES THOMPSON,
GLASGOW, 1885.   *General Manager.*

GLASGOW & SOUTH-WESTERN RAILWAY.

DIRECT ROUTE BETWEEN

SCOTLAND & ENGLAND.

THROUGH TRAINS ARE RUN BETWEEN

GLASGOW (St. Enoch) and LONDON (St. Pancras),

Via the GLASGOW & SOUTH-WESTERN and MIDLAND RAILWAYS,
Giving a Direct and Expeditious Service between

 Glasgow, Greenock, Paisley, Ayr, Ardrossan,
Kilmarnock, Dumfries, &c., and Liverpool,
Manchester, Bradford, Leeds, Sheffield, Bristol, Bath, Birmingham, London, &c.

PULLMAN DRAWING-ROOM AND SLEEPING CARS

Are run by the Morning and Evening Express Trains between GLASGOW and LONDON.

Tourist Tickets are issued from the principal Stations on the Glasgow and South-Western Railway to LONDON, BRIGHTON, ISLE OF WIGHT, BOURNEMOUTH, and numerous places of interest in the South and South-West of England; to BATH, HARROGATE, BUXTON, MATLOCK, MALVERN, and other favourite resorts; also to the English LAKE DISTRICT, ISLE OF MAN, &c., &c.

FIRTH OF CLYDE AND WEST HIGHLANDS, via GREENOCK.

EXPRESS and FAST TRAINS are run at convenient hours between

GLASGOW AND GREENOCK

St. Enoch Station)   (Lynedoch St. and Princes Pier Stations)

IN DIRECT CONNECTION WITH THE

"COLUMBA," "IONA," "LORD OF THE ISLES," "SCOTIA,"

And other Steamers sailing to and from

Kirn, Dunoon, Innellan, Rothesay,
Kyles of Bute, Ardrishaig, Oban,
Inveraray, Largs, Millport, Kilcreggan, Kilmun, Lochgoilhead,
Garelochhead, &c.

Through Carriages are run by certain Trains between GREENOCK (Princes Pier) and EDINBURGH (Waverley), and by the Morning and Evening Express Trains between GREENOCK (Princes Pier) and LONDON (St. Pancras).

RETURN TICKETS issued to COAST TOWNS are available for RETURN AT ANY TIME.

Passengers are landed at Princes Pier Station, from whence there is a Covered Way to the Pier, where the Steamers call; and Passengers' Luggage is conveyed FREE OF CHARGE between the Stations and the Steamers.

ARRAN AND THE AYRSHIRE COAST.

An Express and Fast Train Service is given between GLASGOW (St. Enoch), PAISLEY, and TROON, PRESTWICK, AYR, ARDROSSAN, FAIRLIE, &c.

From ARDROSSAN the Splendid Saloon Steamer "BRODICK CASTLE" sails daily to and from the ISLAND OF ARRAN, in connection with the Express Train Service.

For particulars as to Trains and Steamers see the Company's Time Tables.

Glasgow, April 1885.   ..   W. J. WAINWRIGHT, *General Manager.*

G

GREAT SOUTHERN AND WESTERN RAILWAY, IRELAND.

LAKES OF KILLARNEY.

RAILWAY HOTEL

ADJOINS LORD KENMARE's Demesne, and is situated within easy distance of Ross Castle, Muckross Abbey and Grounds, the Gap of Dunloe, and the principal points of interest.

This Hotel, the largest in the Lake District, possesses unusually good accommodation for Tourists and Families, including spacious and well-furnished Ladies' Drawing Room, Writing, Reception, Billiard, Smoking, Dining, and Private Sitting Rooms. All the Public and Private Sitting Rooms are provided with Pianofortes.

Visitors can arrange to board at the Hotel at a charge of £3 : 3s. per week.

The Porters of the Hotel await the arrival of each Train for the removal of Luggage, &c.

The Manager personally undertakes the formation of Excursion Parties with a view to their comfort and economy.

The Lakes afford excellent Salmon and Trout Fishing.

BOATS, CARRIAGES, PONIES, &c., WITH STEADY ATTENDANTS, ALWAYS READY FOR ENGAGEMENT.

Boatmen, Guides, Drivers, and other Servants of the Hotel are paid ample wages, and are not permitted to solicit Visitors for Gratuities.

A Waggonette will run, from 1st June to 30th September, between the Hotel and Ross Castle. Fare, 6d. each way.

From 1st MAY to 31st OCTOBER 1885

TOURISTS' TICKETS from

DUBLIN TO KILLARNEY &. BACK

Will be issued by the Trains which run direct to Killarney, at the following Fares, viz.—

		FIRST CLASS.	SECOND CLASS.
Single Ticket for One Passenger		£2 10 0	£2 0 0
Do.	Two Passengers	4 10 0	3 12 0
Do.	Three ,,	6 7 6	5 2 0
Do.	Four ,,	8 0 0	6 8 0
Do.	Five ,,	9 7 6	7 10 0
Do.	Six ,,	10 10 0	8 8 0
Do.	Seven ,,	11 7 6	9 2 0
Do.	Eight ,,	12 0 0	9 12 0

AVAILABLE FOR RETURN ON ANY DAY

WITHIN ONE CALENDAR MONTH.

The time of these Tickets can be extended upon the terms stated in the Company's Tourist Programme.

N.B.—Tickets to KILLARNEY can be obtained at the principal Stations on the London and North-Western, Midland, Great Western, Lancashire and Yorkshire, Manchester, Sheffield and Lincolnshire, North Staffordshire, Caledonian, and North British Railways, and Railways in Ireland.

KINGSBRIDGE, DUBLIN.

PLEASURE EXCURSIONS
BY COACH, STEAMER, & TRAIN,
During June, July, August, and September 1885.

OBAN TO OBAN.
Via Pass of Melfort, Lochawe, and Pass of Brander.

BY Coach leaving M'Gregor's Coach Office *every lawful day* at 9.45 A.M. by way of Lochfeochan, Pass of Melfort, Loch Craignish, Carnassary Castle, and Ford, where Passengers join the Steamer " Countess of Breadalbane " for Lochawe Station ; thence per Train due to arrive in Oban at or about 6.15 P.M.; or *vice versa* by Train leaving Oban at 10 A.M. for Lochawe Station, thence per Steamer " Countess of Breadalbane " to Ford, and from Ford by Coach due to reach Oban about 6.15 P.M.

*Fares for the Round :—*First Class, 17s. ; Third Class, 15s. 6d. Coach-driver's and Guard's Fees not included.

Passengers Booked at Coach Office and Railway Station, Oban.

SCENERY SURPASSING GRAND.

SUMMER TOURS IN SCOTLAND.
GLASGOW AND THE HIGHLANDS.
(Royal Route via Crinan and Caledonian Canals.)
Tourists' Special Cabin Tickets issued during the Season,
Giving the *privilege* of the run of *all the undernamed Steamers to any part
of the Highlands* at which they may call during the time specified.
One Week, £3 ; Two Weeks, £5 ; or Six Separate Days, £3 : 10s.

THE
ROYAL

MAIL
STEAMERS

GRENADIER (New Steamship)

COLUMBA	MOUNTAINEER	CLAYMORE	INVERARAY	CASTLE
IONA*	PIONEER	CLANSMAN	LINNET	ISLAY
CHEVALIER	GLENGARRY	CLYDESDALE	LOCHIEL	CAVALIER
GONDOLIER	GLENCOE	LOCHAWE	STAFFA	FINGAL

Sail during the Season for Kyles of Bute, Ardrishaig, Oban, Ballachulish (for Glencoe), Fort William, Banavie, Inverness, Staffa, Iona, Lochawe, Islay, Tobermory, Portree, Strome Ferry, Gairloch (for Lochmaree), Ullapool, Lochinver, Lochmaddy, Tarbert (Harris), Stornoway, etc., affording Tourists an opportunity of visiting the magnificent scenery of Glencoe, the Cuchullin Hills, Quiraing, Loch Coruisk, Loch Scavaig, Lochmaree, the Falls of Foyers, and the famed Islands of Staffa and Iona.

Official Guide, 3·1.; Illustrated, 6d.; Cloth Gilt, 1s. Time Bill, with Map and Fares, free by Post from the owner, DAVID MACBRAYNE, 119 Hope Street, Glasgow.

"ANCHOR LINE."
DIRECT STEAM COMMUNICATION
(Carrying the United States Mails)
By the First-Class Powerful Steam Packet Ships,

	Tons.		Tons.		Tons.		Tons.
ACADIA .	1081	BOLIVIA .	4050	ELYSIA .	2713	OLYMPIA .	2051
ALEXANDRIA	2017	BRITANNIA .	3069	ETHIOPIA	4004	PERSIA .	3547
ALSATIA .	2810	CALEDONIA .	2151	FURNESSIA	5495	ROUMANIA	3387
ANCHORIA	4167	CALIFORNIA	3410	HESPERIA	3037	SCANDINAVIA	1138
ARABIA .	3544	CIRCASSIA .	4272	HISPANIA	3380	SIDONIAN .	1382
ARMENIA .	3395	CITY OF ROME	8415	INDIA .	2476	TRINACRIA	2256
ASIA .	3560	COLUMBIA .	2029	ITALIA .	2248	TYRIAN .	1039
ASSYRIA .	2022	DEVONIA .	4270	KARAMANIA	3148	UTOPIA .	2731
AUSTRALIA	2252	DORIAN .	1038	NUBIA .	3551	VICTORIA .	3358
BELGRAVIA	4976						

GLASGOW TO NEW YORK, *Via* MOVILLE.
Carrying U.S. Mails, every Thursday ; and from **NEW YORK**, Pier 20,
N. River, every Saturday.

LIVERPOOL TO NEW YORK, *Via* QUEENSTOWN.
The Magnificent Steamer "CITY OF ROME," 8415 Tons, sails as follows:—
From Liverpool—Wednesday, May 20, June 17, July 15, August 12,
September 9, October 7.
From New York—Wednesday, June 3, July 1, July 29, August 26,
September 23, October 21.

LONDON TO HALIFAX AND BOSTON EVERY FORTNIGHT.
FARES to NEW YORK, BOSTON, or PHILADELPHIA :—
Saloon, 12 to 25 Guineas. Intermediate, £6 : 6s. and £7. Steerage at
Lowest Rates.

GLASGOW TO BOMBAY AND CALCUTTA,
Via LIVERPOOL AND SUEZ CANAL, every Fortnight.
SALOON PASSAGE £42, and £45 from Liverpool.

GLASGOW AND MEDITERRANEAN SERVICE.
Lisbon, Gibraltar, Genoa, Naples, Messina, Palermo, and
other Ports as required. Every Fortnight.

Glasgow to Lisbon, £6 : 6s. ; Gibraltar, £8 : 8s. ; Genoa, £12 : 12s. ;
Leghorn, £13 : 13s. ; Naples, £14 : 14s. ; Messina or Palermo, £16 : 16s.
Round Voyage and back to Glasgow, 35 Guineas.
Passengers Booked to all parts of the United States and Canada.
Apply to HENDERSON BROTHERS, 18 Leadenhall Street, London ; 17
Water Street, Liverpool ; 1 Panmure Street, Dundee ; Foyle Street,
Londonderry ; 2 Rue Noallis, Marseilles ; 3 Rue Scribe, Paris ; 7 Bowling
Green, New York ; or to   HENDERSON BROTHERS,
47 Union Street, Glasgow.

FLEETWOOD TO BELFAST

AND THE

NORTH OF IRELAND.

EVERY EVENING (SUNDAYS EXCEPTED).

In connection with the Lancashire and Yorkshire and London and North-Western Railways.

THE NORTH LANCASHIRE STEAM NAVIGATION COMPANY'S Royal Mail Steam Ships,

EARL OF ULSTER (New Steamer), | THOMAS DUGDALE,
DUKE OF CONNAUGHT, | PRINCESS OF WALES,

LEAVE FLEETWOOD FOR BELFAST

Every Evening (Sundays excepted), at or after 8.0 p.m., after arrival of trains from London, Birmingham, Hull, Newcastle, Bradford, Leeds, Liverpool, Manchester, Preston, and all parts of the Kingdom; returning

FROM BELFAST TO FLEETWOOD

Every Evening (Sundays excepted), at 8.0 p.m., arriving in Fleetwood in time for early morning trains to the above places.

FARES.—(No Steward's Fee) SINGLE JOURNEY, Saloon, 12s. 6d. ; Steerage, 5s. ; RETURNS (May 1 to Oct. 31), available for two months, and (Nov. 1 to April 30), available for one month, Saloon, 21s. ; Steerage, 8s. 6d. Through Tickets (single and return) are also issued from all the principal Stations of the London and North-Western, Lancashire and York, shire, North-Eastern, Great Western, Great Northern and Manchester, Sheffield and Lincolnshire Railway Companies, to Belfast, and *vice versa.*

SPECIAL TOURISTS' TICKETS AVAILABLE FOR TWO MONTHS

are issued during the Summer Season, *via* the Fleetwood Route, whereby Tourists may visit all places of interest in the North of Ireland and Dublin. For particulars, see the Lancashire and Yorkshire and London and North-Western Companies' Books of Tourists' Arrangements.

At Fleetwood the railway trains run alongside the steamers, and passengers' luggage is carried from the train at the quay on board FREE OF CHARGE.

Fleetwood is unrivalled as a steam packet station for the North of Ireland, and the unexampled regularity with which the Belfast Line of Steamers have made the passage between the two ports for more than forty years is probably without a parallel in steamboat service, and has made this Route the most popular, as it is certainly the most Expeditious and Desirable, for Passengers, Goods, and Merchandise, between the great centres of commerce in England and the North and North-West of Ireland.

For further information, see Bradshaw's Guide, page 382, or apply at any of the stations of the Railway Companies before named ; T. C. HAINES, 20 Donegall Quay, Belfast ; or to THOS. H. CARR, FLEETWOOD.

DUBLIN & GLASGOW STEAM PACKET COMPANY.

THE Company's splendid Saloon Paddle Steamships—DUKE of ARGYLL, DUKE of LEIN-STER, LORD CLYDE, LORD GOUGH, or other Steamers, are intended to Sail, unless prevented by any unforeseen occurrence, to and from GLASGOW & DUBLIN, calling at GREENOCK.

SAILINGS AS PER MONTHLY BILLS.

GLASGOW to DUBLIN.—Every Monday, Wednesday, and Friday, and every alternate Tuesday, Thursday, and Saturday. Train from Central Station, Glasgow, at 6.30 p.m. ; Steamer leaving Greenock about 7.30 p.m.
DUBLIN to GLASGOW.—Every Monday, Wednesday, and Friday, and every alternate Tuesday, Thursday, and Saturday.

Fares.—From Glasgow (including Steward's Fees), Cabin, 15s. ; Ditto (including Rail to Greenock), 16s. 3d: Return Tickets (available for Six Months), £1 : 2 : 6 ; Ditto (including Rail to Greenock), £1 : 5s. Steerage fare from Glasgow, 6s. (including rail to Greenock), 6s. 9d. Return Tickets (available for six months), 10s. (including rail to Greenock), 11s. 6d. Through Express Train (per Caledonian Railway) from Leith at 4.30 p.m., and from Edinburgh (Princes Street Station) at 5 p.m. to Greenock in direct connection with the Dublin Steamer. Passengers are also booked through from the following Railway Stations to Dublin, and *vice versa*, viz.—

	Single.		Return, available for 2 mths.			Single.		Return, available for 2 mths.	
	1st cl.	3 cl. & Strage.	1st cl.	3 cl. & Strage.		1st cl.	3 cl. & Strage.	1st cl.	3 cl. & Strage.
	s. d.	s. d.	s. d.	s. d.		s. d.	s. d.	s. d.	s. d.
Alloa	19 1	8 7	26 4	13 2	Forfar......	30 0	13 10½	40 0	19 10
Arbroath ...	30 8	14 3½	40 10	20 5	Hamilton...	17 3	7 4½	27 0	12 9
Aberdeen ..	39 6	18 8	51 11	25 10	Inverness...	48 6	23 3	73 2	..
Crieff	23 6	10 7½	31 11	15 10	Leith........	20 0	8 6	30 0	14 0
Callander ..	21 0	9 9	28 9	14 8	Montrose...	33 6	15 8	44 5	22 1
Dundee (W.)	28 0	12 11	37 6	18 7	Perth........	24 6	11 3	33 2	16 6
Dumfries...	27 9	12 10	42 11	21 5	Paisley.....	16 3	6 9	25 0	11 6
Edinburgh.	20 0	8 6	30 0	14 0	Stirling.....	19 0	8 5	26 3	13 0

Booking Office at Dublin for Passengers—1 EDEN QUAY. Chief Office and Stores—71 NORTH WALL, DUBLIN. Goods carried at Through Rates from Glasgow and Greenock to Inland Towns in Ireland; and also from a number of the Principal Railway Stations in Scotland to Dublin and Inland Stations in Ireland, and *vice versa*. Further particulars, Monthly Bills, &c., on application to the undermentioned agents:—

JAMES LITTLE & CO., Excise Buildings, Greenock, and

HENRY LAMONT, 93 Hope Street, adjoining Central Station, and Broomielaw, Glasgow.

A. TAYLOR, DUBLIN, *Secretary.*   B. MANN, DUBLIN, *General Manager.*

LOCH LOMOND AND LOCH LONG
SALOON STEAMERS.
(COMMENCING 1st JUNE.)

Loch Lomond.—Leave BALLOCH PIER daily about 8.45 and 10.30* A.M., 12.25 P.M., and 5 P.M. HEAD OF LOCH on Mondays at 6.15 A.M.; daily (except Monday) at 8.30 A.M.; daily at 10.40* A.M., 1.20 and 4.10 P.M.

*Steamers marked thus * will only sail in July and August.*

THOMAS McLEAN, *Manager,* BRIDGE HOUSE, ALEXANDRIA, N.B.

GLASGOW, BELFAST, BRISTOL, CARDIFF, NEWPORT, AND SWANSEA STEAMERS,

'SOLWAY,' 'AVON,' 'SEVERN,' 'PRINCESS ALEXANDRA,'

SAIL with Goods and Passengers from GLASGOW to BRISTOL via BELFAST every Monday and Thursday at 2 P.M.; GLASGOW to CARDIFF and SWANSEA every Friday at 2 P.M.; to NEWPORT every alternate Friday at 2 P.M. From BRISTOL to GLASGOW every Monday and Thursday; SWANSEA to GLASGOW every Wednesday; CARDIFF to GLASGOW every Monday; NEWPORT to GLASGOW every alternate Tuesday.

FARES (GLASGOW)—Cabin, 20s.; Steerage 12s. 6d.; Deck (Soldiers or Sailors), 10s.
  ,, (BELFAST)—Cabin, 17s. 6d.; Steerage, 10s.

RETURNS for Cabin and Steerage issued at Fare and a half available for TWO MONTHS.

These Steamers have superior Cabin accommodation, and offer a good opportunity for parties making a pleasant sea trip to or from West of England.

Goods carried for Newport (Mon.), Exeter, Gloucester, Cheltenham, etc. etc.

For Rates of Freight and other particulars, apply to
MARK WHITWILL & SON, Bristol; M. JONES & BRO., Swansea; E. TAYLOR &' Co., Cardiff; R. BURTON & SON, Newport (Mon.); R. HENDERSON & SON, Belfast; or
WILLIAM SLOAN & CO., 140 Hope Street, Glasgow.

ABERDEEN
AND
LONDON
Average Passage
36 Hours.

THE ABERDEEN STEAM NAVIGATION CO.'S STEAMSHIPS
BAN-RIGH, CITY OF LONDON, or CITY OF ABERDEEN,
will be despatched (weather, etc., permitting) from ABERDEEN, and from The Aberdeen Steam Navigation Co.'s Wharf, Limehouse, LONDON, every Wednesday and Saturday.

FARES—including Stewards' Fees—*Private Cabins* accommodating four passengers, £6.
Private Cabins, if occupied by fewer than four passengers, £5.
Single Tickets—1st Cabin, 30s.; 2d Cabin, 15s.; Children under 14 years, 15s. and 10s.
Return Tickets—available for three months—45s. and 25s.; Children, 25s. and 15s.

Notice to Passengers.—The Co.'s steam tender 'Ich Dien' will attend the Steamers on their arrival in London for the purpose of conveying Passengers to the Temple Pier, Thames Embankment; she will also leave that Pier one hour before the advertised times of sailing, conveying passengers only to the Aberdeen Steamers free of charge. *Friends of passengers wishing to accompany them to the Steamers, may do so on getting written permission from the Company's Agent.* Porters will be in attendance to carry the Luggage on board. For further particulars apply to JOHN A. CLINKSKILL, Agent, The Aberdeen Steam Navigation Co.'s Wharf, Limehouse; and 102 Queen Victoria Street, E.C., London; or to CHARLES SHEPHERD, Manager, Waterloo Quay, Aberdeen.

LEITH AND LONDON.

THE LONDON & EDINBURGH SHIPPING COMPANY'S
SPLENDID FAST-SAILING SCREW-STEAMSHIPS
IONA (New Steamer),

MALVINA, MARMION, MORNA, OR OTHER OF THE COMPANY'S STEAMERS,

Sail from VICTORIA DOCK, LEITH, every *Wednesday, Friday,* and *Saturday* afternoon ; and from HERMITAGE STEAM WHARF, LONDON, every *Tuesday, Wednesday,* and *Saturday* morning.

For Rates of Freight and Fares, apply to THOMAS AITKEN,
8 & 9 Commercial Street, Leith.

NEW ROUTE.
GLASGOW AND THE HIGHLANDS.

THE Steamers "DUNARA CASTLE" and "AROS CASTLE" sail from Glasgow for Oban, Colonsay, and Iona, Tobermory, and Bunessan (Mull), Tyree and Coll, Struan, Carbost, Dunvegan, Stein, and Uig (Skye), Tarbert and Obbe (Harris), Lochmaddy, Kallin, Carnan and Lochboisdale (Uist), and Barra.

. The Tourist who desires (within the limits of a week, and at a reasonable expense) a panoramic view of the general scenery of the Hebrides, with all its varied beauty, sublimity, and grandeur, has no better opportunity afforded him than by taking the round in one of these Steamers.

Further information and Time-bills may be had by applying to
MARTIN ORME, 20 Robertson Street, Glasgow.

CIRCULAR TOURS.
GLASGOW & THE OUTER HEBRIDES.

ONE Week's pleasure-sailing to the West Highlands by the splendid sea-going Steamer "Hebridean," sailing from GLASGOW and GREENOCK on THURSDAYS for OBAN, MULL, SKYE, HARRIS, UIST, BARRA, etc., affords the Tourist a splendid opportunity of viewing the Magnificent Scenery of the West of Skye and the Outer Hebrides.

N.B.—During the Season Special Trips are made to the far-famed ISLAND OF ST. KILDA, where Passengers are given facilities for landing; also to LOCH ROAG, from which the Druidical remains at Callernish may be visited.

Time Bills, Maps of Route, Cabin Plans and Berths, secured at
JOHN M'CALLUM & Co.'s, 12 Ann St. (City), Glasgow.

107

W. & A. K. JOHNSTON'S TOURISTS' MAPS.

(SELECTED FROM JOHNSTON'S "ROYAL ATLAS.")

Mounted on Canvas, and bound in a Pocket-Case.

						s.	*d.*
America (U.S.)	. . .	2 Sheets, with Index of 5675 Names	.	8	0
Australia	. . .	1 ,,	,,	1980 ,,	.	4	6
Austria	. . .	2 ,,	,,	6300 ,,	.	8	0
Belgium and the Netherlands	1 ,,	,,	5300 ,,	.	4	6
Canada	. . . .	2 ,,	,,	3070 ,,	.	8	0
England	. . . .	2 ,,	,,	11,700 ,,	.	8	0
France, in departments	.	1 ,,	,,	4406 ,,	.	4	6
Germany, Empire of, S.W. part	,,	,,	4470 ,,	.	4	6
,, ,, N.	,,	,,	,,	2550 ,,	.	4	6
India	. . . .	2 ,,	,,	7500 ,,	.	8	0
Ireland	. . . .	1 ,,	,,	5270 ,,	.	4	6
Italy	. . . .	2 ,,'	,,	6170 ,,	.	8	0
Mediterranean Shores	.	1 ,,	,,	2170 ,,	.	4	6
Palestine	. . .	1 ,,	,,	3100 ,,	.	4	6
Prussia	. . . .	1 ,,	,,	2550 ,,	.	4	6
Scotland	. . .	2 ,,	,,	11,000 ,,	.	8	0
Spain and Portugal	.	1 ,,	,,	4100 ,,	.	4	6
Sweden and Norway	.	1 ,,	,,	1630 ,,	.	4	6
Switzerland	. . .	1 ,,	,,	4907 ,,	.	4	6

JOHNSTON'S NEW TRAVELLING OR LIBRARY MAPS OF ENGLAND AND SCOTLAND, fully Coloured, on Cloth and in Cases; or on Rollers, Varnished, with complete Indices. Price 12s. 6d. each.

The Publishers have great confidence in recommending these as very useful Reference Maps; they show in complete detail Towns, Villages, Railways, Roads, Country Seats, etc. etc.

THE ATLAS MAP OF SCOTLAND.

SHOWING IN COMPLETE DETAIL

TOWNS, VILLAGES, RAILWAYS, ROADS, COUNTRY SEATS, ETC.

Full Coloured, and bound in Cloth, price 10s. 6d.

NOTE.—All who have travelled, either by Rail, Steamer, or Coach, have found the inconvenience of consulting a large folding map. To obviate this "The Atlas Map of Scotland" has been prepared, by which the Tourist can have before him the part of the country to which he wishes to refer, without finding the other portion of the map in his way.

Dedicated by Special Permission to Her Majesty.

New Edition, 1885, Imperial Folio, hf.-bd. in russia or morocco, with gilt titles and edges, Price £6 : 6s. Full bound, russia or morocco, gilt, Price £10 : 10s. (to order).

THE ROYAL ATLAS OF MODERN GEOGRAPHY.

BY A. KEITH JOHNSTON, LL.D., F.R.G.S.,
Author of the "Physical Atlas," etc.

In a Series of Fifty-two entirely Original and Authentic Maps, Coloured in Outline. With a complete Index of easy reference to each Map, comprising nearly 150,000 Places contained in this Atlas.

The only Atlas for which a Prize Medal was awarded at the International Exhibition, London.

Complete Catalogue of Maps, Atlases, &c., on application.

W. & A. K. JOHNSTON,

Geographers to the Queen, Educational and General Publishers,

EDINA WORKS, EASTER ROAD, & 16 SOUTH ST. ANDREW ST., EDINBURGH.
5 WHITE HART ST., WARWICK LANE, LONDON, E.C.

Dr. Browne coined the word Chlorodyne wherewith to designate his discovery, consequently to apply the word to other compounds is as dishonest as it is absurd.

STORDY & BELL,

ST. LEONARD'S COACH WORKS.

SCOTTISH WIDOWS' FUND.

MAGNITUDE OF THE OPERATIONS.

Policies issued . . . £40,000,000	Claims Paid £14,000,000
Bonus Additions . . 8,100,000	Accumulated Funds . 8,600,000
Policies in Force . . 25,500,000	Annual Revenue . . 1,060,000

PROFITABLE CHARACTER OF THE BUSINESS.

Cash Profit for Seven Years to 31st Dec. 1880 . £1,347,756
Bonus Additions for the Seven Years . . . 2,249,072

This was the LARGEST DISTRIBUTION OF PROFIT made by any Life Office during the period. It yielded Bonuses from £1 : 14s. to £3 : 17 : 5 per cent per annum on the Original Sums Assured, according to the duration of the Policies,—facts which clearly prove

*The Intrinsic Value of the Society's Mutual System, and
The Highly Profitable Character of its Business.*

LIBERAL CONDITIONS OF ASSURANCE.

Surrender Values allowed after payment of one year's premium.
Paid-up Policies allowed in lieu of Surrender Values.

Loans granted within a small margin of the Surrender Value.
Extensive Foreign Residence free of charge from the first.

*Most of the Society's Policies
become Whole-World and Indisputable after the first Five Years.*

THE ATTENTION OF

Persons desiring to effect LIFE ASSURANCES for the benefit of their Families, or in connection with Business Transactions, is called to the above **Financial Results & Conditions of Assurance**, which show how peculiarly suitable the Society's Policies are for Family Provisions, and for all Trust and Security purposes.

EDINBURGH (HEAD OFFICE): 9 ST. ANDREW SQUARE.

London, 28 CORNHILL, E.C. *West End Agency,* 49 PALL MALL.

Dublin, 41 WESTMORELAND STREET.
Glasgow, 114 WEST GEORGE ST.
Manchester, 21 ALBERT SQUARE.
Liverpool, 48 CASTLE STREET.

Birmingham, 12 BENNETT'S HILL.
Leeds, 21 PARK ROW.
Bristol, 40 CORN STREET.
Belfast, 2 HIGH STREET.

Newcastle-on-Tyne, 12 GREY STREET.

Commercial Union Assurance Company

FIRE—LIFE—MARINE.

Capital fully Subscribed £2,500,000
Life Fund in Special Trust for Life Policyholders about £875,000
Other Funds exceed £1,000,000

TOTAL INVESTED FUNDS UPWARDS OF TWO MILLIONS.

Total Net Annual Income exceeds £1,200,000

CHIEF OFFICES: 19 & 20 CORNHILL, LONDON, E.C.

WEST END OFFICE: 8 PALL MALL, LONDON, S.W.

HOME BRANCHES :—Manchester, Liverpool, Newcastle-on-Tyne, Leeds, Nottingham, Birmingham, Norwich, Bristol, Southampton, Dublin, Edinburgh, Glasgow and Aberdeen.

DIRECTORS.

W. Reierson Arbuthnot, Esq.
Robert Barclay, Esq. (Barclay, Bevan, &Co.)
W. Middleton Campbell, Esq. (Hogg, Curtis, Campbell, & Co.)
Jeremiah Colman, Esq. (J. & J. Colman.)
A. Giles, Esq., M.P., 26 Great George St., s.w.
Edmund S. Hanbury, Esq. (Truman, Hanbury & Co.)
Frederick W. Harris, Esq. (Harris & Dixon.)
John Holms, Esq., M.P. (Wm. Holms & Brothers.)
F. Larkworthy, Esq., Bank of New Zealand.
Charles J. Leaf, Esq. (Leaf, Sons & Co.)

William Leask, Esq., Monument Buildgs.
The Right Hon. A. J. Mundella, M.P.
Sir Henry W. Peek, Bart. (Peek Brothers & Co.)
P. P. Rodocanachi, Esq. (P. P. Rodocanachi & Co.)
Thos. Russell, Esq., C.M.G.
P. G. Sechiari, Esq. (Sechiari Bros. & Co.)
Andrew R. Scoble, Esq., Q.C.
D. Cooper Scott, Esq. (Wilson, Sons, & Co., Limited.)
Alexander Sim, Esq.
John P. Tate, Esq.
Henry Trower, Esq. (Trower & Lawson.)

Secretary.—GEO. LYON BENNETT.

FIRE.

Sub-Manager.—JOHN CARSWELL.

Undoubted Security.   Moderate Rates.   Prompt and Liberal Settlements.

LIFE.

Actuary.—T. E. YOUNG, B.A.

Married Women's Property Act (1882).—Policies are issued to husbands for the benefit of their wives and children, thus creating, without trouble, expense, stamp duty, or legal assistance, a Family Settlement, which creditors cannot touch.

The Life Funds invested in the names of Special Trustees. The Assured wholly free from liability.

The Expenses of Management limited by Deed of Settlement.

Fixed Minimum Surrender Values guaranteed; and Claims paid one month after proof of death. New Liberal Conditions.

MARINE.

Underwriter.—J. CARR SAUNDERS.

Rates for Marine Risks on application to the Underwriter.

BRANCH OFFICE, EDINBURGH: 37 HANOVER STREET.
JOHN GRAY, *District Manager.*   W. & J. BURNESS, W.S., *Law Agents.*
BRANCH OFFICE, GLASGOW: 19 ST. VINCENT PLACE.
ARCHD. LAWSON, *District Manager.*
MITCHELLS, COWAN & JOHNSTON, Writers, *Law Agents.*